Getting Things Done

with

Microsoft To Do

Kiet Huynh

Table of Contents

CHAPTER I Introduction to Microsoft To Do 6

1.1 Overview of Microsoft To Do..6

   1.1.1 What is Microsoft To Do? 6

   1.1.2 Key Features and Benefits...10

   1.1.3 How Microsoft To Do Fits into the Microsoft 365 Ecosystem 16

1.2 Getting Started..23

   1.2.1 Setting Up Your Microsoft Account 23

   1.2.2 Navigating the To Do Interface..28

   1.2.3 Syncing Microsoft To Do Across Devices 35

1.3 Understanding the GTD Methodology 40

   1.3.1 Overview of Getting Things Done (GTD)..40

   1.3.2 Applying GTD Principles in Microsoft To Do..43

   1.3.3 Benefits of Using GTD with Microsoft To Do 46

CHAPTER II Setting Up Your Tasks and Lists..51

2.1 Creating and Managing Tasks 51

   2.1.1 Adding New Tasks 51

   2.1.2 Setting Due Dates and Reminders..54

   2.1.3 Organizing Tasks with Tags...59

2.2 Creating Lists and Groups...64

   2.2.1 Building Your First List..64

   2.2.2 Grouping Lists for Better Organization..68

   2.2.3 Using Smart Lists to Automate Task Management 76

2.3 Prioritizing and Sorting Tasks...82

   2.3.1 Setting Task Priorities...82

   2.3.2 Sorting and Filtering Tasks..87

2.3.3 Using Importance and My Day Features 93

CHAPTER III Integrating Microsoft To Do with GTD **98**

3.1 Capturing and Clarifying Tasks 98

3.1.1 The Capture Process in Microsoft To Do 98

3.1.2 Clarifying Tasks and Next Actions 103

3.1.3 Organizing Tasks into Projects and Next Steps 111

3.2 Organizing Your Tasks 116

3.2.1 Creating Projects and Actionable Steps 116

3.2.2 Using Contexts and Tags 121

3.2.3 Managing Reference Material in Microsoft To Do 126

3.3 Reflecting and Reviewing 133

3.3.1 Conducting Weekly Reviews 133

3.3.2 Tracking Progress and Adjusting Plans 138

3.3.3 Using the Completed Tasks View 143

CHAPTER IV Advanced Features and Customization **149**

4.1 Customizing Your Microsoft To Do Experience 149

4.1.1 Personalizing Task Views 149

4.1.2 Changing Themes and Appearance 155

4.1.3 Customizing Notifications and Reminders 162

4.2 Integrating with Other Microsoft 365 Apps 169

4.2.1 Syncing with Microsoft Outlook 169

4.2.2 Using Microsoft To Do with Teams and Planner 174

4.2.3 Automating Workflows with Power Automate 179

4.3 Using Microsoft To Do for Team Collaboration 186

4.3.1 Sharing Lists with Team Members 186

4.3.2 Collaborating on Tasks 190

4.3.3 Tracking Team Progress 198

CHAPTER V Best Practices for Getting Things Done **205**

5.1 Optimizing Your Task Management System 205

5.1.1 Keeping Your Lists Organized 205

5.1.2 Using Recurring Tasks for Routine Actions 211

5.1.3 Breaking Down Large Tasks into Manageable Steps 217

5.2 Time Management and Productivity Techniques 223

5.2.1 Prioritizing Tasks Effectively 223

5.2.2 Combining GTD with Other Productivity Methods 228

5.2.3 Avoiding Common Productivity Pitfalls 234

5.3 Maintaining Balance and Focus 240

5.3.1 Setting Realistic Goals 240

5.3.2 Managing Work-Life Balance with Microsoft To Do 244

5.3.3 Staying Motivated and Avoiding Burnout 250

CHAPTER VI Troubleshooting and Support 255

6.1 Common Issues and How to Fix Them 255

6.1.1 Syncing Problems Across Devices 255

6.1.2 Issues with Task Reminders 261

6.1.3 Handling Duplicated Tasks 266

6.2 Accessing Help and Support 271

6.2.1 Accessing Microsoft Support 271

6.2.2 Using the To Do Community Forums 276

6.2.3 Finding Online Tutorials and Guides 282

6.3 Keeping Microsoft To Do Updated 287

6.3.1 Understanding New Features and Updates 287

6.3.2 Preparing for Major Changes 290

6.3.3 Reporting Bugs and Requesting Features 295

CHAPTER VII Real-World Applications and Case Studies 300

7.1 Case Study: Microsoft To Do in Project Management 300

7.1.1 Managing Project Milestones 300

7.1.2 Coordinating Team Efforts... 304

7.1.3 Tracking Project Progress 308

7.2 Case Study: Personal Productivity with Microsoft To Do 315

7.2.1 Organizing Daily Tasks 315

7.2.2 Managing Personal Goals and Habits... 321

7.2.3 Planning Events and Activities 326

7.3 Real-World Examples.. 334

7.3.1 Using Microsoft To Do in Education... 334

7.3.2 Microsoft To Do for Small Businesses 338

7.3.3 Non-Profit Organization Task Management.. 341

Conclusion... 346

CHAPTER I
Introduction to Microsoft To Do

1.1 Overview of Microsoft To Do

1.1.1 What is Microsoft To Do?

Microsoft To Do is a cloud-based task management application that forms part of the broader Microsoft 365 suite. Launched as the successor to Wunderlist, a popular task management app that Microsoft acquired in 2015, Microsoft To Do was designed to provide a simple, intuitive, and powerful solution for managing tasks, lists, and personal productivity.

At its core, Microsoft To Do is a tool that helps users organize their tasks, track their to-do lists, and manage their time more effectively. The application allows you to create tasks, set due dates, add reminders, categorize tasks with tags, and organize them into lists. Microsoft To Do also supports advanced features like task prioritization, list sharing, and integration with other Microsoft 365 apps, making it a versatile tool for both personal and professional use.

The Evolution from Wunderlist to Microsoft To Do

Wunderlist was widely regarded as one of the best task management apps available, praised for its simplicity and functionality. When Microsoft acquired Wunderlist, the company aimed to integrate its best features into a new application that would be deeply integrated with the Microsoft ecosystem. Microsoft To Do was built from the ground up to incorporate Wunderlist's strengths while taking advantage of the connectivity and scalability of Microsoft 365.

Since its initial release in 2017, Microsoft To Do has undergone significant updates and improvements. The app has gradually introduced more sophisticated features such as My Day, a daily planning tool, and deeper integrations with Microsoft Outlook, Planner, and Teams. These enhancements have positioned Microsoft To Do as a powerful productivity tool that can cater to the needs of both individual users and organizations.

User-Centric Design

One of the key aspects of Microsoft To Do is its user-centric design. The interface is clean, simple, and easy to navigate, making it accessible to users of all skill levels. Whether you are new to task management apps or an experienced productivity enthusiast, Microsoft To Do offers a straightforward experience that allows you to focus on what matters most—getting things done.

The app's design prioritizes clarity and ease of use. For example, when you open Microsoft To Do, you are immediately presented with your tasks for the day through the My Day feature. This helps users avoid feeling overwhelmed by long lists of tasks and instead focus on manageable daily goals. The user interface is also customizable, allowing you to adjust the appearance of lists and tasks to suit your preferences.

Cross-Platform Accessibility

In today's world, where people often switch between multiple devices throughout the day, Microsoft To Do's cross-platform accessibility is a significant advantage. The app is available on a wide range of devices, including Windows PCs, macOS, iOS, Android, and through any web browser. This means you can access your tasks and lists from virtually anywhere, ensuring that you stay on top of your responsibilities no matter where you are.

Microsoft To Do's cloud-based nature ensures that all your tasks, lists, and preferences are synced across all your devices in real-time. Whether you add a task on your phone, update a list on your computer, or check off a completed task in a web browser, the changes are instantly reflected across all your devices. This seamless synchronization ensures that you always have the most up-to-date information at your fingertips.

Security and Privacy

Security and privacy are critical considerations for any productivity tool, especially one that might be used to manage sensitive personal or professional tasks. Microsoft To Do is built on the same secure cloud infrastructure that underpins the entire Microsoft 365 ecosystem, which means it benefits from Microsoft's robust security measures.

Data stored in Microsoft To Do is encrypted both in transit and at rest, ensuring that your information is protected against unauthorized access. Additionally, Microsoft To Do complies with various international data protection regulations, making it a trustworthy choice for users concerned about privacy.

Microsoft also provides enterprise-grade security features, such as multi-factor authentication and conditional access policies, for organizations using Microsoft To Do as part of their Microsoft 365 subscription. These features ensure that only authorized users can access task data and that this access is tightly controlled.

Integration with Microsoft 365

One of the most significant advantages of Microsoft To Do is its integration with the broader Microsoft 365 ecosystem. This integration allows Microsoft To Do to work seamlessly with other productivity tools, such as Outlook, Teams, and Planner, enabling a more unified and efficient workflow.

For example, tasks created in Outlook can automatically appear in Microsoft To Do, allowing you to manage all your tasks in one place. Similarly, Microsoft Planner tasks can be synced with Microsoft To Do, enabling you to manage both personal and team tasks from a single interface. This level of integration is particularly valuable for users who rely heavily on Microsoft's suite of tools for their daily work.

Accessibility Features

Microsoft To Do is designed to be accessible to as many users as possible, including those with disabilities. The app includes a range of accessibility features, such as keyboard shortcuts, screen reader support, and high contrast modes. These features ensure that all users, regardless of their abilities, can effectively use the app to manage their tasks and improve their productivity.

Ongoing Development and Updates

Microsoft To Do is continuously evolving, with regular updates that introduce new features, improve existing functionality, and enhance overall performance. Microsoft is committed to listening to user feedback and incorporating it into the development of the app. This approach ensures that Microsoft To Do remains a cutting-edge tool that meets the evolving needs of its users.

Recent updates have included enhancements such as improved task collaboration features, better integration with other Microsoft 365 apps, and new customization options. Microsoft has also introduced features that support remote work, such as improved sharing and collaboration capabilities, recognizing the changing nature of work in today's digital environment.

Community and Support

Microsoft To Do benefits from a large and active user community. This community is a valuable resource for users looking to learn more about the app, discover new ways to use its features, and troubleshoot any issues they may encounter. Microsoft hosts official forums where users can ask questions, share tips, and connect with other Microsoft To Do users.

Additionally, Microsoft offers extensive documentation and support resources for Microsoft To Do. This includes step-by-step guides, video tutorials, and a comprehensive help center that covers everything from basic setup to advanced features. Whether you're new to Microsoft To Do or looking to master its more complex capabilities, these resources are designed to help you get the most out of the app.

Conclusion

Microsoft To Do is a powerful, versatile, and user-friendly task management tool that can help you stay organized and productive. Whether you're managing personal tasks, coordinating work projects, or simply trying to keep track of your daily to-do list, Microsoft To Do offers the tools you need to get things done.

With its seamless integration into the Microsoft 365 ecosystem, cross-platform accessibility, robust security features, and continuous updates, Microsoft To Do is an ideal choice for anyone looking to improve their task management and productivity. As we explore the rest of this book, you'll learn how to unlock the full potential of Microsoft To Do and use it to achieve your goals.

1.1.2 Key Features and Benefits

Microsoft To Do is a task management application designed to help users organize their personal and professional lives by managing tasks, lists, and reminders. Its intuitive design and seamless integration with other Microsoft 365 applications make it a powerful tool for staying productive. In this section, we will explore the key features of Microsoft To Do and the benefits that make it an essential tool for anyone looking to streamline their workflow.

Task Creation and Management

At the heart of Microsoft To Do is its task creation and management functionality. Users can easily create tasks, assign due dates, set reminders, and add detailed notes or steps to each task. The simplicity of task creation allows for quick entry, which is particularly useful when capturing ideas or to-dos on the go.

- *Simple Task Creation:* Microsoft To Do allows users to create tasks with just a few clicks or taps. Whether you're using the desktop, mobile, or web version, the process is consistent and straightforward. Users can type a task name, and additional details like due dates or reminders can be added immediately or later.

- *Task Prioritization:* One of the standout features is the ability to prioritize tasks by marking them as important. Important tasks are highlighted and can be accessed quickly from the "Important" smart list, ensuring that critical tasks don't get lost among other to-dos.

- *Task Details and Steps:* Users can add additional details to each task, such as notes, links, or files, which can be useful for providing context or storing necessary information. Additionally, tasks can include steps—subtasks that break down larger tasks into more manageable pieces. This feature is particularly useful for complex projects that require multiple actions to complete.

- *Recurring Tasks:* Many tasks in our lives are repetitive, and Microsoft To Do makes it easy to set up recurring tasks. Users can set tasks to recur daily, weekly, monthly, or on custom intervals, ensuring that routine tasks are automatically generated without requiring manual input each time.

List Creation and Organization

Microsoft To Do's list creation and organization features are central to helping users categorize and manage their tasks effectively. Users can create multiple lists to separate personal tasks from work-related ones, or to organize tasks by project or theme.

- *Customizable Lists:* Users can create as many lists as needed, each with its own set of tasks. Lists can be named according to the user's preferences, such as "Work," "Personal," "Shopping," or "Project XYZ." This flexibility allows users to organize their tasks in a way that makes sense to them, keeping their to-do list uncluttered and focused.

- *Grouping Lists:* For users managing multiple projects or areas of responsibility, Microsoft To Do allows the grouping of lists. Groups can contain several lists, providing an additional layer of organization. For example, a user might create a group called "Work Projects" with individual lists for each project they are managing.

- *Smart Lists:* Microsoft To Do automatically generates smart lists such as "My Day," "Important," "Planned," and "Assigned to You," which aggregate tasks from all lists based on certain criteria. These smart lists provide quick access to tasks that require immediate attention, such as tasks due today or tasks that have been flagged as important.

- *List Customization:* Each list can be customized with different themes and colors, making it easy to visually differentiate between them. This feature is particularly helpful when managing multiple lists, as the color-coding adds an extra layer of organization.

My Day Feature

One of the unique and most praised features of Microsoft To Do is the "My Day" list. This feature is designed to help users focus on what needs to be done today by allowing them to plan their day with a handpicked list of tasks.

- *Daily Task Selection:* At the start of each day, users can review their tasks and decide which ones they want to accomplish. These tasks can be added to the "My Day" list, providing a focused view of the day's priorities. This approach helps in reducing overwhelm by narrowing down the list to only what needs attention today.

- *Fresh Start Every Day:* The "My Day" list resets each day, meaning that tasks not completed will not automatically carry over. Instead, they remain in their original lists, allowing users to reassess their priorities daily. This feature encourages users to be intentional about what they choose to work on each day, promoting better time management and focus.

- *Intelligent Suggestions:* Microsoft To Do provides intelligent suggestions for tasks to add to the "My Day" list based on due dates, importance, and previous tasks. This helps users ensure that nothing slips through the cracks and that they are always aware of what needs to be done.

Reminders and Notifications

Reminders and notifications are crucial for ensuring that important tasks and deadlines are not forgotten. Microsoft To Do offers robust reminder and notification features to keep users on track.

- *Customizable Reminders:* Users can set reminders for any task, choosing specific dates and times. This feature is particularly useful for time-sensitive tasks or deadlines. Reminders can be as frequent or as infrequent as needed, from a one-time alert to recurring reminders.

- *Due Dates and Deadlines:* Tasks can be assigned due dates, which helps users manage deadlines effectively. Tasks with due dates appear in the "Planned" smart list, making it easy to see all upcoming tasks at a glance. This is particularly useful for managing long-term projects or ensuring that tasks are completed on time.

- *Push Notifications:* For users on mobile devices, Microsoft To Do provides push notifications that remind them of upcoming tasks. These notifications are customizable, allowing users to choose how far in advance they wish to be reminded. This ensures that users are notified at the most convenient times, avoiding disruptions while still keeping important tasks top of mind.

- *Email Notifications:* When integrated with Outlook, Microsoft To Do can send email notifications for tasks with approaching deadlines. This integration ensures that users who rely heavily on email for communication won't miss important reminders.

Integration with Microsoft 365

One of the key benefits of Microsoft To Do is its seamless integration with the broader Microsoft 365 ecosystem. This integration enhances the functionality of To Do and allows it to work in concert with other tools like Outlook, Teams, and Planner.

- *Outlook Tasks Integration:* Microsoft To Do syncs seamlessly with Outlook, allowing users to manage their tasks across both platforms. Tasks created in Outlook automatically appear in To Do and vice versa. This integration is particularly valuable for users who rely on Outlook for email and calendar management, as it provides a centralized location for all tasks and reminders.

- *Microsoft Teams Integration:* In a team setting, Microsoft To Do integrates with Microsoft Teams, allowing users to share lists and collaborate on tasks within their teams. This integration facilitates better communication and coordination on shared projects, ensuring that everyone stays on the same page.

- *Planner Integration:* For users involved in more complex project management, Microsoft To Do integrates with Microsoft Planner. This integration allows users to see tasks assigned to them in Planner within To Do, ensuring that they can manage both personal and team tasks from a single interface.

- *Microsoft OneNote Integration:* Tasks can also be created from notes in Microsoft OneNote. This feature is especially useful for users who use OneNote for brainstorming or meeting notes, as it allows them to turn their notes into actionable tasks within To Do.

Collaboration Features

In addition to personal task management, Microsoft To Do offers several features that facilitate collaboration, making it a valuable tool for teams and organizations.

- *List Sharing:* Microsoft To Do allows users to share lists with others, making it easy to collaborate on projects or manage shared responsibilities. When a list is shared, all members can add, edit, and complete tasks, ensuring that everyone involved has access to the most up-to-date information.

- *Task Assignment:* Within shared lists, tasks can be assigned to specific team members. This feature is particularly useful for project managers or team leaders who need to delegate tasks and track their progress. Assigned tasks appear in the "Assigned to You" smart list, helping team members stay on top of their responsibilities.

- *Real-Time Syncing:* Changes made to shared lists or tasks are synced in real-time across all devices, ensuring that everyone is always working with the latest information. This real-time syncing is crucial for teams working in dynamic environments where priorities can shift quickly.

Cross-Platform Accessibility

Microsoft To Do is available across multiple platforms, including Windows, macOS, iOS, Android, and the web. This cross-platform accessibility ensures that users can manage their tasks and lists regardless of the device they are using.

- *Consistency Across Devices:* Whether you're on a desktop at work, a tablet at home, or a smartphone on the go, Microsoft To Do offers a consistent experience. The interface is designed to be intuitive and user-friendly across all platforms, ensuring that users can easily switch between devices without a steep learning curve.

- *Offline Access:* Microsoft To Do offers offline access, allowing users to view and edit their tasks even when they don't have an internet connection. Any changes made offline are automatically synced when the device reconnects to the internet, ensuring that tasks are always up-to-date.

- *Web Access:* For users who prefer not to download an app, Microsoft To Do can be accessed via a web browser. This web version provides full functionality and is particularly useful for users who need to access their tasks from public or shared computers.

Security and Privacy

Microsoft To Do benefits from the robust security and privacy features that are a hallmark of Microsoft 365. This makes it a reliable choice for individuals and organizations that need to ensure the security of their task management data.

- *Data Encryption:* All data in Microsoft To Do is encrypted both at rest and in transit. This ensures that your tasks and lists are protected from unauthorized access, whether they are stored on Microsoft's servers or being transmitted between your devices.

- *Compliance with Industry Standards:* Microsoft To Do complies with industry-standard security protocols and regulations, including GDPR. For organizations in regulated industries, this compliance is critical for ensuring that their task management processes meet legal requirements.

- *Control Over Data Sharing:* Microsoft To Do gives users control over how their data is shared. For example, when sharing lists with others, users can control who has access and whether they can edit or only view the list. This control ensures that sensitive tasks are only shared with the appropriate people.

Benefits of Using Microsoft To Do

The key features of Microsoft To Do offer numerous benefits that make it a powerful tool for managing tasks and enhancing productivity.

- *Improved Organization:* With the ability to create multiple lists, prioritize tasks, and set reminders, Microsoft To Do helps users keep their tasks organized and manageable. The smart lists, in particular, provide an easy way to focus on what's important without losing track of other tasks.

- *Enhanced Focus:* The "My Day" feature is designed to help users focus on their most important tasks each day. By allowing users to handpick tasks for the day, it encourages a more intentional approach to task management, reducing overwhelm and increasing productivity.

- *Seamless Integration:* Microsoft To Do's integration with other Microsoft 365 applications means that tasks can be managed across multiple platforms and tools. This integration not only saves time but also ensures that all aspects of a user's workflow are connected, from email to project management.

- *Collaboration and Teamwork:* For teams, the collaboration features of Microsoft To Do make it easier to manage shared tasks and projects. The ability to assign tasks, share lists, and track progress ensures that everyone is aligned and working towards the same goals.

- *Accessibility and Flexibility:* With cross-platform support and offline access, Microsoft To Do is a flexible tool that can be used anytime, anywhere. This accessibility is crucial for users who need to manage their tasks on the go or across different devices.

- *Security and Reliability:* Backed by Microsoft's strong security framework, Microsoft To Do offers users peace of mind that their data is secure. For organizations, this security is essential for maintaining compliance and protecting sensitive information.

In summary, Microsoft To Do is a versatile and powerful tool for managing tasks, whether for personal use or within a team. Its key features—such as task management, list creation, integration with Microsoft 365, and collaboration capabilities—offer significant benefits that can help users stay organized, focused, and productive. Whether you are looking to streamline your daily tasks or manage complex projects, Microsoft To Do provides the functionality and flexibility needed to get things done efficiently.

1.1.3 How Microsoft To Do Fits into the Microsoft 365 Ecosystem

Microsoft To Do is an integral part of the Microsoft 365 ecosystem, providing users with a powerful and versatile task management tool that seamlessly integrates with other Microsoft services and applications. This integration offers several benefits, including enhanced productivity, streamlined workflows, and improved collaboration. In this section, we will explore how Microsoft To Do fits into the broader Microsoft 365 ecosystem and how you can leverage these integrations to maximize your productivity and efficiency.

Integration with Microsoft Outlook

One of the most significant integrations of Microsoft To Do is with Microsoft Outlook. Outlook is a widely used email and calendar application, and its integration with To Do allows users to manage tasks and emails in one cohesive environment. This integration includes the following features:

- Email to Task Conversion: With a simple click, you can convert an email in Outlook into a task in Microsoft To Do. This is particularly useful for managing actionable emails that require follow-up, ensuring that important tasks don't get lost in your inbox.

- Task Synchronization: Tasks created in Microsoft To Do are automatically synchronized with Outlook's task list. This means you can view and manage your tasks from either application, providing flexibility in how you organize your work.

- Reminder and Due Date Syncing: Reminders and due dates set in Microsoft To Do are reflected in Outlook, and vice versa. This ensures that you never miss an important deadline or reminder, regardless of which application you are using.

Integration with Microsoft Teams

Microsoft Teams is a collaboration platform that brings together chat, video meetings, file storage, and app integration. The integration of Microsoft To Do with Teams enhances team collaboration and task management through the following features:

- Task Assignment: Within Teams, you can assign tasks to team members directly from chats or channels. These tasks appear in the assignee's Microsoft To Do list, providing clarity on responsibilities and deadlines.

- Planner Integration: Microsoft To Do integrates with Planner, another task management tool in Microsoft 365 designed for team projects. Tasks from Planner can be viewed and managed in To Do, allowing individual team members to see all their tasks in one place.

- Notifications and Updates: Task-related notifications and updates are displayed within Teams, keeping everyone informed about progress and changes without needing to switch between applications.

Integration with Microsoft OneNote

OneNote is a digital note-taking app that allows users to organize notes, research, and information. The integration of Microsoft To Do with OneNote provides a seamless way to turn notes into actionable tasks:

- Task Creation from Notes: You can create tasks in Microsoft To Do directly from OneNote. This is particularly useful for meeting notes or brainstorming sessions, where you can capture ideas and immediately convert them into tasks.

- Linked Notes and Tasks: Tasks created from OneNote include links back to the original notes, providing context and reference material when working on tasks. This ensures that important information is easily accessible.

- Organization and Tagging: Notes and tasks can be organized and tagged consistently across OneNote and To Do, providing a unified approach to managing information and tasks.

Integration with Microsoft Planner

Microsoft Planner is a task management tool designed for team projects and collaboration. The integration between Microsoft To Do and Planner enhances individual and team productivity through the following features:

- Unified Task Management: Tasks assigned to you in Planner are automatically synchronized with your Microsoft To Do list. This ensures that you can manage both personal and team tasks from a single interface.

- Detailed Task Information: Tasks imported from Planner into To Do include all relevant details, such as descriptions, due dates, and attachments. This ensures that you have all the information you need to complete tasks.

- Progress Tracking: Updates made to tasks in To Do are reflected in Planner, providing team members with real-time visibility into task progress and status.

Integration with Microsoft SharePoint

SharePoint is a web-based collaboration platform that integrates with Microsoft To Do to enhance document and task management:

- Task Linking to Documents: You can link tasks in Microsoft To Do to documents stored in SharePoint. This provides quick access to relevant files and ensures that all necessary resources are easily accessible.

- Collaboration on Documents: Tasks related to document collaboration can be managed in To Do, with updates and progress tracked in SharePoint. This streamlines workflows and ensures that team members are aligned on document-related tasks.

- Project Sites and Task Management: SharePoint project sites can include task lists that are integrated with Microsoft To Do. This provides a centralized location for managing project tasks and tracking progress.

Integration with Microsoft OneDrive

OneDrive is a cloud storage service that integrates with Microsoft To Do to enhance file management and accessibility:

- File Attachments: You can attach files from OneDrive to tasks in Microsoft To Do. This ensures that important documents and resources are linked to relevant tasks, making them easily accessible when needed.

- Document Collaboration: Tasks related to document collaboration can be managed in To Do, with files stored in OneDrive. This enhances team collaboration and ensures that all necessary files are available to team members.

- Cloud Storage Integration: The integration of OneDrive with To Do provides seamless access to cloud-stored files, allowing you to manage tasks and files from anywhere.

Integration with Microsoft Power Automate

Power Automate is a workflow automation tool that integrates with Microsoft To Do to streamline task management and automate repetitive processes:

- Automated Task Creation: You can create automated workflows that generate tasks in Microsoft To Do based on specific triggers, such as receiving an email or updating a file. This reduces manual effort and ensures that tasks are created promptly.

- Workflow Management: Tasks generated through Power Automate are synchronized with To Do, providing a centralized location for managing automated workflows and tasks.

- Custom Automation: Power Automate allows you to create custom workflows that integrate with various Microsoft 365 applications, enhancing productivity and efficiency through automation.

Integration with Microsoft Cortana

Cortana is Microsoft's virtual assistant that integrates with Microsoft To Do to enhance task management through voice commands and natural language processing:

- Voice-Activated Task Management: You can use Cortana to create and manage tasks in Microsoft To Do using voice commands. This is particularly useful for hands-free task management and quick task entry.

- Natural Language Processing: Cortana's natural language processing capabilities allow you to create tasks using conversational language, making task management more intuitive and efficient.

- Reminders and Notifications: Cortana can provide reminders and notifications for tasks in Microsoft To Do, ensuring that you stay on top of important deadlines and commitments.

Integration with Microsoft Dynamics 365

Dynamics 365 is a suite of enterprise resource planning (ERP) and customer relationship management (CRM) applications that integrates with Microsoft To Do to enhance business processes and task management:

- Task Management in CRM: Tasks related to customer interactions and sales processes in Dynamics 365 can be managed in Microsoft To Do. This ensures that important follow-up actions and customer-related tasks are tracked and completed.

- ERP Task Integration: Tasks related to business operations and workflows in Dynamics 365 can be synchronized with Microsoft To Do. This enhances task visibility and management for business processes.

- Unified Business Management: The integration of Dynamics 365 with To Do provides a unified approach to managing tasks across CRM and ERP applications, enhancing productivity and efficiency.

Integration with Third-Party Applications

Microsoft To Do also integrates with various third-party applications, extending its functionality and enhancing task management capabilities:

- Zapier Integration: Zapier is a workflow automation tool that connects Microsoft To Do with hundreds of third-party applications. This allows you to create automated workflows and integrate To Do with other tools you use.

- Trello Integration: You can integrate Microsoft To Do with Trello to manage tasks across both platforms. This is particularly useful for teams that use Trello for project management and To Do for individual task management.

- Slack Integration: Tasks created in Slack can be synchronized with Microsoft To Do, providing a seamless way to manage tasks and communications in one place.

Enhancing Productivity with Microsoft To Do Integrations

The integration of Microsoft To Do with other Microsoft 365 applications and third-party tools provides a comprehensive task management solution that enhances productivity and efficiency. By leveraging these integrations, you can streamline workflows, improve collaboration, and manage tasks more effectively. Here are some tips for maximizing the benefits of these integrations:

- Centralize Task Management: Use Microsoft To Do as your central task management hub, integrating tasks from Outlook, Teams, Planner, and other applications. This provides a single location for managing all your tasks, reducing the need to switch between applications.

- Automate Repetitive Tasks: Leverage Power Automate to create workflows that automate repetitive tasks and processes. This saves time and ensures that tasks are created and managed consistently.

- Enhance Collaboration: Use Teams and Planner integrations to enhance team collaboration and task management. Assign tasks, track progress, and share updates within the tools your team uses most.

- Keep Information Linked: Use OneNote, SharePoint, and OneDrive integrations to link tasks to relevant notes, documents, and files. This ensures that all necessary information is easily accessible when working on tasks.

- Stay Organized and Informed: Use reminders, notifications, and reviews to stay on top of your tasks and commitments. Regularly review and update your tasks to ensure that you are on track to achieve your goals.

In conclusion, Microsoft To Do's integration with the Microsoft 365 ecosystem and third-party applications provides a powerful and versatile task management solution. By leveraging these integrations, you can enhance productivity, streamline workflows, and manage tasks more effectively, helping you to achieve your goals and get things done.

1.2 Getting Started

1.2.1 Setting Up Your Microsoft Account

Before diving into the world of Microsoft To Do and utilizing its powerful task management features, the first and most crucial step is setting up your Microsoft account. A Microsoft account not only allows you to access Microsoft To Do but also integrates with a wide range of Microsoft services, such as Outlook, OneDrive, and Teams, providing a seamless experience across all your devices.

Understanding the Importance of a Microsoft Account

A Microsoft account is a single sign-in service that gives you access to various Microsoft products and services. It enables you to sync your tasks, files, settings, and more across multiple devices, ensuring that your work and personal life are always in sync. With a Microsoft account, you can securely store your data in the cloud, making it accessible from anywhere with an internet connection.

For those using Microsoft To Do in a professional environment, particularly within organizations that use Microsoft 365, your Microsoft account serves as the gateway to collaboration tools like Teams and SharePoint, allowing you to coordinate tasks and projects effortlessly with your colleagues.

Creating a New Microsoft Account

If you don't already have a Microsoft account, creating one is a straightforward process. Here's how you can do it:

1. Visit the Microsoft Account Sign-Up Page:

   To begin, open your web browser and navigate to the Microsoft account creation page at account.microsoft.com. Here, you'll find the option to sign in or create a new account.

2. Choose Your Sign-In Method:

Microsoft allows you to sign in with an existing email address or create a new Outlook.com email account. If you prefer to use an existing email (such as Gmail or Yahoo), click on the "Use a different email address" option. Alternatively, you can create a new Outlook email address by selecting "Get a new email address."

3. Enter Your Email Address or Phone Number:

If you opted to use an existing email, enter it here. Microsoft will send a verification code to this address to confirm your ownership. If you're using a phone number, enter it instead, and you'll receive a verification code via SMS.

4. Create a Strong Password:

Choose a secure password for your Microsoft account. Microsoft recommends using a combination of uppercase and lowercase letters, numbers, and symbols to ensure your account is protected. Remember, your password is the first line of defense against unauthorized access.

5. Verify Your Email or Phone Number:

Once you've entered your email or phone number, Microsoft will send a verification code to confirm your identity. Enter this code on the next screen to proceed. This step is crucial for securing your account and ensuring that you are the rightful owner of the email or phone number associated with it.

6. Enter Your Personal Details:

Microsoft will ask for your name, date of birth, and country or region. This information is used to personalize your account and improve your experience with Microsoft services. It's important to provide accurate details, as they can be useful in account recovery situations.

7. Complete the CAPTCHA:

To verify that you're not a robot, you'll be asked to complete a CAPTCHA challenge. This is a simple task, such as identifying images or entering a code, designed to ensure that a real person is creating the account.

8. Agree to Microsoft's Terms and Conditions:

Before proceeding, you'll need to read and agree to Microsoft's terms of service and privacy policy. These documents outline how your data will be handled and what you can expect from using Microsoft's services. Once you've reviewed and accepted the terms, click "Create account."

9. Set Up Two-Factor Authentication (Optional but Recommended):

For added security, Microsoft offers two-factor authentication (2FA). This means that in addition to your password, you'll need to enter a code sent to your phone or email when signing in from an unrecognized device. Setting up 2FA is highly recommended to protect your account from unauthorized access.

10. Personalize Your Account Settings:

After creating your account, you can personalize it by setting up a profile picture, choosing a theme, and customizing your account settings. These options help tailor your Microsoft experience to your preferences.

Navigating the Microsoft Account Dashboard

Once your account is created, you'll be taken to the Microsoft Account Dashboard. This central hub allows you to manage all aspects of your Microsoft account, from security settings to payment information. Here are some key features you'll find on the dashboard:

- Account Info: View and update your personal information, such as your name, contact details, and preferred language.

- Security: Manage your password, set up two-factor authentication, and review recent sign-ins to ensure your account is secure.

- Devices: View and manage all the devices connected to your Microsoft account. This is particularly useful for keeping track of your smartphones, tablets, and computers.

- Subscriptions: If you have a Microsoft 365 subscription, you can manage your billing information and subscription details here.

- Privacy: Control how Microsoft collects and uses your data. You can review and adjust your privacy settings to align with your preferences.

- Family & Safety: Set up and manage family accounts, including child accounts with parental controls.

Familiarizing yourself with the Microsoft Account Dashboard is important, as it allows you to keep your account secure and personalized to your needs. Additionally, it's where you can access support and recover your account in case you forget your password or encounter other issues.

Syncing Your Microsoft Account Across Devices

One of the major benefits of having a Microsoft account is the ability to sync your settings, files, and tasks across all your devices. Whether you're using a Windows PC, a Mac, an Android device, or an iPhone, your Microsoft To Do tasks and other account data can be seamlessly synchronized. Here's how to ensure your account is set up for syncing:

1. Windows Devices:

  - Sign in to your Windows device with your Microsoft account. This will automatically sync your settings, including your desktop background, browser preferences, and Microsoft To Do tasks.

  - If you're already signed in with a local account, you can switch to your Microsoft account by going to Settings > Accounts > Your Info and clicking on "Sign in with a Microsoft account instead."

2. MacOS:

  - Download and install the Microsoft To Do app from the Mac App Store.

  - Sign in with your Microsoft account to access your tasks and lists. The app will sync your data across all your devices.

  - For broader syncing (e.g., OneDrive files), you can also install the OneDrive app and sign in with your Microsoft account.

3. iOS Devices:

  - Download Microsoft To Do from the App Store.

  - Sign in with your Microsoft account to sync your tasks.

  - Ensure iCloud is enabled for backup, but note that Microsoft To Do uses your Microsoft account for task syncing.

4. Android Devices:

  - Download Microsoft To Do from the Google Play Store.

  - Sign in with your Microsoft account to start syncing tasks.

  - You can also sync your contacts, calendar, and emails by adding your Microsoft account to the device under Settings > Accounts.

By syncing your Microsoft account across devices, you ensure that your tasks and projects are always up-to-date, regardless of which device you're using. This feature is especially useful for professionals who switch between a work computer and a personal smartphone or for anyone who needs to stay organized on the go.

Troubleshooting Account Setup Issues

While setting up your Microsoft account is generally straightforward, you may encounter some issues along the way. Here are common problems and how to resolve them:

1. Verification Code Not Received:

  - Ensure that you've entered the correct email address or phone number. Check your spam or junk folder for the email.

  - If using a phone number, make sure your device has a stable signal. You can also request the code to be resent.

  - If you still don't receive the code, try using a different email address or phone number, or contact Microsoft support for assistance.

2. Password Issues:

  - If you're unable to create a strong password, try using a password manager to generate and store complex passwords.

  - Ensure your password meets Microsoft's security requirements: at least 8 characters, with a mix of letters, numbers, and symbols.

3. Two-Factor Authentication Problems:

  - If you're having trouble setting up 2FA, make sure your phone number is entered correctly and that your device can receive SMS messages.

  - Alternatively, you can use an authenticator app, such as Microsoft Authenticator, to generate verification codes.

4. Account Already Exists:

  - If you receive a message that your email is already associated with a Microsoft account, you may have previously created an account. Try resetting your password using the "Forgot my password" link.

- If you don't remember creating an account, it's possible someone else used your email. Contact Microsoft support to resolve the issue.

5. Device Syncing Issues:

  - Ensure that each device is signed in with the same Microsoft account.

  - Check your internet connection, as a stable connection is required for syncing.

  - For mobile devices, ensure the Microsoft To Do app has the necessary permissions to sync in the background.

Setting up your Microsoft account is the first step toward mastering Microsoft To Do and integrating it into your daily life. Once your account is configured, you'll be able to explore the full potential of Microsoft To Do, from managing simple tasks to orchestrating complex projects. In the next section, we'll guide you through navigating the Microsoft To Do interface, ensuring you're well-equipped to get things done efficiently.

1.2.2 Navigating the To Do Interface

Navigating the interface of Microsoft To Do is a crucial step in mastering the application and leveraging its full potential for productivity and organization. The user interface of Microsoft To Do is designed to be intuitive and user-friendly, ensuring that both new users and seasoned professionals can find their way around with ease. In this section, we will explore the key components of the Microsoft To Do interface, providing detailed descriptions and practical tips for navigating the application efficiently.

1. Home Screen Overview

The home screen is the first thing you see when you open Microsoft To Do. It serves as the central hub from which you can access all of your tasks, lists, and other features. The home screen is divided into several main sections:

- Navigation Pane: Located on the left side of the screen, the navigation pane provides quick access to your lists and smart lists. It includes default lists such as "My Day," "Important,"

"Planned," "Assigned to Me," and "Flagged Email," as well as any custom lists you have created.

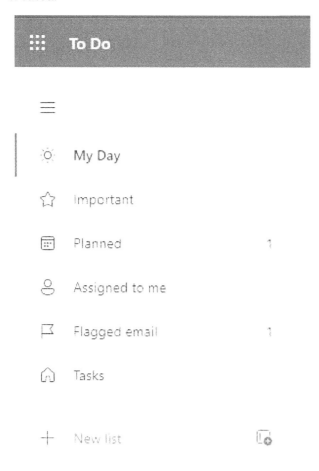

- Task View: The main area of the home screen is the task view, where you can see the tasks for the currently selected list. Each task is displayed with its name, due date, and any associated tags or priorities.

- Command Bar: Situated at the top of the screen, the command bar contains various options for managing your tasks and lists. This includes buttons for adding new tasks, sorting tasks, and accessing settings.

- My Day Pane: On the right side of the screen, the "My Day" pane allows you to focus on tasks you want to accomplish today. You can add tasks to "My Day" from any list and view your daily plan in one place.

2. Navigation Pane

The navigation pane is your primary tool for moving between different lists and views in Microsoft To Do. It provides easy access to all of your tasks and lists, ensuring that you can quickly find what you need. Here's a closer look at the key elements of the navigation pane:

- My Day: This smart list is designed to help you focus on tasks that you want to complete today. You can add tasks to "My Day" from any list by selecting the sun icon next to the task. Tasks in "My Day" are reset at the end of each day, allowing you to start fresh each morning.

- Important: Tasks that you mark as important will appear in this list. You can mark a task as important by clicking the star icon next to the task name. This helps you keep track of high-priority tasks across all of your lists.

- Planned: This list aggregates all tasks that have a due date, providing a consolidated view of your upcoming deadlines. It is automatically organized by due date, helping you to plan your work and avoid missing deadlines.

- Assigned to Me: If you are using Microsoft To Do in conjunction with Microsoft Planner or Microsoft Teams, tasks assigned to you by others will appear in this list. This ensures that you can keep track of all your responsibilities in one place.

- Flagged Email: This list displays emails that you have flagged in Outlook. By integrating your flagged emails into Microsoft To Do, you can manage your tasks and communications more effectively.

- Custom Lists: In addition to the default smart lists, you can create your own custom lists to organize tasks according to your preferences. Custom lists can be named and categorized based on projects, areas of responsibility, or any other criteria that suit your workflow.

3. Task View

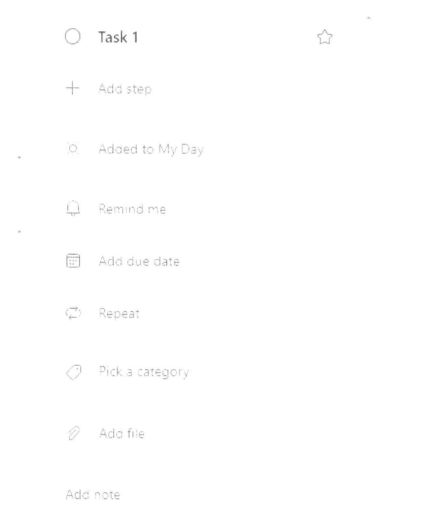

The task view is where you can see and interact with the tasks in the currently selected list. Each task in the task view displays several key pieces of information:

- Task Name: The name of the task is prominently displayed. Clicking on the task name will open the task details pane, where you can add more information and make adjustments.

- Due Date: If a task has a due date, it will be displayed next to the task name. Tasks can be sorted and filtered by due date to help you prioritize your work.

- Tags and Priority: Tasks can be tagged with custom labels and assigned a priority level. Tags help you categorize tasks, while priority levels (low, medium, high) help you focus on the most important tasks.

- Completion Checkbox: Each task has a checkbox next to it. Clicking the checkbox will mark the task as complete, removing it from the active task view and moving it to the completed tasks section.

- Additional Icons: Depending on the task's details, you may see additional icons indicating reminders, attachments, or subtasks. These icons provide quick access to additional task information without needing to open the task details pane.

4. Command Bar

The command bar at the top of the screen contains several important tools and options for managing your tasks and lists. Here are the key features of the command bar:

- Add Task: The "Add Task" button allows you to quickly create a new task in the currently selected list. You can type the task name and press Enter to add it, or click on the task name to open the task details pane for more options.

- Sort and Filter: The sort and filter options help you organize your tasks based on different criteria. You can sort tasks by due date, creation date, importance, or alphabetically. Filters allow you to display only tasks that meet certain conditions, such as tasks with due dates, flagged tasks, or tasks with specific tags.

- List Options: Clicking on the list options button (usually represented by three dots) opens a menu with additional settings for the selected list. This menu includes options to rename the list, change the list theme, share the list with others, and delete the list.

- Settings: The settings button provides access to the general settings for Microsoft To Do. Here, you can customize your preferences, such as notification settings, theme, and connected accounts.

5. My Day Pane

The "My Day" pane is a powerful feature designed to help you focus on the tasks that matter most today. It is a temporary list that resets at the end of each day, allowing you to start fresh with a new plan every morning. Here's how to make the most of the "My Day" pane:

- Adding Tasks to My Day: To add a task to "My Day," click the sun icon next to the task name. You can add tasks from any list, ensuring that your daily plan includes all of your most important tasks.

- Planning Your Day: At the start of each day, take a few minutes to review your tasks and add the ones you want to focus on to "My Day." This helps you create a clear plan for the day and ensures that you stay on track.

- Reviewing Completed Tasks: As you complete tasks throughout the day, they will remain in the "My Day" view with a strikethrough to indicate completion. This helps you keep track of your progress and provides a sense of accomplishment.

- Clearing My Day: At the end of each day, the "My Day" list is automatically cleared. Any tasks that were not completed will remain in their original lists, ensuring that nothing is lost. You can start each new day with a clean slate and a fresh plan.

6. Task Details Pane

The task details pane provides a comprehensive view of all the information related to a specific task. It allows you to add, edit, and manage various task details, ensuring that you can track everything you need to get things done. Here's a closer look at the elements of the task details pane:

- Task Name: The name of the task is displayed at the top of the pane. You can click on the task name to edit it.

- Due Date and Reminders: You can set a due date and time for the task by clicking on the calendar and clock icons. Reminders can also be added to ensure that you don't forget important deadlines.

- Notes: The notes section allows you to add additional information about the task. This can include descriptions, instructions, or any other relevant details.

- Subtasks: Subtasks are smaller steps that need to be completed as part of the main task. You can add subtasks by clicking on the "Add step" button. Each subtask has its own checkbox, allowing you to track progress at a granular level.

- Attachments: You can attach files to a task by clicking on the attachment icon. This is useful for linking documents, images, or other resources directly to the task.

- Tags: Tags help you categorize and filter tasks. You can add tags to a task by clicking on the tag icon and selecting or creating a tag.

- Priority: You can assign a priority level to the task (low, medium, high) to indicate its importance. This helps you focus on high-priority tasks and ensures that critical work is not overlooked.

- Checklist: The checklist feature allows you to create a list of items that need to be completed as part of the task. This is useful for tasks that involve multiple steps or components.

7. Settings and Customization

Customizing the settings of Microsoft To Do allows you to tailor the application to your preferences and workflow. The settings menu provides various options for personalization and configuration:

- General Settings: General settings include options for customizing the theme and appearance of Microsoft To Do. You can choose between light and dark modes, as well as select from various background themes.

- Notifications: Notification settings allow you to manage how and when you receive alerts about your tasks. You can enable or disable notifications for due dates, reminders, and shared lists.

- Connected Accounts: You can connect Microsoft To Do to other accounts, such as Outlook and Microsoft Teams, to integrate your tasks with other tools and services.

- Data and Privacy: The data and privacy settings allow you to manage how your information is stored and shared. You can also export your tasks and lists for backup or transfer purposes.

8. Keyboard Shortcuts

For power users, Microsoft To Do offers a range of keyboard shortcuts that can speed up navigation and task management. Here are some useful shortcuts:

- Add Task: Press `Ctrl + N` to quickly add a new task.

- Complete Task: Press `Ctrl + D` to mark a task as complete.

- Move Task: Press `Ctrl + Up/Down` to move a task up or down in the list.

- Open Task Details: Press `Ctrl + I` to open the task details pane.

- Search: Press `Ctrl + F` to search for tasks across all lists.

By familiarizing yourself with these shortcuts, you can navigate Microsoft To Do more efficiently and enhance your productivity.

9. Summary

Navigating the interface of Microsoft To Do is straightforward, thanks to its intuitive design and user-friendly features. Whether you are creating new tasks, managing existing ones, or customizing the application to suit your needs, understanding the layout and functionality of the interface is key to getting the most out of Microsoft To Do. By mastering the navigation pane, task view, command bar, and task details pane, you can streamline your workflow and focus on what matters most: getting things done.

As you continue to explore and use Microsoft To Do, you'll discover even more ways to customize and optimize your task management system. The interface is designed to adapt to your needs, whether you're managing personal tasks, collaborating with a team, or juggling multiple projects. With a clear understanding of the interface, you're well on your way to becoming a Microsoft To Do power user.

1.2.3 Syncing Microsoft To Do Across Devices

In today's interconnected world, maintaining seamless access to your tasks and lists across multiple devices is crucial for productivity. Microsoft To Do excels in this area by offering robust syncing capabilities that ensure your task management system is always up-to-date, no matter where you are or which device you're using. This section will explore the process of syncing Microsoft To Do across various devices, the underlying technology that supports it, and best practices to ensure a smooth syncing experience.

The Importance of Syncing

Syncing is the process of ensuring that data on one device is replicated on another. For task management apps like Microsoft To Do, syncing means that any changes you make—whether it's adding a new task, updating a deadline, or completing a task—are reflected across all your devices. This ensures consistency and prevents the frustration of managing multiple versions of your task list.

The benefits of syncing Microsoft To Do across devices are numerous:

- Consistency: Your tasks, lists, and reminders are always up-to-date, no matter which device you use.

- Accessibility: Access your tasks from any device, whether it's your smartphone, tablet, or computer.

- Flexibility: Make updates from anywhere and on any device, ensuring that you're always working with the most current information.

- Efficiency: Save time and reduce errors by eliminating the need to manually update your task lists on multiple devices.

Syncing Microsoft To Do with Microsoft Account

To start syncing Microsoft To Do, you'll need to sign in with your Microsoft account. This account acts as a bridge that connects your data across devices. Here's a step-by-step guide on how to ensure your Microsoft To Do is syncing properly:

Sign In to Microsoft To Do

1. Open Microsoft To Do on your device. If you're using the app for the first time, you'll be prompted to sign in.

2. Enter your Microsoft account credentials. If you already use other Microsoft services (like Outlook, OneDrive, or Office 365), you can use the same account to sign in.

3. Follow the on-screen instructions to complete the sign-in process.

Verify Sync Status

1. Once signed in, Microsoft To Do will automatically start syncing your data. To check the sync status, look for the sync icon or indicator within the app.

2. If you see a sync icon with a checkmark or "Up-to-date" message, your device is successfully synced.

3. If you encounter issues, check your internet connection and ensure you're signed in with the correct Microsoft account.

Manage Sync Settings

1. Go to the app settings to review sync options. You can usually find this in the settings or preferences menu.

2. Verify that syncing is enabled and configured according to your preferences. Some devices may have specific settings to manage sync frequency or data usage.

Sync Across Different Platforms

Microsoft To Do supports syncing across various platforms, including Windows, macOS, iOS, and Android. Each platform has its own app, and the syncing process is generally seamless. However, ensure you follow these steps for each device:

- On Windows and macOS: Open the To Do app, sign in with your Microsoft account, and the app will automatically sync your tasks.

- On iOS and Android: Download the Microsoft To Do app from the App Store or Google Play Store. Sign in with your Microsoft account to sync your data.

Troubleshooting Sync Issues

While syncing is generally smooth, occasional issues can arise. Here's how to troubleshoot common sync problems:

1. Check Internet Connection

A stable internet connection is essential for syncing. Ensure you're connected to Wi-Fi or mobile data. If you're experiencing connectivity issues, try restarting your router or checking with your network provider.

2. Confirm Account Details

Ensure you're signed in with the correct Microsoft account. If you have multiple accounts, verify that you're using the one associated with your Microsoft To Do data.

3. Refresh Sync

Sometimes, manually triggering a sync can resolve issues. In the app settings, look for an option to refresh or force a sync. This action can prompt the app to reattempt syncing your data.

4. Update the App

Ensure that you're using the latest version of Microsoft To Do. Updates often include bug fixes and improvements that can resolve syncing issues. Check for updates in the respective app store or update settings.

5. Clear App Cache

On mobile devices, clearing the app cache can sometimes resolve sync problems. Go to your device's settings, find Microsoft To Do, and clear the cache. Note that this action won't delete your data but may require reloading.

6. Contact Support

If you've tried the above steps and still experience syncing issues, contact Microsoft Support for assistance. Provide details about the issue and any error messages you've encountered.

Best Practices for Seamless Syncing

To ensure a smooth syncing experience with Microsoft To Do, consider these best practices:

1. Keep Your Devices Updated

Regularly update the operating system and Microsoft To Do app on all your devices. Updates often include enhancements and fixes that improve syncing performance.

2. Maintain a Stable Internet Connection

A reliable internet connection is crucial for syncing. Avoid making changes to your tasks while offline, as this can cause conflicts when reconnecting.

3. Regularly Check Sync Status

Periodically verify that your tasks are syncing correctly. This proactive approach helps identify and address any issues before they affect your productivity.

4. Use a Single Microsoft Account

To avoid confusion and ensure all your tasks are in one place, use a single Microsoft account across all devices. This approach simplifies syncing and keeps your task data consistent.

5. Backup Your Data

Although Microsoft To Do automatically syncs your data, it's a good practice to periodically back up your tasks and lists. Use Microsoft's cloud storage solutions or export your data if needed.

Syncing Microsoft To Do across devices is an essential aspect of maintaining an organized and productive workflow. By following the steps outlined in this section, troubleshooting common issues, and adhering to best practices, you can ensure that your task management system remains up-to-date and accessible, no matter where you are. As you integrate Microsoft To Do into your daily routine, seamless syncing will become a valuable component of your overall productivity strategy.

1.3 Understanding the GTD Methodology

1.3.1 Overview of Getting Things Done (GTD)

Getting Things Done (GTD) is a time management and productivity methodology developed by David Allen and detailed in his book, Getting Things Done: The Art of Stress-Free Productivity. This methodology is designed to help individuals and organizations achieve greater efficiency and effectiveness in managing their tasks and responsibilities. GTD is built around the principle of capturing and organizing tasks to reduce mental clutter and enhance focus, ultimately allowing users to achieve their goals more systematically.

The Core Principles of GTD

GTD is founded on a few core principles that form the basis of its approach to productivity:

1. Capture Everything: The first principle of GTD is to capture all tasks, ideas, and commitments into a trusted system. This involves recording everything that requires attention, from work projects to personal errands. The goal is to empty your mind of these items, reducing mental clutter and enabling you to focus on the tasks at hand.

2. Clarify and Process: Once tasks are captured, the next step is to clarify and process them. This involves deciding what each item is and determining the next action required to move it forward. For tasks that require more than one step, it's essential to break them down into actionable items and assign them to relevant projects.

3. Organize: After processing, tasks and projects need to be organized into a structured system. This includes creating lists for different contexts (such as work, home, or errands), categorizing tasks by project, and setting priorities. The organization phase ensures that tasks are easy to access and manage, improving overall productivity.

4. Reflect and Review: Regular review is a critical component of GTD. This involves weekly reviews of your lists and projects to ensure that tasks are up-to-date, priorities are aligned, and nothing is falling through the cracks. Reflecting on your progress helps to adjust plans and stay on track with goals.

5. Engage and Execute: The final principle is to engage with your tasks based on the context, time available, and priority. With a well-organized system, you can focus on executing tasks

efficiently, knowing that your system has captured and organized everything you need to address.

The GTD Workflow

The GTD workflow is a step-by-step process that helps manage tasks and projects systematically:

1. Collection: Collect all tasks, ideas, and commitments into an inbox or capture tool. This could be a physical inbox, a digital note-taking app, or any method that allows you to gather everything that needs your attention.

2. Processing: Process each item in your inbox by asking the question, "What is this?" Determine whether it's actionable and, if so, decide the next step. If the task requires less than two minutes, do it immediately. Otherwise, decide if it should be delegated, deferred, or filed for reference.

3. Organizing: Sort actionable items into appropriate lists or categories. Common GTD lists include "Next Actions" for tasks that can be done immediately, "Projects" for tasks requiring multiple steps, and "Waiting For" for items delegated to others.

4. Reviewing: Conduct a weekly review of your lists and projects. Ensure that everything is current, relevant, and properly categorized. Update your lists, reassess priorities, and plan for the coming week.

5. Doing: With your system in place, focus on executing tasks based on the context, time, and energy levels. Use your organized lists to guide your work, making informed decisions on what to tackle next.

Benefits of the GTD Methodology

Implementing GTD can yield several benefits:

- Reduced Stress: By capturing and organizing tasks, you reduce the mental burden of remembering everything. This leads to lower stress levels and a clearer mind.

- Enhanced Focus: GTD helps prioritize tasks, ensuring that you focus on what's most important. With a structured system, you can better manage your time and attention.

- Improved Productivity: The systematic approach to task management promotes efficiency. By breaking tasks into actionable steps and organizing them effectively, you can accomplish more in less time.

- Better Time Management: GTD's emphasis on regular review and organization helps manage time more effectively. You can allocate your time based on priorities and deadlines, leading to better overall productivity.

- Increased Accountability: With a clear system in place, you have a better grasp of your commitments and responsibilities. This leads to increased accountability and follow-through on tasks and projects.

Challenges and Considerations

While GTD offers numerous benefits, it also comes with challenges:

- Implementation: Setting up a GTD system requires initial effort and discipline. It may take time to adapt to new habits and fully integrate the methodology into your routine.

- Consistency: Maintaining a GTD system requires regular updates and reviews. Inconsistent use of the methodology can lead to missed tasks and decreased effectiveness.

- Tool Selection: Choosing the right tools to support GTD is crucial. Whether using digital apps or physical planners, the tools must align with your preferences and workflow.

Conclusion

Getting Things Done (GTD) is a comprehensive productivity methodology that helps individuals and organizations manage tasks effectively. By capturing, clarifying, organizing, reviewing, and executing tasks, GTD provides a structured approach to achieving goals and enhancing productivity. While implementing GTD requires effort and consistency, the benefits of reduced stress, enhanced focus, and improved productivity make it a valuable framework for managing your work and personal responsibilities.

Understanding and applying the GTD methodology within tools like Microsoft To Do can transform how you handle your tasks, leading to a more organized and productive life.

1.3.2 Applying GTD Principles in Microsoft To Do

The Getting Things Done (GTD) methodology, developed by David Allen, is a popular approach to managing tasks and improving productivity. It emphasizes capturing tasks, clarifying their meaning, organizing them into actionable items, reflecting on your progress, and engaging with your tasks effectively. Microsoft To Do is a powerful tool that can help you implement these GTD principles efficiently. In this section, we'll explore how to apply each GTD principle using Microsoft To Do to enhance your productivity and manage your tasks effectively.

Capturing and Collecting Tasks

The first step in GTD is to capture all tasks, ideas, and commitments in a reliable system. Microsoft To Do provides several features to help you capture and collect tasks:

1. Using the My Day Feature

   The My Day feature allows you to focus on a selected set of tasks each day. To capture tasks in My Day, you can add tasks to your list throughout the day, and then review and select the most important ones to include in My Day. This approach helps you concentrate on your daily priorities without being overwhelmed by the entire task list.

2. Creating Quick Add Tasks

   Microsoft To Do's Quick Add feature is designed for fast task entry. By clicking the "+ Add a task" button, you can quickly enter new tasks and set due dates, reminders, and notes. This feature is ideal for capturing tasks on the fly without needing to delve into detailed task management.

3. Using Email Integration

   You can forward emails to Microsoft To Do to create tasks from your email messages. This integration ensures that important tasks and follow-ups from your inbox are captured and added to your task list, helping you stay organized and ensuring nothing falls through the cracks.

Clarifying and Defining Tasks

Once tasks are captured, the next step is to clarify what needs to be done and define actionable steps. Microsoft To Do offers tools to help you clarify and detail your tasks:

1. Adding Details and Subtasks

Microsoft To Do allows you to add details to each task, including descriptions, attachments, and subtasks. By breaking down tasks into smaller, actionable steps, you can clarify what needs to be done and make large projects more manageable. For example, if you have a task like "Plan marketing campaign," you can add subtasks such as "Draft campaign strategy," "Create social media calendar," and "Design promotional materials."

2. Setting Due Dates and Reminders

Assigning due dates and setting reminders in Microsoft To Do helps you clarify deadlines and stay on track. By setting due dates, you establish a timeline for each task, while reminders ensure you are alerted before deadlines. This approach aligns with GTD's focus on clear and actionable tasks.

3. Using Categories and Tags

Organize tasks with categories and tags to clarify their context. Microsoft To Do allows you to assign tags to tasks, making it easier to group and filter tasks based on specific criteria. For instance, you might use tags like "Urgent," "Work," or "Personal" to categorize tasks and quickly identify related items.

Organizing Tasks into Projects and Actionable Steps

Organizing tasks is a critical part of GTD, and Microsoft To Do provides several ways to manage and organize your tasks effectively:

1. Creating and Managing Lists

Microsoft To Do allows you to create multiple lists to organize tasks by project, category, or context. For example, you might create separate lists for "Work Projects," "Personal Goals," and "Shopping." Each list can contain tasks that are relevant to that category, helping you maintain a structured approach to task management.

2. Using Smart Lists

Smart Lists in Microsoft To Do automatically organize tasks based on specific criteria. For instance, the "Important" list aggregates tasks marked with high priority, while the

"Planned" list shows tasks with set due dates. These smart lists help you focus on the most relevant tasks and keep track of deadlines.

3. Grouping Tasks by Project

Organizing tasks into projects or groups is essential for managing complex tasks and ensuring that all related items are addressed. In Microsoft To Do, you can create groups or projects and add tasks to them. This organization helps you keep track of progress on larger projects and ensures that related tasks are managed cohesively.

Reflecting and Reviewing Tasks

Regular reflection and review are key components of the GTD methodology. Microsoft To Do supports these practices through various features:

1. Conducting Daily Reviews

Use the My Day feature to review your daily tasks and plan your day. At the end of each day, reflect on what you've accomplished and adjust your task list for the next day. This regular review helps you stay on top of your tasks and ensures that your daily priorities are aligned with your overall goals.

2. Weekly Reviews

Perform a weekly review to assess your progress, update task lists, and plan for the upcoming week. Microsoft To Do's "Planned" list and completed tasks view can help you review what has been achieved and what still needs attention. Regularly reviewing your tasks helps you stay organized and ensures that you are moving towards your goals.

3. Tracking Progress and Adjusting Plans

Use Microsoft To Do's task completion features to track progress. Completed tasks are moved to the "Completed" list, allowing you to see what you've accomplished. This tracking helps you evaluate your productivity and adjust your plans as needed. If certain tasks or projects are falling behind, you can reorganize and reprioritize them to get back on track.

Engaging with Tasks Effectively

The final principle of GTD is engaging with tasks in a productive manner. Microsoft To Do provides tools to help you stay focused and engaged with your tasks:

1. Setting Up Focus Sessions

Use the "My Day" feature to focus on a select number of tasks each day. By choosing a manageable number of tasks to work on, you can concentrate on completing them without feeling overwhelmed. This focus approach aligns with the GTD principle of engaging with tasks in a deliberate and manageable way.

2. Utilizing Notifications and Reminders

Microsoft To Do's notifications and reminders help you stay on top of deadlines and important tasks. Set reminders for specific tasks to ensure you're alerted at the right time. These reminders help you stay focused and ensure that important tasks are completed on schedule.

3. Integrating with Other Microsoft 365 Tools

Integrate Microsoft To Do with other Microsoft 365 tools, such as Outlook and Teams, to streamline your task management. For example, tasks from Outlook can be synced with Microsoft To Do, allowing you to manage all your tasks in one place. Integration with Teams enables you to collaborate on tasks and share updates with your team.

By applying the GTD principles in Microsoft To Do, you can create a robust task management system that enhances your productivity and helps you stay organized. Microsoft To Do's features and tools are designed to support each stage of the GTD methodology, from capturing and clarifying tasks to organizing, reflecting, and engaging effectively. Implementing these principles in your daily routine will enable you to achieve your goals more efficiently and maintain control over your tasks and projects.

1.3.3 Benefits of Using GTD with Microsoft To Do

Integrating the Getting Things Done (GTD) methodology with Microsoft To Do can transform how you approach task management, productivity, and personal organization. The combination of GTD's structured approach with the practical features of Microsoft To Do offers numerous advantages. Here's a deep dive into the benefits of using GTD with Microsoft To Do:

Enhanced Task Organization

One of the most significant benefits of applying GTD principles in Microsoft To Do is the enhanced organization of tasks. GTD promotes the systematic capture and categorization of tasks, which aligns perfectly with Microsoft To Do's capabilities. By using lists, tags, and priority settings in Microsoft To Do, you can effectively organize tasks into actionable categories.

- Organized Lists and Projects: GTD advocates for breaking tasks into projects and next actions. In Microsoft To Do, you can create separate lists for each project, allowing you to compartmentalize your tasks. For instance, you could have a list for "Marketing Campaign" and another for "Product Launch." Each list can then be populated with specific tasks and subtasks, ensuring that everything is organized and easily accessible.

- Contextual Tags: GTD emphasizes the use of contexts (e.g., "Phone Calls," "Office," "Errands") to group tasks. Microsoft To Do supports tagging, which allows you to assign contextual tags to tasks. This makes it easier to filter and focus on tasks based on where you are or what tools you have available. For example, you can tag tasks as "High Priority" or "Waiting On Others," streamlining your workflow.

Improved Focus and Productivity

GTD helps in maintaining focus by breaking tasks into smaller, manageable actions and setting clear priorities. Microsoft To Do complements this by offering features that support focus and productivity.

- My Day Feature: The "My Day" feature in Microsoft To Do allows you to select tasks from your various lists to focus on for the day. This aligns with GTD's principle of focusing on next actions. By curating your daily tasks, you ensure that your attention is directed towards the most important and immediate tasks, enhancing productivity.

- Prioritization and Due Dates: GTD encourages prioritization and scheduling. Microsoft To Do provides options to set due dates and assign priorities to tasks. This ensures that critical tasks are highlighted and completed on time. Tasks marked with high priority or urgent deadlines will stand out, helping you manage your workload effectively.

Seamless Integration and Synchronization

GTD is about managing tasks across various contexts and timeframes. Microsoft To Do's seamless integration with other Microsoft 365 tools enhances this capability.

- Integration with Outlook: Microsoft To Do integrates with Outlook, allowing tasks and deadlines to sync across platforms. This means that tasks created in Outlook can be viewed and managed in Microsoft To Do, and vice versa. This integration supports GTD's principle of keeping all your tasks and projects in one accessible location, reducing the risk of overlooking important items.

- Cross-Device Synchronization: With Microsoft To Do's cloud-based synchronization, your tasks are updated across all devices. Whether you're using a smartphone, tablet, or computer, your tasks are always up-to-date. This aligns with GTD's emphasis on capturing tasks as they arise and ensures that you can manage your tasks from anywhere, at any time.

Enhanced Review and Reflection

GTD places a strong emphasis on regular reviews to stay on top of tasks and projects. Microsoft To Do's features facilitate these reviews and reflections.

- Completed Tasks View: The ability to review completed tasks is crucial for reflection and tracking progress. Microsoft To Do offers a "Completed" view where you can see tasks that have been finished. This helps in assessing accomplishments, understanding what's been done, and planning for future tasks.

- Customizable Views: You can customize views in Microsoft To Do to match your review needs. For example, creating a view that shows tasks by due date or priority helps in conducting weekly reviews, a core aspect of GTD. This helps in identifying tasks that need immediate attention or adjusting your plans based on current progress.

Streamlined Task Capture

GTD emphasizes capturing tasks as soon as they arise to ensure nothing is forgotten. Microsoft To Do supports this through its user-friendly task capture features.

- Quick Add Feature: Microsoft To Do's quick add functionality allows you to rapidly enter tasks without needing to navigate through multiple screens. This is ideal for capturing tasks on the go, aligning with GTD's principle of immediate task capture.

- Integration with Other Apps: Microsoft To Do integrates with other Microsoft 365 apps, such as OneNote and Teams. This allows you to capture tasks and ideas from various sources and consolidate them in one place, supporting GTD's focus on having a trusted system for all your tasks and projects.

Effective Collaboration and Sharing

GTD is not only about individual productivity but also about managing collaborative projects effectively. Microsoft To Do supports collaboration and sharing, which is essential for team projects.

- Shared Lists: Microsoft To Do allows you to share lists with others, making it easier to collaborate on projects. This feature is beneficial for team-based GTD systems, where tasks are assigned and tracked collectively. Shared lists ensure that everyone involved in a project is on the same page, with tasks and deadlines clearly communicated.

- Task Assignments: For collaborative projects, you can assign tasks to team members. This aligns with GTD's principle of defining clear next actions and accountability. Each team member can see their assigned tasks and track their progress, contributing to overall project success.

Increased Accountability and Motivation

GTD promotes accountability by defining clear next actions and setting achievable goals. Microsoft To Do enhances this by offering features that track progress and motivate completion.

- Task Progress Tracking: Microsoft To Do allows you to track the progress of tasks through completion percentages and status updates. This feature supports GTD's emphasis on tracking and reviewing progress, helping you stay motivated and accountable for completing tasks.

- Reminders and Notifications: Setting reminders and notifications in Microsoft To Do ensures that you don't miss important deadlines. This feature aligns with GTD's principle of timely action, keeping you on track and preventing procrastination.

Adaptability and Flexibility

GTD's principles are adaptable to various workflows and personal preferences. Microsoft To Do's flexibility supports this adaptability.

- Customizable Lists and Categories: You can create and customize lists in Microsoft To Do to fit your specific needs. Whether you follow a traditional GTD approach or adapt it to your unique workflow, Microsoft To Do provides the flexibility to set up your task management system in a way that works best for you.

- Integration with Personal and Professional Tasks: Microsoft To Do allows you to manage both personal and professional tasks in one place. This adaptability supports GTD's holistic approach to task management, where all tasks are captured and managed in a unified system.

By leveraging the benefits of GTD with Microsoft To Do, you can enhance your task management, improve productivity, and achieve your goals more effectively. The integration of GTD's structured approach with Microsoft To Do's practical features creates a powerful combination that supports organized, efficient, and goal-oriented task management.

CHAPTER II
Setting Up Your Tasks and Lists

2.1 Creating and Managing Tasks

2.1.1 Adding New Tasks

Adding tasks in Microsoft To Do is a fundamental feature that helps you get started with organizing your workload. This section will guide you through the various methods and best practices for adding new tasks, ensuring that you can efficiently capture and manage all your tasks within the app.

1. Understanding the Task Input Interface

When you first open Microsoft To Do, you'll see a clean, user-friendly interface with a prominent input field where you can quickly add tasks. This is often located at the top of the task list or in a designated section for new tasks. The interface is designed to be intuitive, allowing you to start typing and hit enter to add a new task. This simplicity is key for quickly capturing tasks as they come to mind.

2. Basic Task Entry

To add a new task, click on the "Add a task" field or the "+" button. Here's a step-by-step process:

- Click or Tap on the Input Field: Depending on whether you're using a desktop or mobile device, click or tap on the area labeled "Add a task" or a similar prompt.

- Type Your Task: Enter a brief description of the task you want to accomplish. Be as specific as possible to make it easier to understand later. For example, instead of writing "Call," specify "Call John about the project update."

- Press Enter or Click Add: Once you've typed in your task, press Enter or click the "Add" button to save it. The task will then appear in your task list.

3. Adding Details to Your Task

Microsoft To Do allows you to add more details to each task to ensure that you have all the necessary information at your fingertips. To do this:

- Select the Task: Click on the task you just created to open the task details pane. This is where you can add more information.

- Add Due Dates: Click on the calendar icon to set a due date for the task. You can select a specific date and time, or simply choose "Today," "Tomorrow," or "Next Week." Setting due dates helps in scheduling and managing deadlines.

- Set Reminders: Click on the bell icon to set a reminder for the task. You can choose a specific date and time for the reminder to alert you, ensuring you don't forget important deadlines.

- Add Notes: Use the notes section to provide additional details about the task. This is helpful for including instructions, links, or other relevant information that you need to complete the task.

- Attach Files: If necessary, you can attach files or documents related to the task by clicking on the attachment icon. This can be useful for tasks that require reference materials or documents.

4. Using Task Lists and Categories

For better organization, you can categorize tasks by adding them to specific lists or assigning them to categories:

- Create a New List: To create a new list, click on "Add a list" or a similar option, then enter a name for the list. For instance, you might create lists for "Work," "Personal," or "Groceries."

- Add Tasks to Lists: When creating a new task, you can assign it to one of your existing lists by selecting the list from a dropdown menu or a selection box.

- Use Categories or Tags: Some versions of Microsoft To Do allow for tagging or categorizing tasks with labels or colors. This can help you quickly identify related tasks and prioritize them accordingly.

5. Task Repetition and Recurrence

For tasks that need to be repeated on a regular basis, Microsoft To Do offers recurrence options:

- Set Recurrence: When adding or editing a task, click on the "Repeat" option. You can choose to repeat the task daily, weekly, monthly, or at custom intervals. This is ideal for tasks such as daily meetings, weekly reports, or monthly reviews.

- Customize Recurrence: You can customize recurrence by specifying exact days of the week, dates, or other patterns. For example, you might set a task to repeat every Monday and Wednesday.

6. Managing Task Priorities

Assigning priorities to tasks helps in distinguishing between tasks based on their importance and urgency:

- Set Priority Levels: To set a priority level, click on the task and select the priority options (e.g., Important, Medium, or Low). This helps in focusing on high-priority tasks first.

- Visual Cues: Microsoft To Do uses visual indicators such as stars or color-coding to represent task priorities, making it easy to see at a glance which tasks are most critical.

7. Keyboard Shortcuts and Quick Add

For users who prefer using keyboard shortcuts, Microsoft To Do supports several shortcuts to streamline task creation:

- Quick Task Addition: Use keyboard shortcuts like `Ctrl + Shift + T` (on some versions) to quickly add a new task without navigating away from your current screen.

- Editing and Managing Tasks: Familiarize yourself with shortcuts for task management, such as `Ctrl + Enter` to save a new task or `Ctrl + Shift + D` to mark a task as complete.

8. Integrating with Other Microsoft Apps

Microsoft To Do integrates seamlessly with other Microsoft 365 applications:

- Outlook Integration: Tasks created in Microsoft To Do can be synced with Outlook, allowing you to manage your tasks directly from your email client.

- Teams Integration: You can also integrate tasks with Microsoft Teams, which enables collaborative task management and keeps everyone on the same page.

9. Synchronizing Tasks Across Devices

One of the advantages of Microsoft To Do is its ability to sync tasks across multiple devices:

- Automatic Syncing: Tasks are automatically synced to the cloud, ensuring that any changes you make on one device are reflected on all your other devices.

- Offline Access: You can still access and modify your tasks offline, and changes will be synced once you reconnect to the internet.

10. Best Practices for Effective Task Management

To make the most out of adding new tasks, consider these best practices:

- Be Specific: Write clear and specific task descriptions to avoid ambiguity.

- Regular Updates: Regularly review and update your tasks to reflect any changes in priorities or deadlines.

- Utilize Reminders: Set reminders for tasks to ensure you stay on track and meet deadlines.

- Organize with Lists: Use lists to categorize and organize tasks based on different projects or areas of your life.

By mastering the art of adding new tasks in Microsoft To Do, you'll be able to keep track of your responsibilities, manage your time effectively, and achieve your goals with greater efficiency. Continue exploring the features and options available to tailor your task management system to suit your needs and preferences.

2.1.2 Setting Due Dates and Reminders

Effective task management goes beyond simply creating tasks. Setting due dates and reminders ensures that tasks are completed on time and helps you stay organized. In

Microsoft To Do, these features are designed to assist you in managing your workload efficiently and preventing tasks from slipping through the cracks.

Understanding Due Dates

A due date is a specific date by which a task needs to be completed. Setting due dates in Microsoft To Do helps you prioritize tasks and ensures that you allocate appropriate time to each task. Here's how to effectively use due dates to manage your tasks:

1. Assigning a Due Date:

   - To assign a due date to a task, open Microsoft To Do and locate the task you want to manage. Click on the task to open its details.

   - In the task details pane, you'll see an option to add a due date. Click on the calendar icon to select a specific date. You can choose from a calendar view or type the date manually.

   - Once selected, the due date will be visible on the task card, helping you track deadlines easily.

2. Using Due Dates to Prioritize Tasks:

   - Assign due dates based on task priority and urgency. Tasks with imminent deadlines should be scheduled earlier in your day or week.

   - Use Microsoft To Do's sorting and filtering features to view tasks by their due dates, making it easier to focus on urgent tasks.

3. Adjusting Due Dates:

   - If a task's deadline changes, you can easily adjust the due date. Open the task details and modify the date as needed. Microsoft To Do will update the task accordingly.

   - Adjust due dates proactively to avoid last-minute rushes. Regularly review your tasks and their due dates to ensure that everything is on track.

4. Recurring Tasks with Due Dates:

   - For tasks that repeat regularly, you can set recurring due dates. In the task details pane, choose the "Repeat" option and select the frequency (daily, weekly, monthly, etc.).

   - Recurring due dates help automate the process of setting deadlines for repetitive tasks, ensuring that you don't forget them.

Setting Reminders

Reminders are notifications that alert you when a task is approaching its due date or requires your attention. Setting reminders helps you stay on top of your tasks and ensures that you meet deadlines. Here's how to use reminders effectively in Microsoft To Do:

1. Adding a Reminder:

  - To add a reminder to a task, open the task details pane by clicking on the task. Look for the reminder icon (a bell symbol).

  - Click on the reminder icon and choose a specific time for the reminder. You can set reminders for the task's due date or choose a custom date and time.

  - Reminders will appear as notifications on your device, helping you remember to complete the task.

2. Customizing Reminder Notifications:

  - Customize the notification settings for reminders to suit your preferences. Microsoft To Do allows you to choose how and when you receive notifications, such as through email or push notifications.

  - Set multiple reminders for a task if necessary. For example, you can set an initial reminder a day before the due date and a final reminder an hour before the task is due.

3. Managing Reminders:

  - Review and manage your reminders regularly. In the Microsoft To Do app, you can view all upcoming reminders and adjust them as needed.

  - Dismiss or snooze reminders if you're not ready to tackle the task immediately. You can choose to be reminded again later, ensuring that you don't miss important deadlines.

4. Using Reminders for Follow-Ups:

  - Set reminders for follow-up actions related to a task. For example, if you need to review a document after completing a task, set a reminder to follow up on that review.

  - Use reminders to track progress on long-term projects. Set periodic reminders to review the status of ongoing tasks and make adjustments as necessary.

Best Practices for Setting Due Dates and Reminders

1. Be Realistic:

   - Set due dates and reminders that are realistic and achievable. Avoid setting overly tight deadlines that may lead to stress or incomplete tasks.

   - Assess your workload and capacity before assigning due dates. Consider factors such as task complexity, dependencies, and your availability.

2. Plan Ahead:

   - Use due dates and reminders as part of your overall planning strategy. Set deadlines well in advance to avoid last-minute pressure and ensure that you have ample time to complete tasks.

   - Plan your day or week by reviewing tasks with upcoming due dates and reminders. Prioritize tasks based on their deadlines and urgency.

3. Regularly Review and Adjust:

   - Regularly review your tasks, due dates, and reminders to ensure that they align with your goals and priorities. Make adjustments as needed to reflect changes in your schedule or task requirements.

   - Conduct periodic reviews to assess your progress and make necessary changes to deadlines and reminders.

4. Leverage Smart Lists:

   - Use Microsoft To Do's Smart Lists to automate task management. Smart Lists can automatically display tasks based on criteria such as due dates, importance, or tags.

   - Create custom Smart Lists to group tasks with upcoming due dates or reminders. This helps you stay focused on tasks that require immediate attention.

5. Avoid Overloading:

   - Be cautious not to overload yourself with too many tasks and reminders. Focus on high-priority tasks and avoid setting excessive reminders that may lead to notification fatigue.

   - Balance your task list and reminders to maintain productivity and reduce stress. Ensure that your reminders are meaningful and relevant to your goals.

Integrating Due Dates and Reminders into Your Workflow

1. Combining Due Dates and Reminders:

 - Use due dates and reminders in conjunction with other task management features. For example, combine due dates with tags and priorities to create a comprehensive task management system.

 - Ensure that reminders align with due dates to provide timely notifications and avoid missing deadlines.

2. Syncing Across Devices:

 - Ensure that due dates and reminders sync seamlessly across all your devices. Microsoft To Do offers cross-platform support, allowing you to access and manage tasks from various devices.

 - Verify that notifications and reminders are configured correctly on each device to receive consistent alerts.

3. Reviewing Task Status:

 - Regularly review the status of tasks with due dates and reminders. Check completed tasks to confirm that deadlines were met and adjust future due dates based on your experience.

 - Use task status reviews to identify patterns and make improvements in your task management approach.

Conclusion

Setting due dates and reminders in Microsoft To Do is crucial for effective task management and achieving your goals. By assigning specific deadlines and configuring timely notifications, you can stay organized, prioritize tasks, and ensure that nothing falls through the cracks. Incorporate these practices into your workflow to enhance productivity and maintain control over your tasks and projects.

As you continue to use Microsoft To Do, remember to regularly review and adjust due dates and reminders to stay aligned with your goals and deadlines. With proper management,

Microsoft To Do can become a powerful tool in your task management arsenal, helping you get things done efficiently and effectively.

2.1.3 Organizing Tasks with Tags

Effective task management in Microsoft To Do is not just about creating tasks and setting due dates; it also involves organizing and categorizing tasks to make them easier to manage and prioritize. Tags are a powerful feature in Microsoft To Do that help you add additional layers of organization to your task management system. In this section, we'll delve into how you can leverage tags to enhance your task organization and improve your productivity.

What Are Tags?

Tags in Microsoft To Do are keywords or labels that you can assign to tasks to categorize them based on context, priority, project, or any other criteria that suit your workflow. Unlike traditional lists and groups, tags offer a flexible way to label tasks with multiple attributes. For example, you might tag tasks with labels like "Urgent," "Meeting," "Follow-up," or "Personal," depending on their nature and urgency.

Benefits of Using Tags

1. Enhanced Organization: Tags allow you to organize tasks across different lists and groups. For instance, you can tag tasks related to a specific project or context, making it easy to filter and view tasks related to that tag.

2. Improved Filtering and Searching: Tags improve your ability to filter and search for tasks. When you apply tags, you can quickly locate tasks associated with a specific tag without needing to manually sift through various lists.

3. Flexibility and Customization: Tags offer a customizable way to categorize tasks beyond the structure of lists and groups. You can create and use tags that fit your personal or professional needs, allowing for a tailored task management system.

4. Quick Access to Related Tasks: By using tags, you can create focused views of tasks that share common characteristics, helping you stay organized and manage your workload more effectively.

Creating and Managing Tags

1. Adding Tags to Tasks

Adding tags to tasks is a straightforward process. Here's how you can do it:

- Open Microsoft To Do: Start by opening the Microsoft To Do app on your device.

- Select a Task: Choose the task you want to tag from your list. If you haven't created the task yet, you can do so by clicking on "Add a task" and entering the task details.

- Edit Task Details: Click on the task to open its details. In the task details view, you will see an option to add tags. This is typically found under the "Add a tag" or "Tags" section.

- Add Your Tags: Type in the tag you want to add. You can use existing tags or create new ones. For example, you might add "Urgent" to indicate that the task needs immediate attention or "Project X" to associate it with a specific project.

- Save Changes: After adding the desired tags, make sure to save or close the task details view to apply the changes.

2. Editing and Removing Tags

If you need to update or remove tags from tasks, follow these steps:

- Open Task Details: Select the task with the tags you want to modify.

- Edit Tags: In the task details view, click on the tag you want to change. You can either type in a new tag or select a different tag from the list.

- Remove Tags: To remove a tag, click on the tag and look for an option to delete or remove it. This will disassociate the tag from the task.

- Save Changes: Ensure that you save any changes made to the tags by closing or updating the task details view.

3. Creating Custom Tags

Custom tags allow you to personalize your task management system based on your specific needs. Here's how to create and use custom tags:

- Identify Your Needs: Think about the various contexts or attributes that are relevant to your tasks. For example, you might want tags for different types of work, urgency levels, or team responsibilities.

- Create Custom Tags: When adding a tag to a task, you can type in any label that fits your needs. For instance, you could create tags like "Client A," "Marketing Campaign," or "Draft Review."

- Use Consistently: To maintain organization, use your custom tags consistently across tasks. This will help you keep track of related tasks and maintain a clear overview of your workload.

Using Tags for Task Prioritization and Organization

1. Filtering Tasks by Tags

One of the key advantages of tags is the ability to filter tasks based on their tags. To filter tasks:

- Open Your Task List: Go to the list where your tasks are stored.

- Use the Filter Option: Look for the filter or search option in the app. This is often represented by a funnel icon or a search bar.

- Select a Tag: Choose the tag you want to filter by. This will display all tasks associated with that tag, allowing you to focus on tasks with similar attributes.

- Review and Manage: Once filtered, you can review the tasks, prioritize them, and manage them accordingly.

2. Creating Tag-Based Views

For enhanced organization, consider creating tag-based views or perspectives. This involves grouping tasks by their tags to create focused views:

- Create a New View: Depending on the features of Microsoft To Do, you might have options to create custom views or use existing ones.

- Apply Tags to View: Set the view to display tasks with specific tags. For example, you could create a view for "High Priority" tasks or tasks associated with a particular project.

- Switch Between Views: Use these views to switch between different contexts or priorities, helping you stay organized and manage your tasks more effectively.

Best Practices for Using Tags

1. Be Consistent: Use a consistent tagging system to avoid confusion. Stick to a set of tags that you use regularly and ensure they are applied consistently across tasks.

2. Limit the Number of Tags: While it's tempting to create many tags, having too many can lead to clutter. Keep your tags focused and relevant to ensure they provide value.

3. Review and Update Tags Regularly: Periodically review your tags to ensure they still meet your needs. Remove or update tags that are no longer relevant to maintain an organized task management system.

4. Combine Tags with Other Features: Use tags in conjunction with other Microsoft To Do features, such as due dates, priorities, and lists, to create a comprehensive task management system.

5. Educate Your Team: If you're using Microsoft To Do for team collaboration, make sure everyone is aware of the tagging system and uses it consistently.

Examples of Effective Tag Use

- Project Management: Tag tasks related to specific projects, such as "Project Alpha" or "Website Redesign." This allows you to easily view all tasks associated with a project.

- Urgency Levels: Use tags like "Urgent," "High Priority," "Medium Priority," and "Low Priority" to categorize tasks based on their urgency.

- Task Types: Apply tags based on the type of task, such as "Meeting," "Research," "Development," or "Follow-up," to quickly identify and manage different types of tasks.

- Personal vs. Professional: Separate tasks into personal and professional categories using tags like "Personal" and "Work" to manage different aspects of your life.

By effectively using tags in Microsoft To Do, you can create a highly organized and efficient task management system that aligns with your personal or professional needs. Tags provide a flexible and customizable way to categorize and manage tasks, helping you stay focused and productive.

2.2 Creating Lists and Groups

2.2.1 Building Your First List

Creating a well-organized list is foundational to mastering task management with Microsoft To Do. Lists allow you to group tasks in a way that reflects your personal or professional priorities, making it easier to track progress and stay focused. In this section, we'll walk you through the steps of building your first list, including key considerations and best practices to ensure your list is effective and easy to manage.

1. Understanding Lists in Microsoft To Do

Before diving into the creation of your list, it's essential to understand what lists are and how they function within Microsoft To Do. Lists are essentially containers for your tasks, allowing you to group related tasks together. Each list can represent a project, a category of tasks, or even a daily or weekly agenda. By organizing your tasks into different lists, you can manage your workload more effectively and keep track of various aspects of your life or work.

2. Creating a New List

To create your first list, follow these steps:

1. Open Microsoft To Do: Launch the Microsoft To Do app on your device. Ensure you're logged in with your Microsoft account to access all features and sync your lists across devices.

2. Navigate to Lists: On the main screen of the app, you'll find the "Lists" section on the left sidebar. This is where all your existing lists will be displayed.

3. Add a New List:

   - Click on the "Add a list" button, usually represented by a plus icon (+) or a similar prompt.

   - A new dialog box or menu will appear, prompting you to enter the name of your list.

4. Name Your List: Choose a clear and descriptive name for your list. For instance, if you're creating a list for a specific project, name it accordingly (e.g., "Project X Tasks" or "Weekly Grocery List"). The name should reflect the purpose of the list to make it easier to identify and use.

5. Customize Your List:

   - Add a Color: You can choose a color for your list to make it visually distinct from others. This is particularly helpful if you have multiple lists and want to quickly identify them.

   - Add an Icon: Some versions of Microsoft To Do allow you to select an icon for your list, adding a visual element that can help you recognize the list at a glance.

3. Organizing Tasks Within the List

Once your list is created, you'll need to start adding tasks to it. Here's how to do that effectively:

1. Add New Tasks:

   - Click on the newly created list to open it.

   - Use the "Add a task" field to enter tasks. You can type the task description directly into the input box and press Enter to add it.

2. Set Due Dates and Reminders:

   - For each task, you can set due dates and reminders. Click on the task to open its details.

   - Use the "Due date" option to set a specific date and time when the task should be completed.

   - Add a reminder to receive a notification before the task is due. This helps you stay on top of deadlines and ensures you don't forget important tasks.

3. Add Notes and Files:

   - In the task details view, you can also add notes to provide additional context or instructions for each task.

   - Attach relevant files if needed, which can be helpful for tasks that involve documents or other resources.

4. Organize Tasks with Tags and Categories:

  - Tags can be used to categorize tasks within your list further. For example, you might use tags like "Urgent," "Follow-Up," or "Personal" to identify different types of tasks.

  - Apply tags by selecting the task and adding the desired tag in the task detail view.

4. Managing and Updating Your List

As you begin using your list, it's important to manage and update it regularly to keep it relevant and useful:

1. Review and Update Tasks:

  - Periodically review the tasks on your list to ensure they are up-to-date. Mark tasks as complete when finished, and adjust due dates or priorities as needed.

  - You can also edit or delete tasks if they are no longer relevant or need modification.

2. Reorganize Tasks:

  - If you find that tasks need to be reordered, you can drag and drop them within the list to rearrange their priority.

  - Use the "Sort" feature to organize tasks based on different criteria, such as due date or priority level.

3. Archive Completed Tasks:

  - To keep your list clean and focused, consider archiving or hiding completed tasks. This can help reduce clutter and make it easier to focus on outstanding tasks.

5. Best Practices for Building Effective Lists

To get the most out of your lists in Microsoft To Do, follow these best practices:

1. Be Specific with Task Descriptions:

  - Use clear and specific descriptions for each task. Vague descriptions can lead to confusion and reduce your efficiency.

2. Break Down Large Tasks:

- For larger projects, break tasks down into smaller, manageable steps. This makes it easier to track progress and stay motivated.

3. Regularly Review and Adjust Your Lists:

  - Make it a habit to review your lists regularly. Adjust priorities, add new tasks, and remove completed or irrelevant tasks to keep your lists current.

4. Use Multiple Lists Strategically:

  - Don't hesitate to create multiple lists to organize different aspects of your life or work. For example, you might have separate lists for personal tasks, work projects, and long-term goals.

5. Leverage Smart Lists and Filters:

  - Utilize smart lists and filters to automatically organize and view tasks based on specific criteria. This helps you stay organized and ensures that important tasks are always visible.

6. Examples of Effective Lists

To illustrate the versatility of lists in Microsoft To Do, here are a few examples:

1. Project Management List:

  - Name: "Project X Tasks"

  - Description: Includes tasks related to a specific project, with due dates, priorities, and assigned team members.

2. Daily To-Do List:

  - Name: "Today's Tasks"

  - Description: A daily list of tasks to be completed today, with reminders and deadlines to ensure timely completion.

3. Personal Goals List:

  - Name: "Personal Goals"

  - Description: A list for tracking personal goals and milestones, such as fitness objectives or learning new skills.

4. Shopping List:

  - Name: "Grocery List"

  - Description: A list for keeping track of items to purchase, organized by category (e.g., fruits, vegetables, dairy).

7. Conclusion

Building your first list in Microsoft To Do is the first step toward a more organized and productive workflow. By following the steps outlined above and applying best practices, you'll be well on your way to managing your tasks efficiently and effectively. Remember, the key to successful task management is consistency and regular updates, so keep refining your lists and adapting them to your needs.

As you become more familiar with Microsoft To Do, you'll find that lists can be a powerful tool in your productivity arsenal, helping you stay on top of your tasks and achieve your goals with ease.

2.2.2 Grouping Lists for Better Organization

In the realm of task management, the ability to group lists effectively is crucial for maintaining clarity, reducing overwhelm, and enhancing overall productivity. Microsoft To Do offers a flexible system that allows users to create groups of lists, making it easier to categorize tasks, manage different areas of life or work, and stay on top of various projects simultaneously.

Understanding the Purpose of Grouping Lists

Grouping lists in Microsoft To Do is more than just a way to keep your tasks in order—it's a strategic method to streamline your workflow. By organizing related tasks into specific groups, you can easily navigate through your tasks, focus on particular areas without distraction, and ensure that nothing falls through the cracks.

For instance, if you're juggling multiple projects at work while also managing personal tasks, grouping lists can help you separate work-related tasks from personal ones. This separation allows you to focus more effectively on the tasks at hand, whether you're working on a major project or planning a weekend getaway.

Strategic Grouping: Approaches and Best Practices

There are several approaches to grouping lists in Microsoft To Do, each tailored to different types of users and work styles. Below are some of the most common strategies, along with their respective advantages and practical tips for implementation.

1. Grouping by Project or Area of Responsibility

One of the most straightforward ways to group lists is by project or area of responsibility. This approach is ideal for professionals managing multiple projects simultaneously, as it allows you to keep all related tasks in one place.

For example:

- Project Alpha: Contains all tasks related to the Alpha project, including research, development, and client meetings.

- Project Beta: Contains all tasks related to the Beta project, such as marketing, design, and implementation.

- Personal Tasks: Group for personal tasks, such as grocery shopping, exercise, and home maintenance.

Within each group, you can create specific lists that focus on different aspects of the project or responsibility. This structure ensures that you have a clear overview of what needs to be done within each area, helping you prioritize and manage your workload more effectively.

2. Grouping by Context

Grouping by context is particularly useful for those following the Getting Things Done (GTD) methodology, where tasks are organized based on the context in which they can be completed. This method ensures that when you're in a specific situation or environment, you can quickly access the tasks that are relevant to that context.

For example:

- @Work: Tasks that need to be completed while at the office or during work hours.

- @Home: Tasks that can be done at home, such as household chores or personal projects.

- @Errands: Tasks that require you to be out and about, like picking up groceries or visiting the post office.

- @Online: Tasks that require internet access, such as researching a topic or sending emails.

By grouping lists by context, you can reduce the mental load of deciding what to do next. When you're at work, you can focus solely on your @Work list, and when you're out running errands, you can check off tasks from your @Errands list.

3. Grouping by Timeframe

Grouping tasks by timeframe is another effective way to organize your lists. This approach is particularly helpful for managing deadlines and ensuring that you're focusing on tasks that are time-sensitive.

For example:

- This Week: Tasks that need to be completed within the current week.

- This Month: Tasks with deadlines later in the month, which require long-term planning.

- Next Month: Tasks that are scheduled for the upcoming month, allowing you to plan ahead.

- Someday/Maybe: Tasks that don't have a set deadline but are ideas or projects you'd like to tackle in the future.

By organizing tasks based on when they need to be completed, you can ensure that you're always on top of your deadlines and aren't overwhelmed by long-term projects that don't require immediate attention.

4. Grouping by Priority

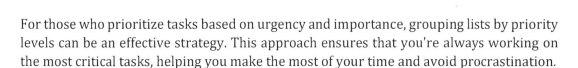

For those who prioritize tasks based on urgency and importance, grouping lists by priority levels can be an effective strategy. This approach ensures that you're always working on the most critical tasks, helping you make the most of your time and avoid procrastination.

For example:

- High Priority: Tasks that are urgent and need immediate attention.

- Medium Priority: Tasks that are important but not time-sensitive.

- Low Priority: Tasks that are neither urgent nor particularly important but still need to be completed.

Grouping by priority allows you to focus your energy on what matters most and ensures that critical tasks are addressed before they become urgent.

5. Grouping by Role or Responsibility

For those who wear multiple hats, whether in a professional or personal capacity, grouping lists by role or responsibility can be a great way to stay organized. This approach is particularly useful for individuals managing different aspects of a business, such as operations, marketing, and finance, or for parents juggling work and family responsibilities.

For example:

- Managerial Duties: Tasks related to overseeing team members, conducting meetings, and strategic planning.

- Marketing Tasks: Tasks focused on marketing efforts, including content creation, social media management, and campaign analysis.

- Finance Tasks: Tasks related to budgeting, financial reporting, and invoice management.

- Family Responsibilities: Tasks such as scheduling appointments, helping with homework, and planning family events.

By grouping tasks according to roles, you can ensure that you're giving appropriate attention to each area of responsibility and not neglecting any particular role.

Creating and Managing Groups in Microsoft To Do

Now that we've explored various strategies for grouping lists, let's dive into the practical steps for creating and managing groups in Microsoft To Do.

1. Creating a New Group

Creating a new group in Microsoft To Do is straightforward:

- Step 1: Open Microsoft To Do and navigate to the left-hand pane where your lists are displayed.

- Step 2: Click on the "New Group" option at the bottom of the pane.

- Step 3: Name your new group according to the strategy you've chosen, such as "Projects," "Contexts," or "Priorities."

- Step 4: Drag and drop existing lists into your new group or create new lists within the group.

This simple process allows you to quickly organize your tasks into cohesive groups, enhancing your ability to manage them effectively.

2. Managing and Rearranging Groups

Once you've created your groups, managing them is easy. You can rearrange groups to reflect changing priorities, rename them as needed, and move lists between groups.

- Rearranging Groups: Click and drag a group to a new position in the list pane. This is particularly useful if you want to keep certain groups, such as "High Priority" or "This Week," at the top of your task list for easy access.

- Renaming Groups: To rename a group, click on the group name, and a text box will appear allowing you to enter a new name.

- Moving Lists Between Groups: To move a list from one group to another, simply drag the list from its current group and drop it into the desired group.

These features make it easy to keep your task management system dynamic and responsive to your evolving needs.

3. Utilizing Subtasks Within Groups

Microsoft To Do also allows you to create subtasks within tasks, which can be an effective way to further organize complex projects or detailed tasks.

For example, within a group labeled "Project Alpha," you might have a list called "Marketing Campaign." Within that list, you can create a task called "Launch Social Media Campaign" and then add subtasks such as "Create Content Calendar," "Design Visual Assets," and "Schedule Posts."

Subtasks are an excellent way to break down larger tasks into manageable steps, making it easier to track progress and ensure that all components of a task are completed.

4. Using Smart Lists for Dynamic Grouping

Microsoft To Do's Smart Lists are a powerful feature that automatically groups tasks based on certain criteria, such as due date, flagged status, or importance. Smart Lists like "My Day," "Important," and "Planned" are automatically updated as you add, modify, or complete tasks.

- My Day: A daily list that helps you focus on tasks you intend to complete today. You can add tasks to My Day from any group or list.

- Important: This Smart List groups all tasks marked as important with a star, regardless of which list or group they belong to.

- Planned: Tasks with due dates are automatically grouped in the Planned list, allowing you to see all time-sensitive tasks at a glance.

Smart Lists provide an additional layer of organization and can be used alongside your manually created groups to ensure that you never miss a critical task.

Examples of Effective Grouping in Different Scenarios

To illustrate the effectiveness of grouping lists, let's explore some practical examples in different contexts.

1. Corporate Project Management

In a corporate environment, where managing multiple projects and team members is common, grouping lists by project is highly effective. For example:

- Group 1: Project Alpha

  - List 1: Research & Development

  - List 2: Marketing & Sales

  - List 3: Client Relations

- Group 2: Project Beta

  - List 1: Product Design

  - List 2: Production & Logistics

  - List 3: Post-Launch Support

Each group contains lists that break down the various phases or departments involved in the project, ensuring that all aspects are accounted for and progress can be tracked within each area.

2. Personal Life Management

For managing personal life tasks, grouping by context or timeframe can help keep everything organized. For example:

- Group 1: This Week

  - List 1: Work Tasks

  - List 2: Personal Errands

  - List 3: Family Activities

- Group 2: Long-Term Goals

  - List 1: Career Development

  - List 2: Financial Planning

  - List 3: Home Improvement Projects

This structure allows you to focus on what needs to be done immediately while keeping long-term goals in view, ensuring that you maintain a balance between urgent tasks and long-term planning.

3. Freelance Work Management

For freelancers who manage multiple clients or projects, grouping lists by client or project can provide clarity and prevent tasks from getting mixed up. For example:

- Group 1: Client A

  - List 1: Content Writing

  - List 2: Social Media Management

  - List 3: Monthly Reporting

- Group 2: Client B

  - List 1: Web Design

  - List 2: SEO Optimization

  - List 3: Analytics & Reporting

By grouping tasks by client, freelancers can easily switch focus between clients and ensure that all deliverables are met on time.

Maximizing Productivity with Well-Organized Groups

Effective grouping of lists in Microsoft To Do can significantly enhance your productivity by providing a clear structure for managing your tasks. Whether you choose to group by project, context, timeframe, priority, or role, the key is to find a system that works for you and stick with it.

By regularly reviewing and adjusting your groups as needed, you can maintain an organized and efficient task management system that supports your goals and helps you achieve success in all areas of life.

Remember, the ultimate goal of grouping lists is to reduce complexity, increase focus, and streamline your workflow. As you continue to use Microsoft To Do, experiment with different grouping strategies to find the one that best fits your unique needs and work style.

2.2.3 Using Smart Lists to Automate Task Management

In the digital age, managing tasks effectively often involves more than just creating lists and setting reminders. To truly optimize productivity, automation becomes a key component. Microsoft To Do's Smart Lists feature is designed to help you streamline your workflow, reduce the manual effort required to manage tasks, and ensure that you stay on top of your priorities without constantly having to remember what needs to be done. Smart Lists are dynamically generated lists that gather tasks based on specific criteria, helping you focus on what matters most at any given time.

Understanding Smart Lists

Smart Lists in Microsoft To Do are pre-configured lists that automatically organize your tasks based on certain attributes. These attributes could be due dates, priority levels, or even tasks that you've marked for follow-up today. The beauty of Smart Lists lies in their ability to present a snapshot of your most critical tasks, allowing you to act on them promptly.

There are several default Smart Lists available in Microsoft To Do, including:

- My Day: A daily planner that encourages you to focus on what you intend to accomplish today.

- Important: A list that compiles tasks marked as important, helping you keep track of your top priorities.

- Planned: This list gathers all tasks with due dates, helping you stay ahead of upcoming deadlines.

- Assigned to Me: A list that consolidates all tasks assigned to you, particularly useful in collaborative environments.

- Tasks: A comprehensive list that includes all tasks across all lists, giving you an overview of everything on your plate.

Each of these Smart Lists plays a unique role in task management, and understanding how to leverage them can significantly enhance your productivity.

Configuring and Customizing Smart Lists

While Smart Lists are pre-configured, Microsoft To Do allows for a degree of customization to better suit your workflow. For instance, you can choose which Smart Lists to display in your navigation pane based on your preferences.

Displaying Smart Lists

To customize the visibility of Smart Lists:

1. Open Settings: Click on your profile picture or the three-dot menu in the top right corner to access the settings.

2. Navigate to Smart Lists: In the settings menu, locate the "Smart Lists" section.

3. Select Visible Smart Lists: Here, you can toggle the visibility of Smart Lists. For example, if you find yourself primarily working with tasks that have due dates, you might want to ensure that the "Planned" Smart List is always visible.

By tailoring the visibility of Smart Lists, you ensure that your Microsoft To Do interface is clean and focused on the areas that matter most to you.

Customizing My Day

The "My Day" feature is perhaps the most interactive of the Smart Lists, as it encourages daily planning and reflection. Unlike other Smart Lists that are automatically populated, "My Day" requires manual selection of tasks each day. This feature not only fosters intentionality in task management but also allows for a daily reset, ensuring that you're always focused on the most relevant tasks.

To customize your "My Day" experience:

1. Start Fresh Every Day: Each morning, your "My Day" list will be empty. This blank slate allows you to intentionally choose tasks that are most critical for the day ahead.

2. Suggestions: Microsoft To Do will suggest tasks based on upcoming due dates, tasks marked as important, or tasks left over from previous days. These suggestions are presented when you click on the "My Day" section, making it easy to populate your list with relevant tasks.

3. Drag and Drop: You can manually drag tasks from other lists into "My Day," giving you complete control over what you focus on each day.

This daily curation process helps you stay adaptable, ensuring that your daily plan reflects both your immediate priorities and any shifts in your workload.

Leveraging Smart Lists for Efficient Workflow Management

Once your Smart Lists are set up and customized, the next step is to integrate them into your daily and weekly routines. Smart Lists are not just about organizing tasks—they're about transforming how you approach your work.

Prioritizing with the Important List

The "Important" Smart List is particularly valuable for managing tasks that require your immediate attention. By marking a task as important, it automatically appears in this list, giving you a clear view of what needs to be prioritized.

Use Case Example: Imagine you're working on a project with multiple deadlines. By marking key tasks as important, you can use the "Important" Smart List to track these high-priority items across various projects, ensuring nothing critical slips through the cracks.

This list acts as a dynamic prioritization tool, allowing you to continually assess and adjust your focus as priorities shift.

Planning Ahead with the Planned List

The "Planned" Smart List is your go-to tool for deadline management. This list aggregates all tasks with due dates, presenting them in chronological order. This feature is especially useful for long-term planning and ensuring that you're always aware of upcoming deadlines.

Use Case Example: Suppose you're juggling several projects with overlapping deadlines. The "Planned" Smart List gives you a timeline view of all upcoming tasks, enabling you to allocate your time effectively and avoid last-minute scrambles.

By regularly reviewing your "Planned" Smart List, you can proactively manage your workload, ensuring that deadlines are met without unnecessary stress.

Managing Collaboration with the Assigned to Me List

In collaborative environments, keeping track of tasks assigned to you can be challenging, especially when working on multiple projects. The "Assigned to Me" Smart List consolidates all tasks assigned to you across different lists, making it easier to manage your responsibilities.

Use Case Example: You're part of a team working on a product launch, with tasks assigned across different departments. The "Assigned to Me" list helps you track your specific responsibilities, ensuring that you contribute effectively to the project's success.

This list not only helps in managing individual responsibilities but also ensures accountability within collaborative projects.

Comprehensive Task Management with the Tasks List

The "Tasks" Smart List provides an overview of all tasks across your lists, giving you a holistic view of your workload. This list is especially useful during weekly reviews, where you assess progress and plan for the week ahead.

Use Case Example: During your weekly review, you open the "Tasks" Smart List to get a complete picture of your workload. This helps you identify any tasks that may have slipped through the cracks and allows you to prioritize for the upcoming week.

By incorporating the "Tasks" Smart List into your routine, you ensure that no task is overlooked, leading to more effective and comprehensive task management.

Advanced Smart List Strategies

For those looking to further enhance their use of Smart Lists, there are several advanced strategies that can be employed to automate and optimize your workflow.

Combining Smart Lists with Filters and Tags

While Smart Lists are powerful on their own, combining them with filters and tags allows for even greater customization and efficiency.

Example: Create a custom view within the "Planned" Smart List that only shows tasks tagged with a specific project name. This allows you to focus on tasks related to a particular project, even if they span multiple lists.

By applying filters and tags, you can create highly tailored Smart Lists that align with your specific workflows and project needs.

Automating Workflows with Microsoft Power Automate

For advanced users, integrating Microsoft To Do with Microsoft Power Automate opens up a world of possibilities for automation. Power Automate allows you to create workflows that automatically add tasks to specific Smart Lists based on triggers or conditions.

Example: Set up a workflow where emails flagged in Outlook are automatically added to the "Important" Smart List in Microsoft To Do. This ensures that critical tasks are captured and prioritized without manual input.

These automations can save time, reduce manual effort, and ensure consistency in how tasks are managed across different platforms.

Creating Custom Smart Lists

While Microsoft To Do's Smart Lists are powerful, there may be times when you need a custom list that isn't covered by the default options. While Microsoft To Do doesn't currently allow for custom Smart Lists in the same way that other tools like Microsoft Planner do, you can simulate this functionality using tags, filters, and custom views.

Example: Create a custom list that shows all tasks tagged with "Urgent" and "High Priority," sorted by due date. This can act as a pseudo-Smart List focused on your most critical tasks.

Although this requires more manual setup, it can be a powerful way to tailor Microsoft To Do to your specific needs.

Conclusion: Maximizing Productivity with Smart Lists

Smart Lists in Microsoft To Do are more than just a feature—they're a fundamental tool for automating and optimizing your task management. By understanding how to configure, customize, and leverage these lists, you can significantly enhance your productivity, ensuring that you're always focused on the right tasks at the right time.

Incorporating Smart Lists into your daily, weekly, and long-term planning routines transforms Microsoft To Do from a simple task manager into a powerful productivity system, fully aligned with the Getting Things Done (GTD) methodology.

As you continue to explore the possibilities offered by Smart Lists, you'll find new ways to streamline your workflow, reduce manual effort, and stay ahead of your tasks. Whether you're managing personal to-dos or coordinating complex projects, Smart Lists provide the automation and organization needed to keep everything on track, allowing you to achieve your goals with greater efficiency and less stress.

2.3 Prioritizing and Sorting Tasks

In any task management system, prioritization is crucial to ensuring that you focus on the most important tasks first. Microsoft To Do provides several features that allow you to set task priorities and sort your tasks accordingly, making it easier to manage your workload and stay on top of your goals. In this section, we'll explore how to effectively prioritize your tasks and how to use sorting features to organize them for optimal productivity.

2.3.1 Setting Task Priorities

Setting task priorities is a fundamental aspect of effective task management. It involves determining the importance of each task in relation to others, enabling you to focus on what needs to be done first. Microsoft To Do offers several tools and techniques that help you prioritize tasks within your lists.

Understanding Task Prioritization

At its core, task prioritization is about making decisions on which tasks are most critical at any given time. Not all tasks carry the same weight or urgency, and recognizing this difference is key to managing your workload effectively. Tasks can generally be categorized based on their importance and urgency:

- High Priority: These are tasks that are both important and urgent. They require immediate attention and should be completed as soon as possible.

- Medium Priority: These tasks are important but not necessarily urgent. They should be addressed after high-priority tasks are completed.

- Low Priority: Tasks that are neither urgent nor critical. They can be deferred until more pressing matters are handled.

By distinguishing tasks in this manner, you can allocate your time and energy more efficiently, ensuring that you're always working on the most important items.

Using the Importance Feature

Microsoft To Do includes a built-in "Importance" feature that allows you to flag tasks based on their priority. You can mark a task as important by clicking the star icon next to the task name. This visually separates high-priority tasks from others, making it easier to identify what needs to be done first.

Tasks marked as important are automatically grouped under the "Important" smart list, which collects all such tasks from across your different lists into one view. This feature is particularly useful when you have multiple projects or lists and want to focus on high-priority tasks without getting distracted by less important ones.

Steps to Mark a Task as Important:

1. Open Microsoft To Do: Navigate to the list that contains the task you want to prioritize.

2. Find the Task: Locate the task in your list.

3. Mark as Important: Click on the star icon next to the task name. The task will be highlighted and added to the "Important" smart list.

Benefits of Using the Importance Feature:

- Immediate Identification: Important tasks are highlighted, making them easily identifiable at a glance.

- Consolidated View: All important tasks across different lists are brought together in the "Important" smart list, allowing you to focus on top priorities.

- Streamlined Workflow: By concentrating on the "Important" list, you can ensure that you're always working on the most crucial tasks.

Setting Due Dates and Reminders for Prioritization

While the Importance feature is a great way to flag tasks, setting due dates and reminders adds another layer of prioritization. Tasks with approaching deadlines naturally take precedence over those with later due dates, and reminders help ensure that you don't forget to complete them on time.

Steps to Set Due Dates:

1. Select the Task: Choose the task you want to set a due date for.

2. Click on the Calendar Icon: This is located next to the task name.

3. Choose a Date: Select the appropriate due date from the calendar. You can choose a specific date or opt for options like "Today," "Tomorrow," or "Next Week."

4. Set a Reminder (Optional): If needed, set a reminder by clicking on the bell icon. You can specify the exact time you want to be reminded about the task.

Benefits of Setting Due Dates and Reminders:

- Time Management: Due dates help you manage your time effectively by creating a clear timeline for task completion.

- Preventing Procrastination: Reminders nudge you to take action, preventing tasks from being forgotten or delayed.

- Prioritization by Deadline: Tasks with sooner due dates automatically become a higher priority, allowing you to focus on what needs to be done next.

Using the "My Day" Feature

The "My Day" feature in Microsoft To Do is a powerful tool for daily prioritization. It allows you to create a customized list of tasks that you intend to complete on a given day. This feature is particularly useful for breaking down your workload into manageable chunks and ensuring that you're focusing on the right tasks each day.

How to Use "My Day":

1. Open the "My Day" Section: On the left-hand side of the Microsoft To Do interface, you'll see the "My Day" section. Click on it to open the daily task planner.

2. Add Tasks to "My Day": You can add tasks from any of your lists to "My Day" by clicking the "Add to My Day" option when viewing a task. You can also manually enter new tasks directly into "My Day."

3. Prioritize Your Day: Arrange tasks within "My Day" based on their importance and urgency. This becomes your action plan for the day.

4. Review and Reflect: At the end of the day, review the tasks in "My Day." Any tasks not completed can be moved to the next day or rescheduled.

Benefits of "My Day":

- Focused Daily Plan: "My Day" helps you concentrate on a specific set of tasks, reducing overwhelm and improving focus.

- Daily Prioritization: By selecting tasks each morning, you actively prioritize what you want to accomplish that day.

- Flexibility: "My Day" resets every day, allowing you to adapt your priorities based on changing circumstances.

Using Categories and Tags for Prioritization

Categories and tags in Microsoft To Do offer another level of task organization, helping you prioritize tasks based on context, project, or other criteria. Tags are particularly useful for grouping tasks that share a common theme, such as "Urgent," "Work," "Personal," or "Follow-up."

Steps to Add Tags to a Task:

1. Open the Task: Select the task you want to tag.

2. Enter a Tag: Type the tag directly into the task notes or use the hashtag symbol () followed by the tag name (e.g., Urgent).

3. Use Tags for Sorting: You can search for tasks by tag or filter your lists to show only tasks with a certain tag.

Benefits of Using Tags:

- Contextual Prioritization: Tags allow you to group tasks based on context or importance, making it easier to find and prioritize related tasks.

- Enhanced Organization: Tags provide an additional layer of organization, especially when managing complex projects with multiple tasks.

- Quick Retrieval: You can quickly retrieve and focus on tasks by searching for a specific tag.

Combining Prioritization Methods

For maximum efficiency, consider combining multiple prioritization methods in Microsoft To Do. For example, you can use the Importance feature to flag critical tasks, set due dates for time-sensitive tasks, and add tags to group tasks by context. This layered approach ensures that you're always working on the right tasks at the right time.

Example Workflow:

1. Flag High-Priority Tasks: Use the Importance feature to identify tasks that require immediate attention.

2. Set Due Dates: Assign due dates to these tasks to ensure timely completion.

3. Tag Tasks by Context: Add tags like Urgent or Follow-up to categorize tasks further.

4. Add to "My Day": Each morning, review your tasks and add the most important ones to "My Day."

Benefits of a Combined Approach:

- Comprehensive Prioritization: By using multiple methods, you cover all aspects of prioritization, from urgency to context.

- Increased Flexibility: A combined approach allows you to adapt your task management strategy to different situations and workloads.

- Improved Focus: Layering prioritization techniques helps you zero in on the most important tasks, improving focus and productivity.

Practical Tips for Effective Prioritization

Effective prioritization requires more than just tools—it also requires a strategic mindset and consistent habits. Here are some practical tips for making the most of Microsoft To Do's prioritization features:

1. Review Regularly: Regularly review your tasks and lists to ensure that priorities are up to date. The dynamic nature of work means that priorities can shift, so make it a habit to reassess your tasks at least once a week.

2. Use Deadlines Wisely: Avoid setting arbitrary due dates for tasks. Instead, use deadlines strategically to highlight genuinely time-sensitive tasks. Overloading your task list with unnecessary deadlines can lead to stress and decreased productivity.

3. Limit Daily Priorities: In "My Day," limit the number of tasks you plan to complete. Focus on 3 to 5 top-priority tasks each day. This helps you maintain focus and prevents your daily plan from becoming overwhelming.

4. Defer Low-Priority Tasks: For tasks that are low priority and not time-sensitive, consider deferring them to a later date. Microsoft To Do allows you to move tasks to future dates, helping you clear your immediate task list without losing track of these tasks.

5. Stay Flexible: While prioritization is important, it's also crucial to stay flexible. Unexpected tasks and changes can arise, so be prepared to adjust your priorities as needed.

6. Reflect on Completed Tasks: Take time to review your completed tasks. This not only gives you a sense of accomplishment but also helps you learn from your prioritization decisions.

2.3.2 Sorting and Filtering Tasks

As you accumulate more tasks in Microsoft To Do, the ability to quickly locate, prioritize, and manage them becomes increasingly important. Sorting and filtering tasks are powerful tools that allow you to navigate your task lists with ease, helping you focus on what's most important at any given moment. Whether you're working on a complex project with multiple components or managing daily chores, effective sorting and filtering ensure that you maintain control over your workflow.

Why Sorting and Filtering Matter

In the context of productivity, clarity and focus are essential. Sorting and filtering your tasks provide this clarity by organizing your tasks based on specific criteria that align with your current priorities. For example, if you're working on a project due by the end of the week, you might want to sort tasks by due date to see what needs immediate attention. Alternatively, if you're in a particular frame of mind and ready to tackle high-effort tasks, you can filter to show only those tasks marked with a high priority.

Effective sorting and filtering reduce cognitive overload, allowing you to focus on the tasks that require your immediate attention, thereby increasing your overall efficiency. Without these tools, you might find yourself overwhelmed by a long list of tasks, struggling to decide where to start. Microsoft To Do's sorting and filtering features are designed to help you cut through the clutter, offering a streamlined way to manage your workload.

Sorting Tasks in Microsoft To Do

Sorting is the process of arranging your tasks in a particular order based on selected criteria. Microsoft To Do offers several sorting options that cater to different needs, allowing you to view your tasks in a way that makes sense for your workflow. The main criteria you can use to sort your tasks include:

- Due Date: This sorts your tasks based on their deadlines. Tasks with the earliest due dates appear at the top of the list, making it easy to see what needs to be completed soonest. This is particularly useful when you're managing multiple deadlines and want to ensure you're meeting them in a timely manner.

- Alphabetical Order: Sorting tasks alphabetically by their title can be helpful if you're managing a large number of tasks and need to quickly locate specific items. This is especially useful when your tasks are labeled with consistent, descriptive titles.

- Creation Date: Sorting by creation date places the most recently added tasks at the top of your list. This is beneficial when you've just brainstormed a series of tasks and want to focus on your latest ideas first.

- Priority: Tasks can be sorted based on their assigned priority levels, from high to low. This allows you to focus on tasks that are most critical to your goals, ensuring that the most important tasks are addressed first.

- Importance: Microsoft To Do includes a feature where you can mark tasks as "important." Sorting by importance will bring these tasks to the forefront, helping you maintain focus on what truly matters.

- My Day: Tasks added to the "My Day" list can be sorted separately. Sorting within "My Day" helps you plan out the sequence in which you want to tackle the day's tasks.

Let's dive deeper into each sorting option and how you can leverage it to optimize your productivity.

Sorting by Due Date

Sorting tasks by due date is perhaps the most commonly used method, especially for those managing tight deadlines or juggling multiple projects. In Microsoft To Do, you can easily sort your tasks so that those with the nearest deadlines appear at the top. This method is ideal for ensuring you stay on top of urgent tasks and avoid last-minute scrambles.

To sort by due date:

1. Open your task list in Microsoft To Do.

2. Click on the three dots (more options) in the upper right corner of the list.

3. Select "Sort by" and choose "Due date."

Once sorted, your tasks will be listed from the earliest to the latest due date. Tasks without a set due date will typically appear at the bottom of the list, keeping the focus on time-sensitive items. This sorting method is particularly effective in high-pressure environments where meeting deadlines is critical.

For example, if you're managing a marketing campaign, you might have tasks like drafting content, scheduling social media posts, and analyzing metrics. By sorting these tasks by due date, you can easily see which ones need to be completed first, ensuring a smooth progression towards your campaign's launch date.

Sorting by Alphabetical Order

Sorting tasks alphabetically is useful when you need to locate a specific task quickly or if you prefer a more structured, name-based organization of your tasks. This method works particularly well in contexts where tasks are given descriptive names that follow a particular pattern or convention.

To sort tasks alphabetically:

1. Go to the task list you wish to organize.

2. Click on the three dots (more options) in the upper right corner.

3. Select "Sort by" and choose "Alphabetically."

Alphabetical sorting can be particularly effective in contexts such as inventory management or client follow-ups, where tasks may be named systematically (e.g., "Follow-up with Client A," "Follow-up with Client B," etc.). By sorting alphabetically, you can ensure that tasks are grouped logically, making it easier to locate and complete them efficiently.

For instance, if you're managing a to-do list for a conference, where tasks include contacting vendors, booking venues, and confirming speakers, alphabetical sorting would group similar tasks together, streamlining the process of managing these activities.

Sorting by Creation Date

Sorting by creation date is a valuable tool when you want to prioritize newly added tasks or ensure that no new ideas slip through the cracks. This method allows you to focus on the most recent tasks first, which is especially helpful in dynamic environments where priorities can change rapidly.

To sort by creation date:

1. Open your task list in Microsoft To Do.

2. Click the three dots (more options) in the upper right corner.

3. Choose "Sort by" and then select "Creation date."

By using this sorting method, you can ensure that recent tasks get the attention they deserve. For example, if you're in a brainstorming session and have added a series of new tasks to your list, sorting by creation date allows you to address these fresh ideas before they are buried under existing tasks.

This method also helps in situations where tasks are continuously added, such as in customer support or sales, where new tasks may be created based on incoming inquiries or leads. Sorting by creation date keeps your most recent responsibilities at the forefront, allowing you to act on them promptly.

Sorting by Priority

Prioritization is a key aspect of effective task management. Sorting tasks by priority ensures that the most critical tasks are handled first, preventing important items from being overshadowed by less urgent ones. Microsoft To Do allows you to assign priority levels to tasks, typically categorized as High, Medium, or Low.

To sort tasks by priority:

1. Navigate to your task list in Microsoft To Do.

2. Click on the three dots (more options) at the top right.

3. Select "Sort by" and then choose "Priority."

Once sorted, tasks with the highest priority will appear at the top of your list. This sorting method is especially useful when managing complex projects where certain tasks are critical to the overall success of the project. By focusing on high-priority tasks, you ensure that the most impactful actions are taken care of first.

For example, in a product development project, tasks like finalizing the product design or securing regulatory approvals would be marked as high priority. Sorting by priority would help keep these critical tasks front and center, ensuring that they are completed before moving on to less urgent tasks.

Sorting by Importance

The "importance" feature in Microsoft To Do allows you to flag tasks that require special attention. Sorting tasks by importance is similar to sorting by priority but offers an additional layer of flexibility. You can mark tasks as important, regardless of their due date or priority level, allowing you to create a custom list of high-focus items.

To sort by importance:

1. Open the desired task list.

2. Click the three dots (more options) in the upper right corner.

3. Select "Sort by" and choose "Importance."

This sorting option is particularly useful when you need to create a "must-do" list within your broader task list. For example, you might have a list of tasks with various due dates and priorities, but you can flag those that are crucial for today or this week as important. Sorting by importance then elevates these tasks, allowing you to focus on them without distraction.

Sorting by My Day

"My Day" is a unique feature in Microsoft To Do that allows you to create a focused list of tasks that you intend to complete within the day. Sorting tasks within "My Day" can help you plan the sequence of your workday more effectively, ensuring that you tackle tasks in a logical and productive order.

To sort tasks within "My Day":

1. Open the "My Day" section in Microsoft To Do.

2. Click on the three dots (more options) in the upper right corner.

3. Choose your preferred sorting option.

You can apply any of the above sorting criteria (due date, priority, importance, etc.) within "My Day" to organize your tasks for the day. This feature is particularly useful for daily planning, as it allows you to start each day with a clear, organized plan of action.

For example, if you've added several tasks to "My Day" but want to ensure you complete the most urgent ones first, sorting by due date or priority within "My Day" will help you stay on track. Alternatively, you might choose to sort alphabetically if your tasks are related to specific

2.3.3 Using Importance and My Day Features

Introduction

In today's fast-paced world, managing your time and prioritizing your tasks effectively are crucial skills. Microsoft To Do provides powerful tools to help you accomplish these goals through its "Importance" and "My Day" features. These features are designed to help you stay focused on what's truly important, ensuring that your productivity aligns with your priorities. In this section, we will explore how to utilize these tools effectively to streamline your task management and make sure that you're not just busy, but productive.

Understanding the Importance Feature

The "Importance" feature in Microsoft To Do allows you to mark tasks as high priority. This simple yet powerful feature helps you quickly identify and focus on the tasks that matter most. By assigning importance to your tasks, you can visually distinguish between critical and less urgent items, making it easier to allocate your time and resources effectively.

How to Mark a Task as Important

Marking a task as important in Microsoft To Do is straightforward:

1. Open Your Task List: Navigate to the task list where your task is located.

2. Identify the Task: Locate the task that you want to mark as important.

3. Mark as Important: Click on the star icon next to the task. The star will turn blue, indicating that the task has been marked as important.

Once a task is marked as important, it will automatically appear in the "Important" smart list. This list aggregates all tasks across your different lists that have been flagged as important, providing a focused view of your most critical tasks.

Benefits of Using the Importance Feature

- Focus on High-Priority Tasks: By using the Importance feature, you can ensure that high-priority tasks stand out. This helps you avoid the common pitfall of working on less critical tasks at the expense of more important ones.

- Efficient Time Allocation: When you clearly identify which tasks are most important, you can allocate your time and energy more effectively, ensuring that you are working on the right tasks at the right time.

- Simplified Decision-Making: In moments of decision fatigue, the Importance feature provides an immediate visual cue, making it easier to decide what to work on next without overthinking.

Strategic Use of the Importance Feature

The Importance feature should be used strategically. Not every task should be marked as important—overusing this feature can dilute its effectiveness. Reserve it for tasks that are genuinely critical to your projects or goals. A good rule of thumb is to consider whether the task has a significant impact on your overall objectives or deadlines. If it does, mark it as important; if not, leave it unmarked.

Introducing the My Day Feature

The "My Day" feature in Microsoft To Do is designed to help you plan and focus on the tasks you want to accomplish today. Unlike the Importance feature, which is more static, My Day is dynamic, allowing you to refresh and reprioritize your tasks on a daily basis. Each day, you can start fresh, choosing tasks from any of your lists to add to My Day. This feature is particularly useful for breaking down larger tasks into manageable daily actions and for keeping your workload realistic and achievable.

How to Use the My Day Feature

Here's how you can effectively use the My Day feature:

1. Start Your Day with a Plan:

   - Open the My Day List: Each morning, begin by opening the My Day list in Microsoft To Do.

- Review Suggested Tasks: Microsoft To Do will suggest tasks based on your upcoming due dates and importance levels. You can add these tasks to your My Day list or dismiss them if they're not relevant for today.

2. Add Tasks to My Day:

- Manual Selection: You can manually add any task from any list to your My Day list. Simply click the "Add to My Day" button found within the task details or drag the task directly to the My Day list.

- Focus on Today's Priorities: Consider the tasks that align with your daily goals and the amount of time you have available. Aim to add a realistic number of tasks that you can reasonably complete within the day.

3. Complete and Review:

- Check Off Completed Tasks: As you complete tasks throughout the day, check them off in the My Day list. This helps you track your progress and provides a sense of accomplishment.

- End of Day Review: At the end of each day, review the tasks in your My Day list. Any incomplete tasks will not automatically roll over to the next day, giving you the opportunity to reassess and decide whether to carry them forward, defer them, or reprioritize.

The Value of a Fresh Start Every Day

The My Day feature provides the psychological benefit of a fresh start each day. Unlike traditional to-do lists that can become overwhelming with unchecked tasks, My Day encourages you to focus on what can realistically be achieved today. This helps prevent the build-up of backlog and reduces the stress associated with an ever-growing task list.

- Daily Focus: My Day narrows your focus to a set of tasks that are most relevant for the current day, promoting a sense of control and clarity.

- Flexibility and Adaptation: Life can be unpredictable, and the My Day feature allows you to adapt to changing circumstances. If something urgent comes up, you can easily adjust your My Day list to reflect your new priorities.

- Encourages Daily Reflection: The end-of-day review process embedded in the My Day feature encourages you to reflect on your productivity, learn from your day, and plan better for tomorrow.

Combining Importance and My Day for Maximum Productivity: While both the Importance and My Day features are powerful on their own, combining them can take your productivity to the next level. Here's how you can leverage both features together:

Morning Routine: Planning Your Day

Start your day by reviewing your Important tasks and considering which ones should be added to your My Day list. Not all important tasks need to be tackled today, but this exercise ensures that you're consciously making decisions about your priorities. Choose a few key tasks that align with your goals for the day and add them to My Day.

- Balancing Priorities: Use the Importance feature to highlight long-term goals and critical deadlines, while using My Day to manage daily tasks that contribute to these broader objectives.

- Avoid Overloading: Be mindful not to overload your My Day list with too many Important tasks. A balanced approach where you mix important tasks with smaller, less critical ones can help maintain your momentum throughout the day.

Midday Check-In: Adjusting Your Focus

Midway through your day, take a moment to check in on your progress. Review your My Day list and the Important tasks that haven't been added to it. This is a good time to adjust your focus if needed—perhaps moving a task from the Important list to My Day if circumstances have changed, or removing a task from My Day if it's no longer a priority.

- Dynamic Adjustment: Stay flexible and responsive to new information or unexpected challenges. The ability to dynamically adjust your tasks ensures that you remain productive, even when things don't go as planned.

- Avoid Distractions: Use the My Day list to keep distractions at bay. By focusing on a pre-selected set of tasks, you're less likely to get sidetracked by lower-priority items.

End-of-Day Reflection: Reviewing and Planning Ahead

At the end of your day, review what you've accomplished in My Day. Any tasks that weren't completed can be reconsidered—decide whether they should be re-added to tomorrow's My Day, left in the Important list, or deprioritized.

- Learning from Today: Reflect on what worked well and what didn't. Did you add too many tasks to My Day? Did you neglect some Important tasks that should have been prioritized? Use these insights to improve your planning for the next day.

- Pre-Planning for Tomorrow: If you already know what your priorities will be tomorrow, you can start pre-populating your My Day list. This allows you to hit the ground running the next morning.

Conclusion

The Importance and My Day features in Microsoft To Do are more than just tools—they are frameworks that can help you manage your tasks with clarity and purpose. By marking tasks as Important, you ensure that your critical work stands out. Meanwhile, the My Day feature allows you to focus on what's most relevant today, providing a fresh start each morning and helping you maintain a balanced, realistic workload.

When used together, these features empower you to not only get things done but to get the right things done, at the right time. They support a dynamic, flexible approach to task management that adapts to your evolving priorities and helps you stay on top of your goals.

Whether you're managing complex projects, daily tasks, or long-term goals, leveraging the power of Importance and My Day can make a significant difference in your productivity and overall effectiveness. As you continue to use Microsoft To Do, these features will become essential components of your daily routine, helping you stay organized, focused, and motivated.

CHAPTER III
Integrating Microsoft To Do with GTD

3.1 Capturing and Clarifying Tasks

3.1.1 The Capture Process in Microsoft To Do

Capturing is the cornerstone of the Getting Things Done (GTD) methodology, and it's the first step toward achieving a clear and organized mind. In essence, capturing involves collecting all the ideas, tasks, and information that demand your attention into a trusted system. The goal is to clear your mind of all the loose ends that might be vying for your attention, ensuring that nothing falls through the cracks.

Microsoft To Do is an excellent tool for the capturing process because it provides a simple yet powerful interface to gather your thoughts, tasks, and commitments all in one place. Whether you're jotting down a fleeting idea, recording an important reminder, or listing out a complex project, Microsoft To Do is designed to handle it all.

Let's explore how to effectively utilize Microsoft To Do for capturing your tasks and information.

The Importance of Capturing

Before delving into the technical details of using Microsoft To Do, it's important to understand why capturing is so crucial. In the GTD methodology, David Allen emphasizes that our brains are for having ideas, not holding them. When we try to keep everything in our heads, we risk cognitive overload, stress, and inefficiency. By offloading these tasks into an external system like Microsoft To Do, we can achieve clarity and focus on what truly matters.

Capturing every task, idea, or commitment, no matter how small, is essential for maintaining a trusted system. When you know that everything you need to do is safely stored and accessible, you can focus on the task at hand without the nagging worry that you're forgetting something. This sense of control and clarity is what makes capturing so powerful.

Setting Up Microsoft To Do for Capturing

To start capturing tasks effectively, it's important to configure Microsoft To Do in a way that aligns with your workflow. Here's a step-by-step guide to setting up your capture process:

1. Install Microsoft To Do Across All Devices: Since you want to capture ideas as they come to you, having Microsoft To Do available on all your devices is crucial. Whether you're at your desk, on the go, or in a meeting, you should be able to quickly jot down a task or idea. Install the app on your smartphone, tablet, and desktop, and ensure that it syncs across all devices.

2. Set Up Quick Add Features: Microsoft To Do allows you to quickly add tasks without navigating through the full app. On mobile devices, you can use widgets or shortcuts. On desktop, the quick add feature can be accessed through the system tray or by using hotkeys. Configuring these quick add features ensures that capturing is as frictionless as possible.

3. Customize Your Default List: When you capture a task in Microsoft To Do, it typically goes into a default list, such as "Tasks" or "Inbox." You can customize this default list according to your preferences. For example, if you prefer a more segmented approach, you might create separate lists for different areas of your life—Work, Personal, Projects, etc. Or, you can use a single list to capture everything and organize it later.

4. Enable Voice Capture and Integration: If you're someone who likes to capture tasks using voice commands, Microsoft To Do integrates with virtual assistants like Microsoft Cortana and Apple Siri. By enabling these integrations, you can simply say, "Add a task to Microsoft To Do," and your voice-captured tasks will be added to your list. This feature is particularly useful when you're driving or multitasking.

5. Integrate with Other Tools: Microsoft To Do integrates well with other tools you might already be using, such as Outlook, Microsoft Teams, and OneNote. If you receive an email that requires action, you can quickly capture it as a task in Microsoft To Do. Similarly, if you're brainstorming in OneNote, you can send key action items directly to your task list.

These integrations ensure that your capture process is seamless and that no task is overlooked.

How to Capture Tasks Effectively

Once your Microsoft To Do is set up, the next step is to develop effective capture habits. Capturing tasks effectively means recording every potential action item as soon as it comes to mind. This section will cover best practices for capturing tasks, including what to capture, how to word your tasks, and tips for making capture a habit.

1. Capture Everything, No Matter How Small: One of the key principles of GTD is to capture everything that has your attention, regardless of size or importance. This could be a major project at work, a reminder to buy groceries, or even an idea for a future blog post. The goal is to get everything out of your head and into Microsoft To Do. By capturing even the smallest tasks, you free up mental space for more significant challenges.

2. Use Clear, Action-Oriented Language: When capturing tasks, it's important to phrase them in a way that makes them actionable. For example, instead of writing "Mom," which is vague and non-actionable, write "Call Mom to discuss weekend plans." Action-oriented language helps ensure that when you review your tasks later, you know exactly what needs to be done without any ambiguity.

3. Capture Context Where Necessary: Sometimes, a task needs additional context to be fully understood later. For example, if you capture a task to "Submit report," it might be unclear which report you're referring to. Adding context like "Submit Q3 sales report to John" provides the necessary details. In Microsoft To Do, you can add notes to tasks for extra clarity, making it easy to include relevant information.

4. Use Microsoft To Do's Natural Language Recognition: Microsoft To Do has a useful feature that allows you to capture tasks using natural language. For example, if you type "Meeting with Sarah tomorrow at 10 AM," Microsoft To Do will automatically recognize the due date and time, setting a reminder accordingly. This makes the capture process quicker and more intuitive.

5. Leverage Smart Lists for Quick Captures: Microsoft To Do's smart lists, such as "My Day" and "Important," can help you capture and organize tasks more efficiently. For instance, when you're adding a task that you know you need to focus on today, you can immediately add it to "My Day." Similarly, if a task is particularly critical, marking it as "Important" during capture ensures that it stands out later.

6. Make Capture a Habit: For capturing to be effective, it must become a consistent habit. This means regularly offloading tasks into Microsoft To Do, whether you're at work, home, or anywhere in between. Consider setting reminders to capture tasks at specific times of the day, like after a meeting or during your evening wind-down. The more you practice capturing tasks immediately, the more natural it will become.

Managing the Capture Inbox

After capturing tasks, the next step is managing your capture inbox. The capture inbox is essentially the list where all your newly captured tasks reside until you have time to process them. For many users, this will be a list named "Tasks" or "Inbox," where all captured tasks initially land. Here's how to effectively manage and process this list:

1. Regularly Review Your Capture Inbox: It's crucial to regularly review your capture inbox to ensure that tasks are not piling up and becoming overwhelming. Schedule time at least once a day to go through your inbox, clarify what each task is, and either complete it or move it to the appropriate list.

2. Process Captured Tasks into Actionable Steps: Not all captured tasks are immediately actionable. Some might need further clarification, while others may be part of a larger project. During your review, take the time to process each task into an actionable step. If a task is too vague or broad, break it down into smaller, more manageable actions. For instance, a task like "Plan vacation" can be broken down into "Research flight options" and "Book hotel."

3. Organize Tasks by Context or Project: Once you've clarified your tasks, it's helpful to organize them by context or project. In Microsoft To Do, you can use tags or create separate lists for different projects or areas of focus. For example, you might have a list for "Work Projects" and another for "Personal Errands." Organizing your tasks in this way ensures that you can easily find what you need when you're ready to work on a specific project or context.

4. Use Due Dates and Reminders Wisely: As you process your captured tasks, consider setting due dates and reminders where appropriate. Microsoft To Do allows you to set specific dates and times for tasks, which is especially useful for time-sensitive items. However, be careful not to overuse due dates, as this can lead to a cluttered and overwhelming task list. Reserve due dates for tasks that truly need them, and use reminders sparingly for high-priority items.

5. Clear Your Capture Inbox Regularly: The goal of managing your capture inbox is to keep it as clear as possible. By regularly processing and organizing tasks, you can ensure that your inbox remains a place for capturing new ideas and tasks, rather than a dumping ground for unprocessed items. Aim to clear your inbox to zero at the end of each day, leaving you with a clean slate for tomorrow.

Capturing on the Go

One of the advantages of Microsoft To Do is its ability to capture tasks on the go. Whether you're in a meeting, commuting, or running errands, you can quickly capture tasks using your mobile device. Here are some tips for capturing on the go:

1. Use Voice Commands:

 As mentioned earlier, voice commands can be a quick and effective way to capture tasks when you're on the move. Simply tell your virtual assistant to add a task to Microsoft To Do, and it will be captured in your inbox. This is particularly useful when you're driving or otherwise occupied.

2. Capture via Email: If you receive an email that requires action, you can forward it to your Microsoft To Do inbox. Microsoft To Do allows you to create tasks directly from emails, ensuring that nothing important slips through the cracks. This feature is especially useful for professionals who receive a high volume of actionable emails each day.

3. Take Advantage of Widgets: If you're using Microsoft To Do on a mobile device, consider adding a widget to your home screen. This allows you to quickly add tasks with a single tap, without needing to open the app. Widgets can be customized to display your most important lists, making it easy to capture tasks at a glance.

4. Capture Offline: Microsoft To Do also supports offline task capture, meaning you can add tasks even when you don't have an internet connection. Your tasks will automatically sync once you're back online, ensuring that you never lose any important information.

Refining Your Capture Process

The capture process is dynamic, and over time, you may find ways to refine and improve how you capture tasks in Microsoft To Do. Here are some strategies for refining your capture process:

1. Regularly Review and Adjust Your Lists: As you capture more tasks, you may find that your initial list setup needs adjustment. Regularly review your lists to ensure they're organized in a way that makes sense for your workflow. Don't be afraid to create new lists or merge existing ones if it helps streamline your process.

2. Experiment with Different Capture Techniques: Everyone's capture process is different, and what works for one person might not work for another. Experiment with different capture techniques—such as using tags, voice commands, or email forwarding—to find what works best for you. The key is to develop a process that feels natural and efficient.

3. Stay Consistent: The most important aspect of capturing is consistency. Make it a habit to capture tasks as soon as they come to mind, and review your capture inbox regularly. Over time, this consistency will lead to a trusted system that you can rely on to manage your tasks and commitments.

4. Seek Feedback and Learn from Others: Finally, don't hesitate to seek feedback from others who use Microsoft To Do or follow the GTD methodology. Joining online communities or forums can provide valuable insights and tips for refining your capture process. Learning from others can help you discover new ways to use Microsoft To Do more effectively.

This section provides an in-depth look at how to effectively capture tasks using Microsoft To Do, aligning with the GTD methodology. It emphasizes the importance of capturing, offers practical tips for setup, and explores various strategies to refine and optimize the capture process.

3.1.2 Clarifying Tasks and Next Actions

Clarifying tasks and determining next actions are essential steps in the Getting Things Done (GTD) methodology, and Microsoft To Do offers powerful tools to support these processes. When tasks are captured in their raw form, they often consist of vague ideas, incomplete thoughts, or general intentions. Without clarification, these tasks can become a source of stress and inefficiency. Clarification is the process of transforming these ambiguous entries into clear, actionable steps, ensuring that each task is defined, organized, and ready for execution.

In this section, we will explore how to use Microsoft To Do to effectively clarify your tasks and identify the next actions required to move projects and goals forward.

The Importance of Clarifying Tasks

Before diving into the practical steps of clarifying tasks in Microsoft To Do, it's essential to understand why clarification is so critical. When tasks remain unclear, they create mental clutter, making it difficult to prioritize and take action. Unclear tasks can also lead to procrastination, as they lack the specificity needed to be actionable. By clarifying tasks, you transform vague thoughts into concrete actions, reducing cognitive load and enhancing productivity.

The process of clarification involves:

- Defining the task: What exactly needs to be done?

- Determining the next action: What is the very next physical or mental step that needs to be taken to move this task toward completion?

- Organizing the task: Where does this task belong in the context of your overall system? Is it a standalone task, or does it belong to a larger project?

By regularly clarifying your tasks, you can maintain a clear and organized to-do list that drives action and results.

Clarifying Tasks in Microsoft To Do

Microsoft To Do is designed to help you manage tasks from the moment they are captured to the moment they are completed. Clarifying tasks in Microsoft To Do involves reviewing your captured tasks and refining them into actionable items. Here's how you can do it:

Step 1: Review Your Captured Tasks

Start by reviewing the tasks you've captured in Microsoft To Do. These tasks might be in the Inbox (if you're using the GTD method of capturing tasks) or scattered across different lists. Your goal in this step is to assess each task and determine what needs to be clarified.

1. Open the To Do App: Navigate to the list where you have captured your tasks.

2. Sort Through the Tasks: Review each task one by one. Ask yourself, "What does this mean?" and "What do I need to do with this?"

During this review, you might find tasks that are:

- Actionable: These are tasks that can be acted upon immediately.

- Non-actionable: These could be reference materials, ideas for future projects, or tasks that require further thought.

Step 2: Define the Task

Once you've identified that a task is actionable, the next step is to clearly define it. This involves breaking down the task into its most essential elements so that it is clear what needs to be done.

1. Rename the Task (if necessary): If the task's name is vague or unclear, rename it to reflect the specific action that needs to be taken. For example, change "Call John" to "Call John to discuss project timelines."

2. Add Details: If the task requires additional information or context, use the Notes section in Microsoft To Do to add those details. This could include meeting details, reminders of what needs to be discussed, or links to relevant documents.

Defining the task clearly is crucial for ensuring that you know exactly what to do when you see it on your list. A well-defined task reduces decision-making time and helps you move directly into action.

Step 3: Determine the Next Action

The heart of the GTD method is the concept of next actions. A next action is the very next physical or mental step you need to take to move a task toward completion. Determining the next action is about making your tasks as actionable as possible.

1. Ask the Right Questions: To determine the next action, ask yourself, "What is the very next thing I need to do to move this forward?" This could be making a phone call, drafting an email, researching a topic, or setting up a meeting.

2. Break Down Complex Tasks: If a task seems overwhelming, it may need to be broken down into smaller, more manageable steps. For example, instead of "Complete report," your next actions might be "Draft report outline," followed by "Research key data points," and then "Write introduction."

In Microsoft To Do, you can break down tasks into smaller steps by using Subtasks. Subtasks allow you to list all the necessary actions required to complete a larger task. This feature is especially useful for complex tasks that involve multiple steps.

Step 4: Organize the Task

After clarifying and defining the next action, it's time to organize the task within your overall task management system. This involves assigning the task to the appropriate list, setting a due date, and adding any necessary tags.

1. Assign to a List: Decide where this task belongs within your system. Microsoft To Do allows you to create multiple lists, so you can assign tasks to the relevant list based on context, project, or area of responsibility.

2. Set Due Dates and Reminders: If the task has a specific deadline, set a due date. Microsoft To Do also allows you to set reminders, ensuring that you won't forget to take action at the appropriate time.

3. Add Tags for Context: Tags in Microsoft To Do help you categorize tasks based on context, priority, or any other criteria that are important to you. For example, you might tag a task with "@Work" if it's related to your job or "@Home" for personal tasks.

By organizing tasks in this way, you ensure that everything is in its place, making it easier to manage your workload and focus on the right tasks at the right time.

Applying the Clarification Process in Daily Practice

To make the most of Microsoft To Do and the GTD methodology, it's important to integrate the clarification process into your daily routine. Here's how you can do that:

1. Daily Review of Captured Tasks

Make it a habit to review your captured tasks daily. This can be done at the start of your workday or during a dedicated planning session. By consistently clarifying tasks as they come in, you prevent them from piling up and becoming overwhelming.

During your daily review:

- Go through the tasks in your Inbox or Captured Tasks list.

- Clarify each task by defining it, determining the next action, and organizing it into the appropriate list.

- Prioritize tasks based on urgency, importance, and deadlines.

2. Weekly Review and Reflection

In addition to daily reviews, a weekly review is a cornerstone of the GTD system. During your weekly review, you can take a more comprehensive look at your tasks, projects, and goals.

In your weekly review:

- Review all your lists in Microsoft To Do.

- Clarify any tasks that haven't been fully defined or organized.

- Reflect on your progress over the past week and adjust your tasks and priorities accordingly.

The weekly review is an opportunity to ensure that your system is up-to-date, all tasks are clear, and you're on track to achieve your goals.

3. Use the My Day Feature for Daily Focus

Microsoft To Do's My Day feature is a powerful tool for maintaining focus on the tasks that matter most. Each day, you can select tasks from your lists and add them to My Day for a focused, prioritized view of what you need to accomplish.

To use My Day effectively:

- At the start of each day, review your tasks and add the most important ones to My Day.

- Ensure that each task in My Day has been clarified, with a defined next action and a clear purpose.

- As you complete tasks, check them off in My Day and feel the satisfaction of making tangible progress.

4. Contextual Task Management

Another powerful feature in Microsoft To Do is the ability to manage tasks based on context. Contexts are categories or tags that indicate where, when, or with whom a task can be completed.

For example:

- Use the tag @Office for tasks that need to be done at work.

- Use @Calls for tasks that involve making phone calls.

- Use @Errands for tasks that require you to be out of the house.

By organizing tasks by context, you can easily filter and focus on the tasks that are relevant to your current situation. Microsoft To Do's filtering options make it simple to view tasks by tag, ensuring that you're always working on the most appropriate tasks at any given moment.

Clarification and Project Management

In the context of project management, the process of clarifying tasks takes on additional importance. Projects often involve multiple tasks, dependencies, and collaborators, making it essential to have a clear and organized task list.

1. Breaking Down Projects into Tasks

When managing a project, start by breaking it down into individual tasks. Each task should represent a specific action or deliverable that contributes to the completion of the project.

- Use Microsoft To Do's Lists to create a dedicated list for each project.

- Add tasks to the project list, ensuring each one is clearly defined and actionable.

- Use Subtasks for tasks that require multiple steps, providing a detailed roadmap for project completion.

2. Clarifying Dependencies and Sequencing

Projects often involve tasks that are dependent on the completion of other tasks. Clarifying these dependencies is crucial for effective project management.

- Identify tasks that need to be completed before others can begin.

- Use tags or notes to indicate dependencies within Microsoft To Do.

- Sequence tasks in the correct order to ensure smooth progress through the project.

3. Regular Project Reviews

Regularly reviewing your project tasks ensures that everything is on track and that any issues are addressed promptly.

- Conduct a Weekly Review of your project tasks, clarifying and updating them as needed.

- Monitor progress and adjust deadlines or priorities based on the current state of the project.

- Use the Completed Tasks View in Microsoft To Do to track what has been accomplished and what still needs attention.

By applying these principles to project management, you can ensure that your projects are well-organized, that tasks are clear and actionable, and that you're consistently moving toward project completion.

Overcoming Common Challenges in Clarifying Tasks

While clarifying tasks is a straightforward process, there are common challenges that can arise. Understanding these challenges and how to overcome them will help you maintain an effective task management system.

1. Vague Tasks and Procrastination

One of the most common challenges is dealing with vague tasks that lead to procrastination. When a task is unclear, it's easy to put it off, leading to delays and reduced productivity.

- Solution: Make it a rule that every task must be actionable. If you find a task that's vague, take a moment to clarify it before moving on. Use the strategies discussed earlier to rename the task, add details, and determine the next action.

2. Overwhelming Projects

Large projects can be overwhelming, especially when they're represented by a single, broad task on your list.

- Solution: Break down large projects into smaller, manageable tasks. Use Subtasks in Microsoft To Do to outline each step required to complete the project. This not only makes the project more manageable but also provides a clear path forward.

3. Maintaining Consistency in Clarification

It's easy to start strong with the task clarification process but then lose consistency over time, especially during busy periods.

- Solution: Build a routine around task clarification. Set aside time each day for reviewing and clarifying tasks. Use the Weekly Review to catch any tasks that may have slipped through the cracks. Consistency is key to maintaining a clear and organized task list.

The Benefits of a Well-Clarified Task List

By consistently clarifying tasks in Microsoft To Do, you'll experience several benefits:

- Reduced Stress: Clear, actionable tasks reduce mental clutter, making it easier to focus on what needs to be done.

- Increased Productivity: When tasks are well-defined, you spend less time deciding what to do and more time actually doing it.

- Improved Focus: With a clear task list, you can focus on the most important actions, leading to better time management and more effective work.

- Better Project Management: Clarified tasks provide a clear roadmap for projects, helping you manage complex workflows with ease.

In summary, clarifying tasks and identifying next actions are critical components of the GTD methodology, and Microsoft To Do provides the tools you need to master these processes. By applying the strategies outlined in this section, you can transform your task management system into a powerful engine for productivity and success.

3.1.3 Organizing Tasks into Projects and Next Steps

In the Getting Things Done (GTD) methodology, organizing tasks into projects and identifying the next actionable steps is a critical phase in ensuring that your workflow is streamlined and productive. This section will guide you through the process of transforming your captured tasks into organized projects and actionable next steps using Microsoft To Do.

Understanding the Importance of Projects and Next Steps

In GTD, a project is any outcome that requires more than one action step to complete. It's not just about listing tasks—it's about seeing the bigger picture, breaking it down into manageable components, and understanding the sequence in which these components need to be addressed. Each project should have a clear outcome, and each task should represent a concrete action that moves you toward that outcome.

The idea of "Next Steps" or "Next Actions" is equally important. The GTD system emphasizes that every project needs a next action to keep it moving forward. A next action is the very next physical or visible thing you need to do to move a project toward completion. By defining these next steps, you prevent projects from stagnating and ensure that you always know what needs to be done next.

Step 1: Identifying Projects in Microsoft To Do

The first step in organizing your tasks into projects is to identify which tasks belong together as part of a larger project. This might seem straightforward, but it requires thoughtful consideration of your tasks and their broader context.

1. Review Your Captured Tasks: Start by reviewing all the tasks you've captured in Microsoft To Do. This includes tasks you've entered manually, tasks forwarded from email, and those created through integrations with other tools like Microsoft Teams or Outlook.

2. Group Related Tasks Together: As you review, start grouping related tasks together. For example, if you have tasks like "Draft project proposal," "Research competitor strategies,"

and "Prepare budget estimate," these likely belong to a larger project like "New Product Launch."

3. Create a New List for Each Project: In Microsoft To Do, each project should have its own dedicated list. To create a new list, simply click the "New List" button on the left-hand side of the interface. Name the list after the project, such as "New Product Launch" or "Website Redesign."

4. Move Tasks to the Appropriate Project List: Once your project lists are created, move the grouped tasks from your general task list to the corresponding project list. This can be done by dragging and dropping the tasks or by selecting the task, clicking on the three-dot menu, and choosing "Move to" followed by the project list.

5. Review and Refine Your Project Lists: After organizing tasks into their respective projects, take a moment to review each list. Ensure that all relevant tasks are included and that no tasks are misplaced. This step is crucial for maintaining clarity and focus within your projects.

 Step 2: Defining Next Steps for Each Project

Once you've organized your tasks into projects, the next step is to define the "Next Steps" for each project. Remember, the goal is to identify the very next physical action that needs to be taken to move the project forward.

1. Identify the Immediate Action Required: Within each project list, identify the task that needs to be done first. This might be something like "Schedule kickoff meeting" or "Draft initial concept." This task should be clear and actionable, leaving no ambiguity about what needs to be done.

2. Set Due Dates and Priorities: Once you've identified the next step, assign a due date and, if necessary, a priority level. This helps in maintaining momentum and ensures that you don't lose track of what needs to be done next. In Microsoft To Do, you can set due dates and reminders by clicking on the task and selecting the appropriate options. Setting a priority can be done by marking the task as "Important" by clicking on the star icon.

3. Add Notes and Context: For more complex next steps, consider adding notes or context to the task. This could include a brief description of the task, links to relevant documents, or any other information that might help when it comes time to complete the action. Microsoft To Do allows you to add notes directly to each task, which can be accessed by clicking on the task and typing in the notes field.

4. Identify Subsequent Actions: Once the immediate next step is identified, think about what comes after it. While you should focus on the next action, having a rough idea of subsequent steps can help you plan more effectively. You can list these as subtasks in Microsoft To Do by opening the task and clicking "Add step." This feature allows you to break down a task into smaller, more manageable actions, keeping everything organized within the main task.

5. Assign Next Steps to Team Members: If you're working on a collaborative project, use Microsoft To Do's sharing features to assign next steps to specific team members. Shared lists allow you to delegate tasks, track progress, and ensure that everyone knows their responsibilities. To share a list, click on the list's title and select "Share list." You can then invite team members by email.

Step 3: Continuously Reviewing and Updating Projects and Next Steps

Organizing tasks into projects and identifying next steps is not a one-time activity. It requires continuous review and updating to ensure that your projects are progressing smoothly.

1. Conduct Regular Reviews: Make it a habit to regularly review each of your project lists. During these reviews, check the status of ongoing tasks, adjust due dates if necessary, and ensure that each project has a clearly defined next step. A weekly review is recommended, where you can assess the overall progress of your projects and make any necessary adjustments.

2. Update Next Steps as Projects Progress: As you complete tasks and move projects forward, new next steps will emerge. Update your Microsoft To Do lists accordingly by moving completed tasks to the "Completed" section and identifying the new next action. This keeps your project lists dynamic and ensures that you always have a clear plan of action.

3. Reflect on Task Organization: Periodically, reflect on how well your tasks are organized within projects. Are there tasks that no longer align with the project's goals? Are there new tasks that need to be added? Microsoft To Do's flexibility allows you to easily rearrange tasks, create new lists, and adjust priorities as needed.

4. Use Tags and Categories for Enhanced Organization: As your projects grow in complexity, consider using tags and categories to further organize your tasks. Microsoft To Do allows you to tag tasks with keywords that can help you filter and find tasks across different projects. For example, you might tag tasks related to client communication with

"Client" or tasks related to design work with "Design." Tags can be added by clicking on a task, typing the tag into the notes field, or using the "Hashtags" feature if supported.

Step 4: Leveraging Microsoft To Do Features for Enhanced Project Management

Microsoft To Do offers several advanced features that can enhance your project management capabilities. By leveraging these tools, you can streamline your workflow and ensure that your projects are managed efficiently.

1. Use Smart Lists for Efficient Task Management: Smart Lists in Microsoft To Do, such as "My Day" and "Important," provide an overview of tasks that require immediate attention. By adding your next steps to these lists, you can ensure that they are front and center when you start your day. This is particularly useful for keeping track of high-priority tasks or tasks that are due soon.

2. Integrate with Microsoft Planner for Complex Projects: If your projects involve multiple team members and require more detailed tracking, consider integrating Microsoft To Do with Microsoft Planner. Planner allows you to create detailed project plans, assign tasks to team members, and track progress in a more structured way. You can sync tasks between Planner and To Do to keep everything in one place.

3. Utilize Power Automate for Workflow Automation: For repetitive tasks or tasks that depend on external triggers, use Microsoft Power Automate to create automated workflows. For example, you can set up a flow that automatically creates a new task in Microsoft To Do whenever an email with a specific subject line is received in Outlook. This can save time and ensure that nothing falls through the cracks.

4. Take Advantage of Cross-Platform Accessibility: Microsoft To Do is available on multiple platforms, including Windows, Mac, iOS, and Android. Use this cross-platform accessibility to manage your tasks on the go. Whether you're at your desk or on the move, you can update your projects and next steps, ensuring that your task management system is always up to date.

Step 5: Reflecting on the Organization Process

Organizing tasks into projects and defining next steps is a process that can greatly enhance your productivity and project management efficiency. By using Microsoft To Do effectively, you can ensure that your tasks are well-organized, your projects are clearly defined, and your next steps are always actionable.

However, it's important to remember that task organization is an ongoing process. As projects evolve, your task management system will need to adapt. Regular reviews, continuous updates, and the strategic use of Microsoft To Do's features will help you maintain a clear and focused approach to managing your work.

In conclusion, organizing tasks into projects and identifying next steps is a critical component of the GTD methodology. Microsoft To Do provides the tools and flexibility needed to implement this system effectively. By following the steps outlined in this section, you can ensure that your projects are always moving forward and that you're always clear on what needs to be done next.

3.2 Organizing Your Tasks

3.2.1 Creating Projects and Actionable Steps

In the Getting Things Done (GTD) methodology, the concept of a "project" is key to managing complex tasks that require multiple steps to complete. Unlike simple to-dos that can be done in one action, projects involve a series of steps, each of which must be completed to achieve the desired outcome. Microsoft To Do is well-equipped to help you manage these projects effectively, breaking them down into actionable steps that are both manageable and trackable.

Understanding Projects in GTD and Microsoft To Do

In GTD, a project is defined as any desired outcome that requires more than one action step. This broad definition means that a project could be anything from "Plan a Marketing Campaign" to "Organize the Annual Company Retreat." The key to effectively managing projects is to break them down into specific, actionable steps that can be tracked individually. Microsoft To Do provides a flexible and intuitive interface for managing these projects, allowing you to organize tasks, set priorities, and keep track of progress.

When thinking about projects in Microsoft To Do, it's essential to consider both the end goal and the individual steps needed to achieve it. The application allows you to create a new list specifically for your project, or you can incorporate your project into an existing list by adding relevant tasks and subtasks. The advantage of using lists is that they allow you to group related tasks together, making it easier to manage and track your progress.

To start creating projects in Microsoft To Do, it's helpful to first list out all the projects you are currently working on. This exercise will give you a clear overview of what needs to be done and allow you to prioritize accordingly. Once you have a list of projects, the next step is to break each one down into actionable steps. These steps should be specific, measurable, and have a clear outcome.

For example, if your project is "Launch a New Product," your actionable steps might include "Conduct Market Research," "Develop a Marketing Strategy," "Design Packaging," and "Organize a Launch Event." Each of these steps represents a smaller task that contributes to the overall project. In Microsoft To Do, these steps can be entered as individual tasks within a project list. You can then set deadlines, assign priorities, and add notes or attachments to each task to ensure that everything is on track.

Setting Up Projects in Microsoft To Do

To begin creating a project in Microsoft To Do, start by creating a new list specifically for that project. This list will serve as the central hub for all the tasks associated with the project. For example, if your project is "Plan a Corporate Training Program," you could create a list titled "Corporate Training Program" in Microsoft To Do.

Once your list is created, you can start adding tasks that represent the individual steps needed to complete the project. For each task, consider the following elements:

- Task Name: This should be a brief but descriptive name that clearly indicates what needs to be done. For example, "Book Venue for Training" or "Prepare Training Materials."

- Due Date: Setting a due date helps you stay on track and ensures that the project progresses according to schedule. Microsoft To Do allows you to set due dates for each task, and you can also set reminders to alert you when a task is approaching its deadline.

- Priority: Not all tasks are equally important, so it's helpful to assign priorities to each task. Microsoft To Do offers a simple priority system where you can mark tasks as "Important" or leave them as normal. Prioritizing tasks ensures that you focus on the most critical aspects of the project first.

- Subtasks: If a task is complex and requires multiple steps to complete, you can break it down into subtasks. Subtasks are a great way to manage the finer details of a project without overwhelming your main task list. For example, the task "Prepare Training Materials" might include subtasks like "Create PowerPoint Presentation," "Print Handouts," and "Order Training Manuals."

- Notes and Attachments: Microsoft To Do allows you to add notes and attachments to each task, providing a convenient way to store additional information or documents related to the project. This feature is particularly useful for keeping track of ideas, instructions, or any other information that might be relevant to the task.

Breaking Down Projects into Actionable Steps

The process of breaking down a project into actionable steps is one of the most critical aspects of effective task management. In the context of GTD, each step should be a specific action that moves you closer to completing the project. The key here is to ensure that each step is clear and concise, with no ambiguity about what needs to be done.

Let's consider an example project: "Launch a New Product." At first glance, this project might seem daunting, but by breaking it down into smaller, actionable steps, you can make the process more manageable. Here's how you might approach it:

1. Conduct Market Research:

   - Define the target audience

   - Analyze competitors

   - Gather customer feedback

   - Identify market trends

2. Develop a Marketing Strategy:

   - Create a marketing plan

   - Set marketing goals and KPIs

   - Determine marketing channels

   - Allocate budget for marketing activities

3. Design Packaging:

   - Brainstorm packaging ideas

   - Select packaging materials

   - Design the packaging layout

   - Approve the final design

4. Organize a Launch Event:

   - Choose a venue

   - Plan the event schedule

   - Send out invitations

- Arrange catering and logistics

Each of these tasks can be added as individual items in your Microsoft To Do project list. By breaking the project down in this way, you can focus on one step at a time, making steady progress toward your ultimate goal. Additionally, by setting due dates and assigning priorities, you can ensure that the project stays on track and that each task is completed in a timely manner.

Utilizing Contexts and Tags for Organization

In the GTD methodology, "contexts" are used to group tasks based on the tools, locations, or people required to complete them. For example, you might have contexts like "Phone Calls," "Emails," "Office," or "Home." Microsoft To Do allows you to use tags as a way to implement contexts in your task management system.

Tags are a powerful tool for organizing your tasks and projects. By tagging tasks with relevant contexts, you can easily filter your task list based on what you can do in a particular context. For example, if you're at the office, you can filter your tasks by the "Office" tag to see only the tasks that can be completed there. Similarly, if you have some time to make phone calls, you can filter by the "Phone Calls" tag to see a list of all the calls you need to make.

To add a tag to a task in Microsoft To Do, simply type the tag in the notes section of the task, prefixed with a hashtag (e.g., Office, PhoneCalls). You can then search for or filter tasks based on these tags. Using tags in this way allows you to organize your tasks more effectively and ensures that you can always find the tasks you need to focus on at any given time.

Managing Reference Material in Microsoft To Do

In addition to actionable tasks, projects often involve reference material that you need to keep track of. This could include documents, links, notes, or any other information related to the project. Microsoft To Do allows you to store reference material directly within your task list, making it easy to access everything you need in one place.

For example, if you're working on a project to "Organize a Conference," you might have reference material such as vendor quotes, venue options, and speaker bios. You can attach these documents directly to the relevant tasks in your Microsoft To Do list. Alternatively, you can create a separate task specifically for storing reference material, where you can add notes and attachments related to the project.

By keeping your reference material organized within Microsoft To Do, you can ensure that everything you need is easily accessible when you need it. This helps to reduce the time spent searching for information and allows you to focus more on completing the tasks at hand.

Best Practices for Project Management in Microsoft To Do

To get the most out of Microsoft To Do when managing projects, it's important to follow some best practices:

1. Keep Tasks Actionable: Each task in your project list should represent a specific, actionable step that moves you closer to completing the project. Avoid vague or broad tasks that don't clearly indicate what needs to be done.

2. Use Subtasks for Complex Tasks: If a task involves multiple steps, break it down into subtasks. This allows you to track progress more effectively and ensures that no detail is overlooked.

3. Set Realistic Deadlines: Assign due dates to each task to keep your project on track. Be realistic about how long each task will take, and avoid setting deadlines that are too tight or too far in the future.

4. Prioritize Wisely: Not all tasks are equally important, so prioritize them based on their impact on the overall project. Focus on completing high-priority tasks first, and use Microsoft To Do's importance feature to highlight these tasks in your list.

5. Review and Adjust: Regularly review your project list to track progress and make any necessary adjustments. This might involve rescheduling tasks, adding new tasks, or re-prioritizing based on changing circumstances.

By following these best practices, you can use Microsoft To Do to manage your projects more effectively, ensuring that each project is completed on time and to a high standard.

Conclusion

Creating projects and actionable steps in Microsoft To Do is a powerful way to manage complex tasks and achieve your goals. By breaking down projects into specific, manageable tasks, you can ensure that every aspect of the project is covered and that progress is tracked effectively. Microsoft To Do's features, such as task prioritization, subtasks, tags, and attachments, provide a flexible and intuitive platform for managing projects of any size or complexity. By integrating the principles of GTD with Microsoft To Do, you can enhance your productivity and ensure that your projects are completed efficiently and successfully.

3.2.2 Using Contexts and Tags

Organizing tasks effectively is a key element of the Getting Things Done (GTD) methodology. One of the primary ways to achieve this is by using contexts and tags within Microsoft To Do. This section will explore how to implement these tools to streamline your task management process, making it easier to identify, prioritize, and complete tasks based on your current situation, available resources, and mental focus.

Understanding Contexts in GTD

In the GTD system, contexts refer to the specific conditions or environments required to complete a task. A context could be a physical location, a specific tool, a particular person, or even a state of mind. The purpose of assigning contexts to tasks is to filter and organize your to-do list based on what can be done given your current circumstances. This allows you to focus on tasks that are actionable right now, minimizing decision fatigue and maximizing productivity.

For example:

- @Office: Tasks that require you to be physically present in the office.

- @Home: Tasks that can only be completed at home.

- @Computer: Tasks that need a computer.

- @Calls: Tasks that involve making phone calls.

- @Errands: Tasks that involve running errands outside.

Contexts are a way to segment your workload into manageable chunks, helping you to focus on what's possible in a given moment. When properly implemented, they enable you to quickly adapt to changes in your environment and make better decisions about how to use your time and energy.

Implementing Contexts in Microsoft To Do

Microsoft To Do doesn't have a native feature explicitly labeled as "contexts" like in some other task management apps. However, you can effectively implement contexts using tags. Tags are a versatile feature in Microsoft To Do that allows you to label tasks with keywords or phrases that describe important aspects of the task. By using tags to represent contexts, you can easily filter your tasks based on the current context.

Step-by-Step Guide to Using Contexts via Tags in Microsoft To Do:

1. Identify Your Contexts:

   Begin by identifying the primary contexts that are relevant to your work and personal life. These contexts should be aligned with the environments, tools, and conditions that frequently affect your ability to complete tasks. Start with a manageable number of contexts, and expand as necessary.

2. Create Tags for Each Context:

   In Microsoft To Do, you can create tags by simply typing `` followed by your chosen context name in the task title or notes section. For example, if you have a context for tasks that require you to be at the office, you would tag those tasks as `Office`. Do this for each of your contexts, ensuring that the tags are consistent across all tasks.

3. Assign Context Tags to Tasks:

   As you create or review tasks in Microsoft To Do, assign the appropriate context tags to them. This can be done when you initially capture the task or during your daily or weekly reviews. Make sure each task has at least one context tag, but remember that a task might have multiple relevant contexts.

4. Use the Search Bar to Filter by Context:

   Microsoft To Do allows you to search for tasks by their tags. Use the search bar at the top of the app to filter tasks by a specific context. For example, typing `Calls` into the search bar will display all tasks tagged with `Calls`, allowing you to focus only on tasks that can be done over the phone.

5. Create Custom Lists for Each Context (Optional):

If you find that you frequently work within certain contexts, consider creating separate lists in Microsoft To Do for each context. While this isn't necessary for everyone, it can help to further segment tasks and provide an easy way to focus on specific types of work. For example, you could have a list titled "@Office Tasks" that only includes tasks with the `Office` tag.

6. Review and Adjust Contexts Regularly:

Your contexts may evolve over time, especially as your work environment or personal responsibilities change. Regularly review your contexts during your weekly review process to ensure they remain relevant. Add new contexts or remove obsolete ones as needed to keep your system streamlined and effective.

Example of Contexts in Action:

Imagine you have a busy day ahead, filled with meetings and tight deadlines. In the morning, you check your `Calls` context and see that you have several phone calls to make. You can quickly handle these tasks in a batch, saving time and energy. Later, when you're at the office, you filter by `Office` to focus on tasks that require being at your desk, such as reviewing documents or attending in-person meetings. By the end of the day, you've effectively used contexts to organize your work, ensuring that you're always working on the most appropriate tasks given your circumstances.

Using Tags Beyond Contexts

While contexts are a powerful use of tags in Microsoft To Do, tags can also be used for other organizational purposes. Let's explore additional ways you can leverage tags to enhance your productivity and task management.

1. Project Tags:

Projects often consist of multiple tasks spread across different contexts. By tagging tasks with the project name, you can easily track and review all tasks related to a specific project, regardless of their context.

- Example: Suppose you're working on a project called "Website Redesign." Tag all related tasks with `WebsiteRedesign` so you can quickly see everything that needs to be done for that project, whether it's a design review (`Office`), a meeting with the client (`Calls`), or brainstorming new ideas (`Computer`).

2. Priority Tags:

In addition to using Microsoft To Do's built-in priority feature, you can create tags to signify levels of urgency or importance. This can help you make quick decisions about which tasks need immediate attention and which can be deferred.

- Example: Use tags like `Urgent`, `HighPriority`, `MediumPriority`, and `LowPriority` to categorize tasks based on their urgency. During your daily review, focus on `Urgent` tasks first to ensure you're addressing the most critical items.

3. Time-Based Tags:

For tasks that need to be completed within a specific timeframe, consider using tags that represent time requirements. This can include tags for tasks that can be completed quickly or those that require extended focus.

- Example: Use tags such as `QuickWin` for tasks that can be completed in less than 15 minutes, and `DeepWork` for tasks that require longer periods of concentrated effort. This allows you to match tasks with the time you have available.

4. Energy-Level Tags:

Some tasks require high levels of energy and concentration, while others can be done with less mental effort. By tagging tasks based on the energy required, you can match your tasks to your current energy level.

- Example: Use tags like `HighEnergy` for tasks that require creativity or intense focus, and `LowEnergy` for routine tasks like filing paperwork or responding to emails. This way, you can choose tasks that align with your energy level throughout the day.

5. Resource Tags:

If certain tasks require specific resources, tools, or people, use tags to note these requirements. This helps ensure you have everything you need before starting a task.

- Example: Tag tasks with `MeetingRoom` if they require a specific space or `JohnDoe` if they require input from a particular person. This ensures that you're fully prepared to complete the task when the time comes.

Best Practices for Using Tags

To make the most of tags in Microsoft To Do, consider the following best practices:

1. Keep Tags Consistent:

   Consistency is key when using tags. Make sure to use the same spelling and format for each tag across all tasks. This avoids confusion and ensures that all related tasks are easily searchable.

2. Avoid Tag Overload:

   While tags are useful, over-tagging can lead to clutter and reduce efficiency. Stick to a manageable number of tags that serve a clear purpose. If you find that certain tags are not being used regularly, consider removing them.

3. Use Tags in Combination:

   Don't hesitate to combine tags to create powerful filters. For example, searching for `HighPriority Office` will show you tasks that are both high priority and can be done at the office. This helps you focus on the most critical tasks in the right context.

4. Regularly Review and Update Tags:

   During your weekly reviews, take the time to review and update your tags. This ensures that your tagging system remains aligned with your current work and personal circumstances.

5. Leverage Tags for Reflection:

   Use tags as a way to reflect on your task management habits. For example, you might tag tasks that frequently get deferred or postponed with `Deferred`. Over time, you can review these tags to identify patterns and improve your task management strategies.

Conclusion

Using contexts and tags in Microsoft To Do is a powerful way to enhance your task management, making it easier to stay organized and focused in any situation. By thoughtfully implementing these tools, you can better align your tasks with your current environment, energy level, and resources, ensuring that you're always working on the right tasks at the right time.

Remember, the key to successful task management is not just capturing and completing tasks but organizing them in a way that makes them actionable and relevant. Contexts and tags are essential elements in this process, offering a flexible and customizable approach to managing the complexities of modern work and life.

By applying the principles outlined in this section, you'll be well on your way to mastering the art of getting things done with Microsoft To Do.

3.2.3 Managing Reference Material in Microsoft To Do

Managing reference material is a crucial part of the Getting Things Done (GTD) methodology. In GTD, reference material includes any non-actionable information that you need to keep for future use. This could be anything from documents, notes, and web links to emails and contact information. In Microsoft To Do, managing reference material efficiently helps you stay organized and ensures that all the information you need is readily accessible when you need it.

Understanding Reference Material

Before diving into how to manage reference material in Microsoft To Do, it's essential to understand what constitutes reference material. Reference material is typically non-actionable. This means it doesn't require any immediate action but might be useful for future projects or tasks. Examples include:

- Meeting notes

- Research documents

- Project guidelines

- Contact lists

- Inspirational quotes

- Educational articles

Having a systematic approach to manage this material helps avoid clutter and ensures that actionable tasks are not buried under piles of information.

Creating a Reference List

The first step in managing reference material in Microsoft To Do is to create a dedicated list for it. This list acts as a central repository for all your reference materials. Here's how to do it:

1. Create a New List:

   - Open Microsoft To Do.

   - Click on "New List" at the bottom of the sidebar.

   - Name this list "Reference Material" or any other name that clearly indicates its purpose.

2. Add Sections:

   - Within the Reference Material list, you can create sections to categorize different types of reference materials. For example, you could have sections for "Project Documents," "Meeting Notes," "Inspirational Quotes," and so on.

   - To add a section, click on the three dots next to the list name and select "Add section."

3. Organize by Categories:

   - Within each section, you can create individual tasks that act as placeholders for different reference items. Use meaningful titles for these tasks so you can easily find the information you need.

Adding and Managing Documents

Microsoft To Do allows you to attach files to tasks, making it a convenient way to store documents and other reference materials. Here's how you can manage documents:

1. Attach Files to Tasks:

   - Open a task in your Reference Material list.

- Click on the paperclip icon to attach a file.

- Select the file from your device. This could be a PDF, Word document, image, or any other file type.

2. Use Cloud Storage Integration:

- Microsoft To Do integrates with OneDrive, allowing you to link to files stored in the cloud. This is particularly useful for larger files or for documents that you need to share with others.

- To add a link to a OneDrive file, copy the shareable link from OneDrive and paste it into the task notes or comments section.

3. Organize Files within Tasks:

- For tasks with multiple attachments, use the task description or comments to provide context. This makes it easier to remember why you saved the document and how it relates to your projects.

Managing Web Links and Articles

In addition to documents, you may need to manage web links and online articles. Microsoft To Do provides a straightforward way to organize this type of reference material:

1. Add Links to Tasks:

- Open a task in your Reference Material list.

- Copy the URL of the web page or article you want to save.

- Paste the URL into the task notes or comments section.

2. Use Descriptive Titles:

- When adding a link, use the task title to describe the content. For example, if you're saving an article on project management, the task title could be "Article on Project Management Best Practices."

3. Categorize Links:

- Just like with documents, categorize your web links within the appropriate sections of your Reference Material list. This helps keep your reference material organized and easy to navigate.

Incorporating Notes and Ideas

Notes and ideas are another form of reference material that can be efficiently managed in Microsoft To Do. These could include brainstorming ideas, meeting summaries, or personal insights. Here's how to handle them:

1. Create Tasks for Notes:

   - For each note or idea, create a new task in your Reference Material list.

   - Use the task title to summarize the note or idea, and use the task description for more detailed information.

2. Organize by Context:

   - Group your notes and ideas by context or project. For example, you could have a section for "Project A Notes" and another for "Meeting Summaries."

3. Use Tags for Easy Retrieval:

   - Microsoft To Do allows you to add tags to tasks. Use tags to categorize notes by topic, making it easier to find them later. For example, tag notes with keywords like "brainstorming," "meeting," or "idea."

Storing Contact Information

Contact information can be a valuable part of your reference material. This might include details of colleagues, clients, or other important contacts. Here's how to manage contacts in Microsoft To Do:

1. Create a Contacts Section:

   - In your Reference Material list, create a section named "Contacts."

2. Add Contact Details:

- For each contact, create a new task. Use the task title for the contact's name and the task description for details like phone number, email address, and any other relevant information.

3. Link to Contacts:

- If you have contact information stored in other apps like Outlook, you can include links to those contacts in the task description. This provides quick access without duplicating information.

Maintaining and Reviewing Reference Material

Managing reference material is not a one-time task. It requires regular maintenance and review to ensure that the information remains relevant and useful. Here are some tips for maintaining your reference material:

1. Regular Reviews:

- Schedule regular reviews of your Reference Material list. During these reviews, check for outdated or irrelevant information and remove it. This keeps your reference list lean and useful.

2. Update and Revise:

- As you gather new reference material, add it to the appropriate sections. Update existing tasks with new information as needed. This ensures that your reference material is always current.

3. Archiving Old Material:

- For reference material that you no longer need but want to keep for historical purposes, consider creating an "Archive" section. Move outdated tasks to this section instead of deleting them. This way, you keep your main reference list clean while retaining access to older information.

Leveraging Microsoft To Do Features for Reference Material

Microsoft To Do offers several features that can enhance the management of reference material. Here are some additional tips to leverage these features effectively:

1. Using My Day for Quick Access:

  - If there are specific reference materials you need for the day, add them to My Day. This feature provides quick access to the information you need without searching through your lists.

2. Utilizing Task Comments:

  - Use the comments section in tasks to add context or updates to your reference material. This is particularly useful for tracking changes or adding insights over time.

3. Integrating with Other Tools:

  - Microsoft To Do integrates seamlessly with other Microsoft 365 tools. Use OneNote for detailed notes and link them to your tasks. Use Outlook to manage emails and link relevant emails to tasks in your Reference Material list.

Examples of Managing Reference Material

To illustrate the process, let's consider a few examples of managing reference material in Microsoft To Do:

Example 1: Managing Project Documents

- Scenario: You are working on a project that requires several important documents, including the project charter, timeline, and stakeholder communication plan.

- Steps:

  - Create a "Project Documents" section in your Reference Material list.

  - Add tasks for each document (e.g., "Project Charter," "Project Timeline").

  - Attach the relevant documents to each task or link to files in OneDrive.

  - Use the task description to note any important details or context.

Example 2: Organizing Meeting Notes

- Scenario: You attend regular meetings and need to keep track of notes and action items.

- Steps:

  - Create a "Meeting Notes" section.

  - For each meeting, create a new task titled with the meeting date and topic.

  - Use the task description to write your notes.

  - Add tags like "action items" or "discussion points" for easy reference.

Example 3: Saving Inspirational Quotes

- Scenario: You come across inspirational quotes that you want to keep for motivation.

- Steps:

  - Create an "Inspirational Quotes" section.

  - For each quote, create a new task with the quote in the title.

  - Use the task description for the author and any personal reflections.

Conclusion

Managing reference material is a vital aspect of staying organized and productive. By creating a dedicated Reference Material list in Microsoft To Do and organizing it effectively, you can ensure that all your important information is at your fingertips. Regular reviews and updates will keep your reference material relevant and useful, helping you stay on top of your tasks and projects. Microsoft To Do's features, such as file attachments, tags, and integrations, make it a powerful tool for managing reference material efficiently. With a well-organized system, you can focus on getting things done without the distraction of searching for information.

3.3 Reflecting and Reviewing

Reflecting and reviewing are essential components of the Getting Things Done (GTD) methodology. While capturing, clarifying, and organizing your tasks help you to keep track of what needs to be done, reflecting and reviewing ensure that you're on the right path. These steps are crucial for maintaining clarity, staying focused, and making necessary adjustments to your plans. In this section, we will explore how to effectively reflect and review your tasks within Microsoft To Do.

3.3.1 Conducting Weekly Reviews

The Weekly Review is a cornerstone of the GTD methodology. It is the time you set aside to review your tasks, projects, and commitments, ensuring that everything is captured, organized, and aligned with your goals. Conducting a thorough Weekly Review within Microsoft To Do helps you stay on top of your responsibilities, reduces stress, and enhances your overall productivity.

Understanding the Importance of the Weekly Review

Before diving into the steps, it's important to understand why the Weekly Review is vital. Life and work are dynamic, and things change quickly. Tasks might get completed, new priorities might emerge, and goals may shift. Without regular reflection, it's easy to lose sight of what's important and fall behind on your commitments. The Weekly Review serves as a checkpoint that allows you to:

- Regain Control: It's easy to feel overwhelmed when tasks pile up. The Weekly Review is your chance to regain control by ensuring that everything is in its proper place.

- Stay Focused: By reviewing your tasks and projects, you can identify what's most important and ensure that your actions are aligned with your goals.

- Adapt to Change: Life is unpredictable, and plans often need to be adjusted. The Weekly Review helps you adapt by giving you the opportunity to reassess your priorities.

- Reduce Stress: Knowing that you've captured and reviewed everything helps to reduce mental clutter, allowing you to focus on what really matters.

With these benefits in mind, let's explore how to conduct a Weekly Review in Microsoft To Do.

Step 1: Prepare for Your Weekly Review

Preparation is key to conducting an effective Weekly Review. Set aside a specific time each week for this process. Ideally, choose a time when you're unlikely to be interrupted and can focus without distractions. This could be at the end of your workweek, on a Sunday evening, or any other time that works best for you.

Before you begin, gather any tools or materials you might need, such as:

- Your Microsoft To Do app: Ensure that it's updated and synced across all your devices.

- A notebook or journal: Some people find it helpful to jot down thoughts or insights that come up during the review.

- Any relevant documents: If you have physical or digital documents related to your projects, have them ready.

Once you're prepared, you're ready to begin the review.

Step 2: Review Your Captured Tasks

The first step in the Weekly Review is to go through your inbox and other capture points to ensure that all your tasks have been clarified and organized. In Microsoft To Do, this typically involves reviewing your "Tasks" or "My Day" list, where you might have quickly captured tasks throughout the week.

1. Open Your To Do App: Start by opening the Microsoft To Do app and navigating to the list where you capture tasks. This might be your general "Tasks" list or a specific list you use for incoming tasks.

2. Review Each Task: Go through each task in your capture list. Ask yourself the following questions:

  - Is this task still relevant?

  - Have I already completed this task?

  - Does this task need to be broken down into smaller, actionable steps?

- Is there a specific due date or context that needs to be assigned?

3. Clarify and Organize: For each task, clarify what needs to be done and organize it accordingly. This might involve assigning the task to a specific project, setting a due date, or adding tags for context. If a task is no longer relevant, delete it.

4. Move to Appropriate Lists: Once a task has been clarified, move it to the appropriate list. If it's part of a larger project, place it in the corresponding project list. If it's something you plan to do soon, consider adding it to your "Next Actions" or "My Day" list.

This step ensures that all your captured tasks are organized and ready for action.

Step 3: Review Your Project Lists

After processing your captured tasks, the next step is to review your project lists. In Microsoft To Do, project lists are the lists that represent ongoing projects or larger goals that require multiple steps to complete.

1. Open Your Project Lists: Navigate to the lists in Microsoft To Do that represent your ongoing projects. If you have many projects, you might want to review them one at a time.

2. Check Project Progress: For each project list, review the tasks you've completed and those that are still pending. Ask yourself:

  - Is the project on track?

  - Are there any tasks that need to be added, updated, or removed?

  - Are there any obstacles or issues that need to be addressed?

3. Identify Next Actions: For each project, ensure that you have a clear next action. This is the next specific task that will move the project forward. If you don't have a next action, create one.

4. Reassess Priorities: Review the overall priority of each project. Are there projects that have become more or less important? If so, adjust your focus and priorities accordingly.

5. Update Deadlines: If any tasks or projects have deadlines, make sure they are up-to-date. Adjust deadlines as needed based on the current status of the project.

This step ensures that your projects are progressing smoothly and that you have a clear plan for moving forward.

Step 4: Review Your Calendar

Your calendar is an essential part of the Weekly Review process, as it helps you see the bigger picture of your commitments and time management.

1. Check Past Appointments: Start by reviewing your calendar for the past week. Reflect on any meetings, events, or deadlines you had. Did anything important come up that requires follow-up? Are there any tasks that need to be added based on these appointments?

2. Review Upcoming Commitments: Next, review your calendar for the upcoming week (and beyond, if necessary). Identify any important meetings, deadlines, or events that require preparation.

3. Schedule Tasks: Based on your review, schedule any tasks or activities that need to be done in the upcoming week. For example, if you have an important meeting, you might need to schedule time to prepare an agenda or gather materials.

4. Block Time for Focus Work: Consider blocking out time on your calendar for focused work or specific tasks. This helps ensure that you have dedicated time to work on your most important tasks.

Reviewing your calendar helps you stay aware of your commitments and ensures that your tasks are aligned with your schedule.

Step 5: Review Your Next Actions and Waiting For Lists

Your "Next Actions" and "Waiting For" lists are critical components of the GTD system. These lists represent tasks that are actionable now and tasks that you're waiting on others to complete.

1. Review Next Actions: Open your "Next Actions" list in Microsoft To Do and review each task. Ensure that each task is still relevant and that it's something you can act on. If any tasks are no longer necessary, remove them. If a task needs to be broken down further, do so.

2. Prioritize Your Next Actions: Identify the most important tasks in your "Next Actions" list. Consider adding these to your "My Day" list or flagging them for attention. This will help you focus on what's most important in the coming week.

3. Review Waiting For: Next, review your "Waiting For" list. This list contains tasks that you're waiting for someone else to complete. For each task, ask yourself:

  - Has the person completed the task?

  - Do I need to follow up with them?

  - Should I reassign or delegate this task to someone else?

4. Follow Up as Needed: If there are tasks on your "Waiting For" list that require follow-up, make a note to contact the relevant person. You might also consider setting reminders in Microsoft To Do to follow up at a specific time.

By reviewing these lists, you ensure that you're staying on top of your actionable tasks and following up on any dependencies.

Step 6: Review Your Goals and Long-Term Projects

While the Weekly Review focuses on immediate tasks and projects, it's also important to review your long-term goals and projects periodically. This helps you stay aligned with your bigger objectives and ensures that your daily actions are contributing to your long-term success.

1. Review Long-Term Goals: Open any lists or documents where you've captured your long-term goals. Reflect on your progress and consider whether your current tasks and projects are aligned with these goals.

2. Break Down Long-Term Projects: If you have long-term projects, ensure that they are broken down into manageable steps. Identify the next actions for these projects and add them to your relevant lists.

3. Adjust Your Focus: Based on your review, you might need to adjust your focus or reallocate your time and resources. If a long-term goal has become more urgent, consider prioritizing it in the upcoming week.

4. Reflect on Your Vision: Take a moment to reflect on your overall vision and values. Are your current projects and tasks helping you move towards your desired future? If not, consider making adjustments.

This step helps you maintain a balance between short-term tasks and long-term objectives, ensuring that your actions are always contributing to your overall vision.

Step 7: Celebrate Your Progress

The final step in the Weekly Review is to acknowledge and celebrate your progress. It's easy to get caught up in what's left to do, but it's equally important to recognize what you've accomplished.

1. Review Completed Tasks: Take a moment to review the tasks and projects you've completed over the past week. Reflect on how far you've come and the progress you've made.

2. Celebrate Wins: Identify any significant wins or milestones you've achieved. Whether it's completing a major project, overcoming a challenge, or simply staying consistent with your tasks, take time to celebrate these achievements.

3. Express Gratitude: Consider expressing gratitude for the opportunities, support, and resources that have helped you progress. This could be a simple moment of reflection or a note of thanks to someone who has supported you.

4. Motivate Yourself: Use this moment of reflection to motivate yourself for the upcoming week. Remind yourself of your goals, your progress, and the exciting challenges ahead. Celebrating your progress helps to boost your motivation, reinforce positive habits, and maintain a sense of accomplishment.

By following these steps, you can conduct an effective Weekly Review within Microsoft To Do, ensuring that your tasks, projects, and goals are always aligned and that you're on track to achieving your objectives. Regular reflection and review are essential for maintaining productivity, reducing stress, and staying focused on what matters most.

3.3.2 Tracking Progress and Adjusting Plans

Tracking progress and adjusting plans are essential components of the GTD (Getting Things Done) methodology when using Microsoft To Do. By regularly assessing your progress and making necessary adjustments, you can ensure that you stay on track with your goals and maintain a high level of productivity. This section will explore various strategies and techniques for effectively tracking progress and adjusting plans in Microsoft To Do.

Setting Clear and Measurable Goals

The first step in tracking progress is to set clear and measurable goals. When goals are specific and quantifiable, it becomes easier to monitor progress and determine whether you are on track to achieve them. In Microsoft To Do, you can create tasks that represent your goals and use due dates, reminders, and priority levels to keep them front and center.

For example, if your goal is to complete a project by a specific date, you can break down the project into smaller, actionable tasks and set deadlines for each task. This approach allows you to monitor your progress towards the larger goal by tracking the completion of individual tasks.

Using Lists and Tags for Organization

Microsoft To Do allows you to organize your tasks into lists and use tags to categorize them. This feature is particularly useful for tracking progress, as it enables you to group related tasks and monitor the completion of tasks within each category.

For instance, if you are working on multiple projects simultaneously, you can create separate lists for each project and use tags to indicate the status of each task (e.g., "In Progress," "Completed," "Pending Review"). By regularly reviewing these lists and tags, you can quickly assess your progress and identify any areas that may require adjustment.

Leveraging the My Day Feature

The My Day feature in Microsoft To Do is designed to help you focus on the tasks that need to be completed today. Each day, you can add tasks to My Day, providing a clear and manageable list of priorities.

To use My Day effectively, start by reviewing your tasks and selecting the most important or urgent ones to add to My Day. As you complete each task, mark it as done. At the end of the day, review any unfinished tasks and decide whether to carry them over to the next day or reschedule them for a later date.

By consistently using the My Day feature, you can maintain a clear focus on your daily priorities, track your progress, and ensure that you are making steady progress towards your larger goals.

Monitoring Task Completion

One of the simplest yet most effective ways to track progress is to monitor the completion of tasks. Microsoft To Do provides several features that make it easy to see which tasks have been completed and which are still pending.

As you complete tasks, mark them as done by clicking the checkbox next to each task. Completed tasks will be moved to the "Completed" section, where you can review them at any time. This visual representation of your progress can be highly motivating and provide a sense of accomplishment.

Additionally, you can use the "Completed Tasks View" to review your progress over a specific period. This feature allows you to filter completed tasks by date, providing a clear picture of your achievements and helping you identify any patterns or trends in your productivity.

Adjusting Plans Based on Progress

Tracking progress is only part of the equation; you also need to adjust your plans based on the insights you gain from monitoring your progress. This process involves evaluating your current status, identifying any obstacles or delays, and making necessary adjustments to your tasks and timelines.

Conducting Regular Reviews

Regular reviews are a cornerstone of the GTD methodology and are essential for maintaining an effective task management system in Microsoft To Do. By conducting weekly, monthly, and quarterly reviews, you can assess your progress, identify any areas that need improvement, and make necessary adjustments to your plans.

During a weekly review, for example, you can:

- Review your completed tasks from the past week and celebrate your achievements.

- Assess any incomplete tasks and determine whether they need to be rescheduled, delegated, or broken down into smaller steps.

- Update your task lists and prioritize your tasks for the upcoming week.

- Reflect on any challenges or obstacles you encountered and brainstorm solutions to overcome them.

Monthly and quarterly reviews follow a similar process but focus on a longer time frame. These reviews provide an opportunity to assess your progress towards larger goals, evaluate your overall productivity, and make strategic adjustments to your plans.

Using Insights and Analytics

Microsoft To Do does not currently offer built-in analytics or reporting features, but you can still track your progress using external tools and techniques. For example, you can export your tasks to Excel or another spreadsheet application and create custom reports to analyze your progress over time.

Additionally, you can use third-party integrations, such as Power BI, to create detailed visualizations and gain deeper insights into your productivity. By leveraging these tools, you can identify trends, measure your performance, and make data-driven decisions to improve your task management system.

Adapting to Changing Priorities

In any dynamic work environment, priorities can change rapidly. It is important to remain flexible and adapt your plans accordingly. Microsoft To Do makes it easy to adjust your tasks and timelines based on changing priorities.

For instance, if a new project or urgent task arises, you can quickly add it to your task list and adjust the due dates and priorities of your existing tasks. Use the drag-and-drop feature to rearrange tasks within your lists and ensure that your most important tasks are always at the top.

By regularly reviewing and adjusting your plans, you can stay aligned with your current priorities and ensure that you are always working on the most important tasks.

Collaborating with Team Members

If you are working on projects that involve collaboration with others, tracking progress and adjusting plans becomes even more critical. Microsoft To Do offers features that facilitate collaboration and help you stay on track with your team.

You can share task lists with team members, assign tasks to specific individuals, and use comments to communicate updates and provide feedback. By collaborating effectively, you can ensure that everyone is on the same page, monitor the progress of shared tasks, and make adjustments as needed.

Regular team check-ins and progress meetings can also help you stay coordinated and ensure that any adjustments to the plan are communicated clearly to all team members.

Automating Progress Tracking

Automation can be a powerful tool for tracking progress and adjusting plans. Microsoft To Do integrates with various automation platforms, such as Microsoft Power Automate, allowing you to create automated workflows that streamline your task management process.

For example, you can set up automated reminders for upcoming tasks, create workflows that update task statuses based on specific triggers, or integrate Microsoft To Do with other productivity tools to centralize your task management.

By leveraging automation, you can reduce manual effort, ensure consistency in tracking progress, and quickly adapt your plans based on real-time data.

Staying Motivated and Avoiding Burnout

Tracking progress and adjusting plans is not just about maintaining productivity; it's also about staying motivated and avoiding burnout. Microsoft To Do provides several features that can help you stay engaged and motivated as you work towards your goals.

Use the "Completed Tasks View" to celebrate your achievements and recognize the progress you have made. Setting realistic and achievable goals can also help you maintain a sense of accomplishment and avoid feeling overwhelmed.

Additionally, be mindful of your workload and ensure that you are not overloading yourself with too many tasks. Prioritize self-care and take regular breaks to recharge and maintain your productivity over the long term.

Conclusion

Tracking progress and adjusting plans are essential components of an effective task management system. By setting clear and measurable goals, organizing your tasks, leveraging the My Day feature, and conducting regular reviews, you can monitor your progress and make necessary adjustments to stay on track.

Microsoft To Do offers a range of features that support these practices, from task organization and prioritization to collaboration and automation. By consistently applying these strategies and techniques, you can ensure that you are working efficiently, staying aligned with your priorities, and ultimately achieving your goals.

Remember, the key to successful task management is not just about getting things done but getting the right things done at the right time. By tracking your progress and making informed adjustments, you can create a productive and balanced workflow that supports your personal and professional success.

3.3.3 Using the Completed Tasks View

The Completed Tasks View in Microsoft To Do is a powerful tool that allows you to reflect on your progress, evaluate your productivity, and maintain a record of your accomplishments. This feature is integral to the GTD methodology, which emphasizes the importance of regularly reviewing completed tasks to ensure that you remain on track with your goals and projects. This section will delve into the benefits of using the Completed Tasks View, how to access and use it effectively, and strategies for leveraging this feature to enhance your productivity.

Understanding the Importance of Reviewing Completed Tasks

In the context of GTD, reviewing completed tasks serves several purposes. First and foremost, it provides a sense of accomplishment and motivation. Seeing the tasks you've completed can reinforce positive behaviors and encourage you to continue working towards your goals. It's a visual representation of your progress and can be particularly motivating when you feel overwhelmed by the tasks ahead.

Secondly, the Completed Tasks View allows you to conduct a retrospective analysis of your work. By reviewing what you've done, you can identify patterns in your productivity, recognize tasks that may have taken longer than expected, and pinpoint areas where you might need to improve your workflow. This analysis is crucial for making informed adjustments to your planning and task management strategies.

Lastly, keeping a record of completed tasks is essential for accountability, especially in a professional setting. Whether you're working on a team or managing personal projects, being able to review and report on what you've accomplished can be invaluable during performance reviews, project debriefs, or when you simply need to recall specific details of a past task.

How to Access the Completed Tasks View in Microsoft To Do

Accessing the Completed Tasks View in Microsoft To Do is straightforward. Each list in Microsoft To Do allows you to toggle between active tasks and completed tasks, making it easy to review what you've accomplished.

1. Navigating to the List: Open the list that contains the tasks you want to review. This could be a specific project list, a daily to-do list, or any other list you've created in Microsoft To Do.

2. Viewing Completed Tasks: At the bottom of the list, you'll find an option to show or hide completed tasks. By default, completed tasks are hidden to keep your view uncluttered. Click on the "Show completed tasks" option to reveal the tasks you've marked as done.

3. Reviewing Task Details: Once you've revealed your completed tasks, you can click on each task to review the details. This includes the original due date, any notes or attachments you added, and the exact date and time the task was marked as complete.

4. Filtering Completed Tasks: If you're working with a large number of completed tasks, you might want to filter them by date, priority, or other criteria. While Microsoft To Do doesn't offer advanced filtering options within the Completed Tasks View, you can use tags or custom lists to organize and review specific sets of completed tasks.

Best Practices for Reflecting on Completed Tasks

To get the most out of the Completed Tasks View, it's essential to incorporate regular reflection into your workflow. Here are some best practices for using this feature effectively:

1. Weekly Reviews: Dedicate time each week to review your completed tasks. This aligns with the GTD practice of conducting weekly reviews, where you reflect on what you've accomplished, assess your progress towards goals, and plan the upcoming week. During this review, consider what went well, what challenges you encountered, and what adjustments you can make to improve in the future.

2. Categorize and Analyze: If you have a significant number of completed tasks, categorize them by project, priority, or context. This can help you identify trends, such as which types of tasks are taking up most of your time or which projects are progressing smoothly. Use this analysis to optimize your future task management strategies.

3. Document Key Insights: As you review your completed tasks, take notes on any key insights or lessons learned. This could include recognizing a pattern of procrastination on certain types of tasks, identifying tasks that consistently take longer than expected, or noting strategies that helped you complete tasks more efficiently. Documenting these insights can be invaluable for continuous improvement.

4. Celebrate Milestones: Use the Completed Tasks View to celebrate your achievements. Whether you've completed a major project or simply had a particularly productive day, taking the time to acknowledge your accomplishments can boost your motivation and help you maintain a positive mindset.

5. Plan for Future Action: The reflection process isn't just about looking back—it's also about planning for the future. Based on your review of completed tasks, identify any next actions that need to be added to your lists, adjust your priorities, and refine your goals. This ensures that your task management system remains dynamic and responsive to your changing needs.

Leveraging Completed Tasks for Long-Term Goals

One of the key advantages of Microsoft To Do's Completed Tasks View is its ability to help you track long-term goals. By regularly reviewing your completed tasks, you can ensure that you're making consistent progress towards larger objectives. Here's how to leverage this feature for long-term goal achievement:

1. Linking Tasks to Goals: For each long-term goal, break it down into smaller, actionable tasks and create a list or project in Microsoft To Do. As you complete these tasks, review them in the Completed Tasks View to ensure that each step is moving you closer to your goal.

2. Tracking Milestones: Use the Completed Tasks View to track when you've reached key milestones in your long-term projects. This helps you maintain momentum and provides a clear record of your progress over time.

3. Adjusting Strategies: As you review your completed tasks, consider whether your current strategies are effectively moving you towards your long-term goals. If you notice that certain tasks are not contributing as much as expected, or if progress is slower than anticipated, use this information to adjust your approach.

4. Maintaining Focus: Reflecting on completed tasks related to long-term goals can help you stay focused and motivated. By regularly reviewing what you've accomplished, you can keep your goals top of mind and ensure that your daily actions are aligned with your broader objectives.

Using Completed Tasks for Team Collaboration

If you're using Microsoft To Do in a team setting, the Completed Tasks View can also be a valuable tool for collaboration. It allows team members to review each other's progress, ensure that everyone is on track, and identify any areas where additional support might be needed.

1. Shared Lists: In a shared list, team members can view completed tasks to see what others have accomplished. This transparency fosters accountability and helps the team stay aligned on project goals.

2. Project Debriefs: After completing a project, use the Completed Tasks View to conduct a debrief with your team. Review the tasks that were completed, discuss what went well and what challenges were encountered, and document any lessons learned for future projects.

3. Continuous Improvement: Encourage team members to regularly review their own completed tasks and share insights with the group. This can lead to continuous improvement in team workflows and task management practices.

Maintaining a Balanced Perspective

While the Completed Tasks View is an excellent tool for reflection and analysis, it's important to maintain a balanced perspective. Here are a few considerations to keep in mind:

1. Avoiding Perfectionism: Reflecting on completed tasks can sometimes lead to over-analysis or a desire for perfection. While it's important to learn from your experiences, try not to dwell on minor mistakes or inefficiencies. Focus on the overall progress and the lessons learned, rather than striving for unrealistic standards.

2. Recognizing All Achievements: It's easy to focus on the most significant tasks or projects when reviewing your completed tasks, but don't overlook the smaller achievements. Every task completed, no matter how small, contributes to your overall progress. Acknowledge and appreciate these smaller wins as part of your reflection process.

3. Balancing Reflection with Action: While reflection is crucial, it's also important to balance it with action. Spend enough time reviewing your completed tasks to gain valuable insights, but don't get stuck in analysis mode. Use your reflections to inform your future actions and keep moving forward.

Conclusion

The Completed Tasks View in Microsoft To Do is more than just a log of what you've accomplished—it's a powerful tool for reflection, learning, and continuous improvement. By regularly reviewing your completed tasks, you can gain valuable insights into your productivity, identify areas for improvement, and stay motivated on your path to achieving your goals.

Incorporating this reflective practice into your weekly routine, whether through formal reviews or casual check-ins, will help you stay aligned with the principles of the GTD methodology. It ensures that your task management system remains effective, dynamic, and responsive to your changing needs.

Ultimately, the Completed Tasks View is a reminder of what you're capable of achieving. It's a testament to your progress, a source of motivation, and a guide for your future endeavors. As you continue to use Microsoft To Do to organize your work and achieve your goals, let the Completed Tasks View be a central part of your reflective practice—helping you to get things done, one task at a time.

CHAPTER IV
Advanced Features and Customization

4.1 Customizing Your Microsoft To Do Experience

Customizing your Microsoft To Do experience is essential to making the app work best for your individual needs and preferences. Microsoft To Do offers a variety of customization options that allow you to tailor your task management process, helping you stay organized, focused, and productive. In this chapter, we'll delve into the various ways you can personalize your Microsoft To Do experience, starting with how to personalize your task views.

4.1.1 Personalizing Task Views

One of the most powerful features of Microsoft To Do is its flexibility in allowing you to personalize how you view and interact with your tasks. Personalizing your task views can help you focus on what matters most, organize your workload more effectively, and ultimately increase your productivity. This section will cover the different ways you can customize your task views, including setting up your task lists, adjusting your view settings, and creating a system that works for you.

Understanding Task Views in Microsoft To Do

Before we dive into the customization options, it's important to understand the basic task views available in Microsoft To Do. These views include:

1. My Day: A dynamic list that resets every day, allowing you to choose tasks to focus on each day.

2. Planned: A view that shows tasks with due dates, sorted by date.

3. Important: A view of tasks you've marked as important.

4. Flagged Email: A view that displays emails you've flagged in Outlook, synced as tasks in To Do.

5. Assigned to You: A view showing tasks that others have assigned to you via shared lists or Microsoft Planner.

6. Tasks: A general view that shows all tasks, unsorted.

These default views provide a starting point for organizing and managing your tasks. However, to truly optimize your productivity, you'll want to customize these views according to your workflow.

1. Setting Up Custom Lists

Creating custom lists is one of the most effective ways to personalize your task views in Microsoft To Do. Custom lists allow you to categorize and group tasks based on different projects, areas of focus, or contexts, making it easier to manage and track your work.

Steps to Create Custom Lists:

1. Create a New List: Click the "+ New List" option on the sidebar, name your list, and hit Enter.

2. Organize Tasks by Context: Create lists based on contexts (e.g., Work, Personal, Shopping, Projects).

3. Use Emojis and Icons: Add emojis or icons to your list names to make them visually distinctive and easier to recognize at a glance.

4. Group Lists: You can group related lists together by creating a "Group" and dragging your lists into it. For example, create a "Work" group and add all work-related lists inside.

Benefits of Custom Lists:

- Focused Organization: Tailor your lists to match specific areas of your life, making it easier to switch contexts when necessary.

- Quick Access: Custom lists allow you to quickly access tasks relevant to your current focus or activity, minimizing distractions.

- Better Task Management: By categorizing tasks into specific lists, you can avoid clutter and better manage your workload.

2. Customizing the My Day View

The My Day feature in Microsoft To Do is a powerful tool for focusing on the tasks that matter most each day. By default, the My Day view resets every day, encouraging you to start fresh and intentionally select tasks that align with your priorities.

Personalizing My Day:

1. Add Tasks to My Day: Each morning, review your tasks and add the ones you want to focus on to My Day by clicking the sun icon next to the task.

2. Prioritize Tasks: Within My Day, reorder tasks based on priority. Drag and drop tasks to rearrange them, placing the most important or time-sensitive tasks at the top.

3. Use Suggestions: Microsoft To Do provides task suggestions based on your previous activity. Review these suggestions daily to identify tasks that might need attention.

4. Combine with Other Views: While My Day is your main focus, don't forget to glance at other views (like Planned or Important) to ensure you're covering all bases.

Benefits of Customizing My Day:

- Daily Focus: By deliberately choosing tasks for My Day, you ensure that your focus remains on what's most important.

- Flexibility: My Day adapts to changing priorities, allowing you to adjust your focus as needed.

- Encourages Reflection: The daily reset encourages you to reflect on your priorities and start each day with a clear plan.

3. Sorting and Filtering Tasks

Sorting and filtering tasks are crucial customization options that can drastically improve how you view and manage your tasks in Microsoft To Do. By organizing tasks based on specific criteria, you can quickly locate what you need and focus on relevant tasks.

Sorting Tasks:

1. Sort by Due Date: Organize tasks based on their due dates, with the earliest at the top. This is useful for deadline-driven work.

2. Sort by Creation Date: Arrange tasks in the order they were created, which can help you address newer tasks first.

3. Sort by Importance: Prioritize tasks by their importance. Tasks marked as "Important" can be sorted to appear at the top of your list.

4. Custom Sorting: Drag and drop tasks to create a custom order that reflects your unique priorities.

Filtering Tasks:

1. Filter by Tags: If you've tagged tasks with specific keywords, you can filter your list to show only tasks with those tags.

2. Filter by List: Focus on tasks within a specific list or group, filtering out tasks from other areas.

3. Filter by Due Date: View tasks due today, tomorrow, or this week, helping you focus on immediate priorities.

4. Filter by Completion Status: Toggle between viewing all tasks or only incomplete tasks to maintain focus on what's still pending.

Benefits of Sorting and Filtering:

- Clarity: Sorting and filtering bring clarity to your tasks, making it easier to focus on what's important and what needs to be done next.

- Time Management: By sorting tasks by due date or importance, you can better manage your time and avoid last-minute rushes.

- Personalization: These features allow you to tailor your task view to suit your working style and preferences.

4. Utilizing Smart Lists

Smart Lists in Microsoft To Do are automatically generated lists that aggregate tasks based on specific criteria, such as due dates or importance. While they come with default settings, you can customize which Smart Lists are visible and how they're used in your workflow.

Enabling/Disabling Smart Lists:

1. Access Settings: Go to Settings > Smart Lists to view the available options.

2. Enable/Disable Specific Lists: Toggle the visibility of Smart Lists like "Important," "Planned," or "All" based on your needs.

Customizing Smart Lists:

1. Using the Important List: Customize the Important list to only include tasks from certain lists, ensuring it remains focused on what's truly important.

2. Using the Planned List: Customize the Planned list to show only tasks due within a specific time frame, such as this week, rather than all future tasks.

3. Hiding Unused Lists: If you don't use certain Smart Lists (e.g., Assigned to You), you can hide them to reduce clutter in your sidebar.

Benefits of Customizing Smart Lists:

- Tailored Task Management: Customize Smart Lists to reflect how you organize and prioritize your tasks, making them more relevant to your workflow.

- Simplified Workflow: By hiding unnecessary lists and focusing on those that matter, you can streamline your task management process.

- Enhanced Focus: Smart Lists help you concentrate on the most pressing tasks without being overwhelmed by everything else.

5. Adjusting Task Details for Personalization

Every task in Microsoft To Do has a range of details that can be customized to better suit your needs. From due dates and reminders to notes and attachments, tailoring these details can enhance how you manage and complete your tasks.

Personalizing Task Details:

1. Due Dates and Reminders: Set specific due dates and reminders for tasks, aligning them with your schedule. For recurring tasks, customize the frequency of repetition to match your workflow.

2. Adding Notes: Use the Notes section to add context, instructions, or additional information relevant to the task. This can be particularly useful for tasks that require multiple steps or collaboration with others.

3. Attachments and Links: Attach relevant files or links to tasks, ensuring that everything you need to complete the task is in one place.

4. Using Subtasks: Break larger tasks into subtasks to track progress on individual components, making complex tasks more manageable.

Benefits of Adjusting Task Details:

- Increased Efficiency: Customizing task details allows you to organize tasks more effectively, reducing the time spent searching for information.

- Better Task Management: By tailoring due dates, reminders, and subtasks, you can ensure that tasks are completed on time and to a high standard.

- Enhanced Collaboration: Adding detailed notes and attachments improves communication and collaboration, particularly in shared lists or team projects.

6. Personalizing Notifications and Reminders

Notifications and reminders are key to staying on top of your tasks, but they need to be set up in a way that works best for you. Overly frequent reminders can be distracting, while too few can lead to missed deadlines. Microsoft To Do allows you to customize notifications and reminders to fit your preferences.

Customizing Notifications:

1. Setting Reminder Times: Adjust the default reminder times to match when you're most likely to act on them (e.g., setting reminders for the start or end of your workday).

2. Choosing Notification Types: Decide which types of notifications you want to receive (e.g., due dates, reminders, shared list updates) and on which devices.

3. Snoozing Reminders: Customize the snooze duration for reminders, allowing you to temporarily delay a notification without forgetting the task.

Personalizing Reminder Settings:

1. Context-Specific Reminders: Set reminders based on specific contexts or locations, ensuring you're reminded of tasks when you're in the right place to complete them.

2. Recurring Reminders: For recurring tasks, customize how often reminders appear, ensuring they're frequent enough to keep you on track without becoming a nuisance.

3. Managing Notification Preferences Across Devices: Sync your notification preferences across devices to ensure consistency, or customize notifications for different devices based on how you use them.

Benefits of Customizing Notifications and Reminders:

- Avoiding Overload: By fine-tuning notifications, you can avoid becoming overwhelmed by alerts, allowing you to focus on what matters most.

- Timely Task Completion: Custom reminders help ensure that you complete tasks on time, without the need to constantly check your task lists.

- Greater Flexibility: Personalized reminders and notifications give you more control over your time and attention, leading to increased productivity.

Conclusion: The Power of Personalization

Customizing your task views in Microsoft To Do is more than just a matter of aesthetics; it's about creating a system that supports your unique workflow and productivity needs. By setting up custom lists, adjusting task details, personalizing your My Day view, and fine-tuning notifications, you can transform Microsoft To Do into a powerful tool that helps you get things done with greater efficiency and ease. The time you invest in personalization will pay off in the form of a more streamlined, focused, and productive task management experience.

4.1.2 Changing Themes and Appearance

Microsoft To Do is more than just a task management tool; it's an environment where you spend significant time organizing your work and personal life. Customizing the appearance of your Microsoft To Do app allows you to create a workspace that is visually appealing and tailored to your preferences, which can enhance your overall productivity and satisfaction. This section will guide you through the various options available to change themes and appearance, and how these adjustments can impact your user experience.

Why Customize Themes and Appearance?

Before diving into the how-to, it's important to understand why you might want to customize the appearance of Microsoft To Do. Personalization isn't just about aesthetics; it's about creating an environment that suits your workflow and mental state. The right color scheme, theme, and layout can:

1. Improve Focus and Productivity: Certain colors and visual arrangements can help reduce eye strain, improve focus, and make it easier to navigate and manage tasks.

2. Reflect Your Personality: Customizing your workspace can make it feel more personal, comfortable, and aligned with your unique style or brand.

3. Enhance Mood and Motivation: A workspace that you enjoy looking at can positively impact your mood and motivation, making it more enjoyable to plan and execute tasks.

Exploring Theme Options

Microsoft To Do offers a variety of theme options that allow you to change the overall look and feel of the application. These themes can be applied globally across the app or set individually for each task list.

1. Default Themes

   - Light Theme: This is the standard theme with a clean, bright look. It's ideal for users who prefer a minimalist and straightforward interface. The Light Theme enhances readability in well-lit environments and is often favored during daytime use.

   - Dark Theme: The Dark Theme offers a more subdued, low-light option. It's easier on the eyes during nighttime or in low-light settings. This theme is also popular among users who prefer a modern, sleek look and is known to reduce eye strain over long periods.

   - System Theme: The System Theme adapts to the current theme of your operating system (Windows or macOS). If your system switches between light and dark modes based on the time of day, Microsoft To Do will automatically adjust to match. This dynamic theme option is perfect for those who like their apps to seamlessly integrate with their overall system environment.

2. Custom Themes

- Color Themes: Microsoft To Do allows you to apply specific color themes to individual task lists. For instance, you can assign a blue theme to work-related tasks and a green theme to personal tasks. These color themes make it easy to visually distinguish between different categories of tasks at a glance. To set a color theme, simply select a list, click on the three dots (more options), and choose "Theme" from the menu. A palette of colors will appear, allowing you to select the one that best suits your needs.

- Custom Backgrounds: In addition to color themes, you can customize the background of your task lists with images. Microsoft To Do offers a selection of background images to choose from, ranging from abstract designs to nature scenes. If none of the provided images suit your style, you can upload your own. This feature allows for even greater personalization and can help you create a workspace that is visually inspiring.

How to Change Themes and Appearance

Now that you understand the different options available, let's go through the steps to change themes and appearance in Microsoft To Do.

1. Changing the Overall App Theme

- Step 1: Open the Microsoft To Do app on your device.

- Step 2: Click on your profile picture or initials in the upper right-hand corner of the app to open the settings menu.

- Step 3: In the settings menu, scroll down to the "Theme" section.

- Step 4: Choose between the Light, Dark, or System theme. Your selection will be applied immediately across the entire app.

2. Setting a Custom Theme for Individual Lists

- Step 1: Navigate to the task list you want to customize.

- Step 2: Click on the three dots (more options) located in the upper right-hand corner of the list.

- Step 3: Select "Theme" from the dropdown menu.

- Step 4: Choose a color from the available palette. This color will now be applied to the header and various accents within the list.

- Step 5 (Optional): To add a custom background image, select the "Background" option and either choose from the provided images or upload your own.

3. Syncing Themes Across Devices

- One of the great features of Microsoft To Do is that your theme and appearance settings sync across all your devices. If you set a dark theme on your desktop, it will automatically apply to your mobile app as well, provided you are logged into the same Microsoft account. This ensures a consistent experience, no matter where you access your tasks.

Impact of Themes on Productivity

While themes and appearance settings might seem purely cosmetic, they can have a significant impact on your productivity and task management. Here's how different themes can influence your work habits:

1. Light Theme for Clarity and Focus

- The Light Theme is often associated with clarity and focus. The high contrast between text and background in this theme can make it easier to read and organize your tasks, which is particularly beneficial in bright environments. If you find yourself working in well-lit spaces or during the day, the Light Theme might help you maintain focus and prevent distractions.

2. Dark Theme for Comfort and Extended Use

- The Dark Theme is designed for comfort, especially in low-light conditions. It reduces the amount of blue light emitted by your screen, which can be beneficial for those who spend long hours in front of the computer. The Dark Theme is also less likely to cause eye fatigue, making it a good choice for evening work sessions or if you prefer a more relaxed visual experience.

3. Color Themes for Quick Task Identification

- Using color themes for different lists helps in quickly identifying tasks related to specific projects or categories. For example, assigning a red theme to high-priority tasks can help you spot urgent items at a glance. This method of color-coding can enhance your ability to prioritize and manage tasks effectively.

4. Custom Backgrounds for Inspiration and Motivation

- Custom backgrounds allow you to inject personality and inspiration into your workspace. A background image that resonates with you can serve as a motivational tool, helping to create a positive emotional response when you open your task list. Whether it's a serene landscape, an abstract design, or a personal photo, the right background can set the tone for your workday and keep you motivated.

Considerations for Accessibility

When customizing themes and appearance, it's important to consider accessibility. Microsoft To Do is designed with accessibility in mind, and certain themes might be better suited for users with specific needs:

1. High Contrast for Better Visibility

- For users with visual impairments, high-contrast themes can make it easier to read text and distinguish between different elements on the screen. While the Light Theme typically offers high contrast, some custom color themes might not. It's important to test different options to find the one that provides the best visibility.

2. Font Size and Spacing Adjustments

- Although theme customization in Microsoft To Do doesn't directly change font size or spacing, these can be adjusted through your operating system's accessibility settings. Ensuring that text is large enough to read comfortably is key to maintaining productivity, particularly for those with visual challenges.

3. Screen Reader Compatibility

- Microsoft To Do is compatible with screen readers, and changing themes shouldn't impact the effectiveness of these tools. However, users relying on screen readers should choose themes that maintain a clear visual hierarchy to ensure smooth navigation and task management.

Common Issues and Troubleshooting

While changing themes and appearance is generally straightforward, you might encounter some issues along the way. Here are a few common problems and how to resolve them:

1. Theme Settings Not Syncing

   - If your theme settings don't appear to be syncing across devices, ensure that you are logged into the same Microsoft account on all devices. Additionally, check that sync is enabled in the app settings. If the issue persists, try signing out and back into the app to force a sync.

2. Custom Background Not Displaying Correctly

   - If your custom background image isn't displaying as expected, ensure that the image meets the required file format and size. Large images might take longer to load, especially on mobile devices, so consider resizing the image to optimize performance.

3. Difficulty Changing Themes on Mobile

   - On mobile devices, theme settings might be located in a different part of the app. If you're having trouble finding the theme options, check under the "Settings" menu, usually accessible from your profile icon or the app's main menu. If you're still unable to locate the theme settings, consider checking for app updates or reinstalling the app.

Leveraging Themes for Different Workflows

Different workflows might benefit from different theme settings. Here are some suggestions for how to match your theme choice with your work style:

1. Project Management

   - If you manage multiple projects, consider using different color themes for each project list. This will help you quickly switch between projects and stay organized. A Dark Theme might be beneficial if you're working on complex projects that require extended focus and screen time.

2. Personal Task Management

   - For personal tasks, a Light Theme combined with calming background images can create a relaxing and inviting space for managing daily chores, personal goals, and hobbies. Color themes can also be used to distinguish between different areas of your life, such as fitness, home maintenance, and leisure activities.

3. Team Collaboration

   - When collaborating with a team, consistent use of themes can help create a unified appearance across shared lists. For example, using a specific color theme for all shared lists can foster a sense of cohesion and make it easier for team members to navigate shared tasks.

Future of Customization in Microsoft To Do

As Microsoft continues to develop and enhance its products, we can expect to see more customization options in future updates to Microsoft To Do. Potential enhancements might include:

1. Advanced Theme Settings

   - Future updates could introduce more granular control over themes, such as custom color palettes, advanced background settings, and even animated backgrounds for a more dynamic user experience.

2. Integration with Personalization Tools

   - Microsoft To Do might integrate with other Microsoft personalization tools, allowing users to sync themes across multiple apps or even create custom themes that apply to their entire Microsoft 365 environment.

3. Enhanced Accessibility Features

   - As accessibility continues to be a priority, we can anticipate more options designed to accommodate a wider range of needs, such as customizable font styles, additional high-contrast themes, and further screen reader optimizations.

Conclusion

Customizing themes and appearance in Microsoft To Do is more than just a way to make the app look good—it's a tool to enhance your productivity, focus, and overall experience. By taking the time to personalize your workspace, you can create an environment that not only meets your functional needs but also inspires and motivates you to achieve your goals.

Whether you prefer a clean, minimalist look or a vibrant, colorful interface, Microsoft To Do offers the flexibility to make your task management experience truly your own.

4.1.3 Customizing Notifications and Reminders

Microsoft To Do is a powerful task management tool that helps you stay on top of your tasks and deadlines. One of the key features that makes it so effective is its ability to send you notifications and reminders. These alerts ensure that you never miss an important deadline, meeting, or task. In this section, we will explore the various ways you can customize notifications and reminders in Microsoft To Do to suit your specific needs and preferences.

Understanding the Role of Notifications and Reminders

Before diving into customization, it's important to understand the difference between notifications and reminders in Microsoft To Do:

- Notifications: These are alerts that pop up on your device to inform you about a task or event. They are designed to catch your attention and can be triggered by a variety of events, such as the start of a task, a due date approaching, or a task being completed.

- Reminders: These are specific types of notifications that you set for individual tasks. Reminders can be set to alert you at a particular time, such as a few hours or days before a task is due. They serve as prompts to ensure you remember to complete the task on time.

Effective use of notifications and reminders can significantly boost your productivity by keeping you informed and on track. Customizing these alerts allows you to tailor them to your workflow, ensuring they are as helpful as possible without being disruptive.

Setting Up Basic Notifications

Microsoft To Do allows you to configure notifications at both the app level and the task level. Here's how you can set up and customize basic notifications:

1. Configuring App-Level Notifications

App-level notifications are general alerts that apply to the entire Microsoft To Do app. These include notifications for due dates, reminders, and task completions. To customize app-level notifications:

- Access Notification Settings: Open Microsoft To Do on your device. Navigate to the settings menu, which can typically be accessed by clicking on your profile picture or the gear icon in the upper-right corner of the screen.

- Enable or Disable Notifications: In the settings menu, you will find an option for notifications. You can choose to enable or disable notifications for due dates, reminders, and completed tasks. If you find that you're receiving too many notifications, you may choose to disable some of them to reduce distractions.

- Customize Notification Timing: You can also adjust when you receive notifications. For example, you might prefer to receive notifications only for tasks that are due within the next 24 hours, rather than for every task with an upcoming due date. This helps you focus on the most urgent tasks without being overwhelmed by alerts.

 2. Customizing Task-Level Notifications

Task-level notifications are more specific and allow you to tailor alerts for individual tasks. Here's how to customize them:

- Setting Task Reminders: When creating or editing a task, you can set a reminder by clicking on the task and selecting the reminder icon (usually depicted as a bell). You can then choose the date and time when you want to be reminded of the task. For example, if you have a meeting at 3 PM, you might set a reminder for 2:30 PM to ensure you have time to prepare.

- Choosing Recurring Reminders: For tasks that occur regularly, such as daily or weekly reports, you can set recurring reminders. When setting a reminder, select the recurrence option and choose the appropriate frequency (daily, weekly, monthly, etc.). This ensures you're alerted for each occurrence of the task without having to manually set new reminders each time.

- Adjusting Notification Preferences for Specific Tasks: For tasks that require more attention, you might choose to receive multiple reminders leading up to the due date. Conversely, for less critical tasks, you might only want one reminder shortly before the task is due. Microsoft To Do allows you to set multiple reminders for a single task, each at a different time, giving you flexibility in how you're notified.

Advanced Notification Customization

Beyond the basic settings, Microsoft To Do offers advanced customization options that allow you to fine-tune how and when you receive notifications. This can be particularly useful for managing complex workflows or collaborating with a team.

1. Integrating with Calendar Apps

One powerful way to enhance your notification system is by integrating Microsoft To Do with your calendar app. This allows you to see your tasks alongside your scheduled events, providing a comprehensive view of your day.

- Syncing with Outlook Calendar: If you use Microsoft Outlook, you can sync your To Do tasks with your Outlook calendar. This integration allows your tasks to appear in your calendar view, and you can set reminders directly from your calendar app. To set this up, go to your To Do settings and enable the calendar sync option.

- Using Third-Party Calendar Integrations: If you use a different calendar app, such as Google Calendar, you can still integrate your tasks by exporting your Microsoft To Do tasks and importing them into your calendar. While this method might require more manual setup, it ensures that all your reminders and notifications are consolidated in one place.

2. Customizing Notification Sounds and Alerts

Sometimes, the standard notification sounds might not be enough to catch your attention, especially if you receive a lot of alerts throughout the day. Microsoft To Do allows you to customize notification sounds to make them more noticeable.

- Changing Notification Sounds: On most devices, you can change the sound that plays when you receive a notification. This can be done through your device's notification settings, where you can select a different sound for Microsoft To Do alerts. Choose a sound that you associate with urgency to help you prioritize tasks.

- Enabling Vibrations or LED Alerts: If you often keep your phone on silent, consider enabling vibration or LED alerts for Microsoft To Do notifications. This ensures you still receive a physical prompt when a task reminder goes off, even if you're in a meeting or in a quiet environment.

3. Using Location-Based Reminders

One of the more advanced features in Microsoft To Do is the ability to set location-based reminders. These reminders trigger notifications when you arrive at or leave a specific location, making them ideal for tasks that are tied to a particular place.

- Setting Up Location-Based Reminders: To set a location-based reminder, select a task and choose the reminder option. Instead of setting a time, choose the location option and enter the address or location where you want to be reminded. For example, you might set a reminder to pick up groceries when you leave work or to call a client when you arrive at the office.

- Managing Location Permissions: To use location-based reminders, you need to ensure that Microsoft To Do has permission to access your device's location services. This can be configured in your device's privacy settings. Be mindful of battery usage, as continuous location tracking can drain your device's battery faster.

Optimizing Notification Workflow for Teams

If you're using Microsoft To Do within a team, notifications and reminders can play a crucial role in ensuring everyone stays aligned and on schedule. Here are some tips for optimizing notifications in a collaborative environment:

 1. Coordinating Task Assignments with Notifications

When working in a team, assigning tasks and setting corresponding notifications can help ensure that everyone is aware of their responsibilities and deadlines.

- Assigning Tasks with Notifications: When you assign a task to a team member, consider setting a reminder for them. This can be done by adding a due date and selecting the option to notify the assignee. This ensures that the person responsible for the task receives a timely reminder, reducing the chances of missed deadlines.

- Using Shared Lists for Team Visibility: By sharing task lists with your team, everyone can see which tasks have reminders set. This transparency helps team members understand the timeline of a project and coordinate their efforts more effectively.

 2. Managing Notification Overload

In a busy team environment, it's easy to become overwhelmed by notifications, especially if you're juggling multiple projects. Here's how to manage notification overload:

- Prioritizing Important Alerts: Not all tasks require immediate attention. Use Microsoft To Do's priority settings to filter notifications so that only high-priority tasks trigger alerts. This helps you focus on what's most important without being distracted by less urgent tasks.

- Setting Quiet Hours: If you need uninterrupted time to focus, consider setting quiet hours during which notifications are muted. This can be particularly useful during meetings or focused work periods. Quiet hours can be configured in your device's Do Not Disturb settings, ensuring that only the most critical alerts break through.

3. Leveraging Power Automate for Custom Alerts

For advanced users, Microsoft's Power Automate can be a game-changer in creating custom workflows that include notifications and reminders. Power Automate allows you to set up automated flows that trigger alerts based on specific conditions.

- Creating Automated Flows: For example, you could create a flow that sends an email reminder to a team member if a task is not marked as complete by a certain date. Or, you might set up a flow that posts a notification in a Microsoft Teams channel when a high-priority task is added to a shared list.

- Using Templates for Common Scenarios: Power Automate offers a variety of templates that can help you quickly set up common workflows. These templates can be customized to fit your team's needs, saving you time while ensuring that your notification system is as effective as possible.

Balancing Notifications for Personal Productivity

While notifications are essential for staying on track, too many alerts can be counterproductive. It's important to strike a balance between being informed and avoiding notification fatigue. Here's how to maintain that balance:

1. Reviewing and Adjusting Notification Settings Regularly

Your needs may change over time, so it's important to periodically review and adjust your notification settings in Microsoft To Do. Take the time to evaluate which alerts are helpful and which ones might be unnecessary.

- Conducting Regular Reviews: Set aside time every few weeks to review your notification settings. Ask yourself whether the alerts you're receiving are contributing to your productivity or if they're becoming a distraction. Adjust your settings accordingly to keep your workflow optimized.

- Experimenting with Different Settings: Don't be afraid to experiment with different notification settings. You might find that reducing the number of alerts or changing the timing of reminders helps you stay focused. The goal is to find a setup that keeps you informed without overwhelming you.

2. Incorporating Breaks into Your Notification Schedule

Continuous notifications can lead to burnout, especially if you're constantly being reminded of tasks throughout the day. To prevent this, consider incorporating breaks into your notification schedule.

- Scheduling Breaks from Notifications: Use Microsoft To Do's scheduling features to block off time for breaks during the day. During these periods, you can mute notifications, allowing yourself time to recharge without the pressure of constant reminders.

- Using Notifications to Promote Healthy Habits: On the flip side, you can also use reminders to promote healthy habits, such as taking a walk or stretching. By setting reminders for these activities, you can ensure that you're taking care of your well-being while staying productive.

3. Integrating with Focused Work Techniques

To maximize productivity, consider integrating notifications with focused work techniques like the Pomodoro Technique or time blocking.

- Using Reminders for Pomodoro Sessions: If you use the Pomodoro Technique, where you work in focused intervals with short breaks, set reminders for the start and end of each session. This helps you stay disciplined and ensures that you're taking regular breaks to maintain your focus.

- Time Blocking with Notifications: If you practice time blocking, where you allocate specific blocks of time for different tasks, use Microsoft To Do to set reminders at the beginning and end of each block. This keeps you on schedule and helps you transition smoothly between tasks.

Conclusion

Customizing notifications and reminders in Microsoft To Do is an essential step in creating a task management system that works for you. By understanding the different types of alerts available, configuring them to suit your needs, and integrating them with your workflow, you can ensure that you're always informed without being overwhelmed.

Whether you're managing personal tasks, collaborating with a team, or working on complex projects, Microsoft To Do's notification features offer the flexibility and control you need to stay productive and achieve your goals.

4.2 Integrating with Other Microsoft 365 Apps

Integration is one of the most powerful features of Microsoft To Do. By seamlessly connecting with other Microsoft 365 applications, To Do can become an even more effective tool for task management, allowing users to synchronize tasks across platforms, collaborate more effectively, and automate routine processes. In this section, we'll explore how Microsoft To Do integrates with other key apps in the Microsoft 365 suite, starting with Microsoft Outlook.

4.2.1 Syncing with Microsoft Outlook

Microsoft Outlook is a widely-used email and calendar application that forms the backbone of communication and scheduling in many organizations. Integrating Microsoft To Do with Outlook allows users to manage their tasks directly from their email inbox and calendar, ensuring that nothing slips through the cracks. This integration is particularly useful for professionals who rely on Outlook to keep track of their daily responsibilities, as it helps unify task management across platforms.

Understanding the Integration

The integration between Microsoft To Do and Outlook is designed to be intuitive and seamless. When you sync the two applications, tasks from Outlook's "Tasks" section automatically appear in Microsoft To Do, and any changes made in one application will reflect in the other. This means that whether you prefer working directly from your Outlook inbox or using the dedicated To Do app, you'll always have access to the most up-to-date information.

Setting Up the Sync

To get started with syncing Microsoft To Do and Outlook, follow these steps:

1. Access Microsoft To Do Settings:

   - Open the Microsoft To Do app on your device.

- Click on your profile picture or initials in the upper-right corner of the screen to open the account settings menu.

- Select "Settings" from the dropdown list.

2. Enable Task Syncing:

- In the settings menu, locate the "Connected Apps and Services" section.

- You should see an option labeled "Outlook" or "Outlook Tasks." Click on it to enable syncing.

- If prompted, sign in with your Microsoft account credentials.

3. Customize Sync Preferences:

- Once syncing is enabled, you can customize how tasks are synced between the two apps.

- Choose whether you want all tasks to sync automatically or if you'd prefer to manually select which tasks to sync.

- Set preferences for how tasks are displayed, including due dates, reminders, and categories.

4. Confirm Sync:

- After setting your preferences, click "Save" or "Confirm" to finalize the integration.

- Your tasks should now appear in both Microsoft To Do and Outlook.

Using the Integration in Daily Workflows

Now that you've set up the sync, it's important to understand how to effectively use the integration in your daily workflows. Here are some key ways to make the most of the Microsoft To Do and Outlook integration:

1. Managing Email Tasks:

- Many tasks originate from emails. With the To Do and Outlook integration, you can easily convert emails into tasks.

- In Outlook, simply drag and drop an email into the Tasks section, or right-click on an email and select "Add to Microsoft To Do." This will create a new task in To Do with the email subject as the task title.

- You can then set due dates, reminders, and priorities directly in Microsoft To Do.

2. Synchronizing Calendar Events:

   - Outlook's calendar is a central hub for scheduling meetings, deadlines, and events. With the integration, any tasks associated with these calendar events can be easily managed in To Do.

   - For example, if you schedule a meeting in Outlook, you can create a corresponding task in To Do to prepare for the meeting, set reminders, and track related actions.

   - This ensures that you're always prepared for upcoming events and deadlines.

3. Tracking Project Tasks:

   - For project managers and team members, syncing tasks between Outlook and Microsoft To Do can be invaluable for keeping track of project progress.

   - Use Outlook's email and calendar functions to communicate and schedule, and rely on Microsoft To Do to manage the specific tasks associated with these projects.

   - You can also share task lists with other team members to ensure everyone is aligned and aware of their responsibilities.

4. Prioritizing Tasks Across Platforms:

   - One of the challenges of using multiple apps is ensuring that your priorities are consistent across platforms. With the Outlook and To Do integration, you can prioritize tasks in either application, and the changes will be reflected everywhere.

   - Use Outlook's categories and flags to mark important tasks, and then refine these priorities in Microsoft To Do using the "My Day" feature or custom lists.

5. Using Reminders and Notifications:

   - Both Outlook and Microsoft To Do offer robust reminder and notification systems. By integrating the two, you can ensure that you receive timely alerts for all your tasks, regardless of where they were created.

   - Set reminders in To Do for tasks that need to be completed by a specific time, and sync these with Outlook to get notifications on your email and calendar.

Advanced Tips for Syncing Microsoft To Do with Outlook

Once you're comfortable with the basic integration, you can explore more advanced features and tips to further optimize your workflow:

1. Creating Recurring Tasks:

  - If you have tasks that repeat on a regular basis, you can set them up as recurring tasks in either Outlook or Microsoft To Do.

  - For example, if you have a weekly meeting, you can create a recurring task to prepare for the meeting each week. This task will automatically appear in both To Do and Outlook, ensuring you're always prepared.

2. Using Categories and Tags:

  - Both Outlook and Microsoft To Do allow you to categorize tasks using tags or labels. These categories can help you organize your tasks by project, priority, or context.

  - When you sync tasks between the two apps, make sure to use consistent categories to maintain organization across platforms.

3. Leveraging Smart Lists:

  - Microsoft To Do offers a feature called "Smart Lists," which automatically groups tasks based on certain criteria, such as due dates, importance, or completion status.

  - By using Smart Lists, you can quickly see tasks that are due soon, tasks you've flagged as important in Outlook, or tasks that need to be completed today.

4. Automating Task Creation:

  - With the integration in place, you can automate the creation of tasks based on specific email triggers in Outlook.

  - For instance, you can use Outlook rules to automatically create a task in Microsoft To Do when you receive an email from a particular sender or with a specific keyword in the subject line. This is especially useful for managing recurring requests or following up on important communications.

Troubleshooting Sync Issues

While the integration between Microsoft To Do and Outlook is generally smooth, there may be times when you encounter sync issues. Here are some common problems and how to resolve them:

1. Tasks Not Syncing:

  - If tasks are not syncing between Outlook and Microsoft To Do, first ensure that you are signed into the same Microsoft account on both apps.

  - Check your internet connection, as syncing requires a stable connection.

  - Try refreshing the To Do app or restarting Outlook to see if the tasks appear.

2. Duplicate Tasks:

  - Duplicate tasks can occur if you accidentally sync the same task from multiple accounts or platforms.

  - To resolve this, review your task lists in both Outlook and Microsoft To Do, and delete any duplicates.

  - Ensure that you are only syncing tasks from one account at a time to avoid future duplicates.

3. Missing Tasks:

  - If a task you created in Outlook is missing in Microsoft To Do (or vice versa), check your sync settings to make sure all tasks are being synced.

  - Also, ensure that the task was saved properly in the original app before checking the synced app.

Conclusion

Syncing Microsoft To Do with Outlook is a powerful way to streamline your task management process, ensuring that you never miss an important task or deadline. By integrating these two applications, you can manage your email, calendar, and tasks in a unified way, making it easier to stay organized and productive.

Whether you're managing personal tasks, team projects, or a combination of both, the Microsoft To Do and Outlook integration offers the flexibility and functionality you need to keep everything on track. With this integration in place, you can focus on getting things done, confident that your tasks are always up-to-date and accessible wherever you are.

Next, we'll explore how Microsoft To Do can be integrated with other Microsoft 365 apps like Teams and Planner, further expanding its capabilities and usefulness in a collaborative work environment.

4.2.2 Using Microsoft To Do with Teams and Planner

As the digital workplace evolves, the need for integrated tools that facilitate seamless collaboration and task management becomes increasingly crucial. Microsoft To Do, when combined with Microsoft Teams and Planner, provides a robust solution for managing tasks within a collaborative environment. This section explores how you can leverage the strengths of Microsoft To Do in conjunction with Teams and Planner to create a cohesive and efficient workflow that supports both individual and team productivity.

Understanding the Role of Microsoft Teams and Planner

Before diving into the integration process, it's important to understand the distinct roles of Microsoft Teams and Planner within the Microsoft 365 ecosystem:

- Microsoft Teams: Primarily a communication and collaboration platform, Microsoft Teams enables team members to chat, hold meetings, and collaborate on files in real-time. It serves as a hub for teamwork, integrating with various Microsoft 365 apps to streamline workflows.

- Microsoft Planner: A task management tool designed for team collaboration, Planner allows teams to create plans, organize and assign tasks, and track progress visually through boards and charts. It is particularly useful for managing projects, ensuring that everyone is on the same page.

While Microsoft To Do is focused on individual task management, Teams and Planner cater to group-based task management and communication. Integrating these tools enables a unified approach where individual tasks (managed in To Do) and team tasks (managed in Planner and Teams) coexist and complement each other.

Setting Up the Integration

The integration between Microsoft To Do, Teams, and Planner allows you to synchronize tasks across platforms, ensuring that nothing falls through the cracks. Here's how you can set up and maximize the use of this integration:

1. Linking Microsoft To Do with Teams

Microsoft Teams is not just a chat platform; it's a powerful tool for managing tasks and projects. Integrating To Do with Teams brings your personal tasks into the collaborative space of Teams, making it easier to keep track of what you need to do both individually and as part of a team.

- Adding Microsoft To Do as a Tab in Teams: To integrate Microsoft To Do with Teams, you can add To Do as a tab within any channel. This allows team members to access their personal tasks directly from Teams. To do this:

1. Open Microsoft Teams and navigate to the channel where you want to add To Do.

2. Click on the "+" (plus) icon at the top of the channel to add a new tab.

3. In the list of apps, search for "Tasks by Planner and To Do" and select it.

4. Choose the "My Tasks" option to display personal tasks from Microsoft To Do.

5. Once added, the tab will show tasks, allowing you to manage them directly within Teams.

- Task Notifications in Teams: You can configure Teams to send notifications for tasks created or updated in Microsoft To Do. This ensures that you stay informed about your tasks while collaborating with your team. Notifications can be customized to alert you based on task priority, due dates, or changes made by team members.

- Using the To Do Bot in Teams: Microsoft Teams also supports bots, including the To Do bot, which allows you to add and manage tasks directly from the chat interface. By interacting with the To Do bot, you can quickly create new tasks, mark tasks as complete, or get reminders about your tasks without leaving the Teams environment.

2. Integrating Microsoft To Do with Planner

While Microsoft To Do excels at managing personal tasks, Planner is designed for managing team tasks. By integrating the two, you can have a complete view of both your individual and team responsibilities.

- Viewing Planner Tasks in Microsoft To Do: Microsoft To Do allows you to view and manage tasks from Planner within the To Do interface. This integration ensures that you don't need to switch between apps to stay on top of your responsibilities. To enable this:

1. Open Microsoft To Do and navigate to the "Planned" or "Assigned to Me" list.

2. Tasks that are assigned to you in Planner will automatically appear in these lists.

3. You can manage these tasks in To Do, including setting reminders, due dates, and marking them as complete.

- Managing Tasks Across Both Tools: While tasks created in Planner are intended for team management, integrating with To Do means you can manage these tasks alongside your personal ones. For instance, you can add Planner tasks to your "My Day" list in To Do, helping you prioritize them alongside personal tasks.

- Creating Planner Tasks from Microsoft To Do: Although To Do is mainly for personal task management, there are scenarios where you might want to convert a personal task into a team task managed in Planner. While this feature is somewhat limited, you can manually create a corresponding Planner task and link it to your To Do task for better tracking.

- Using Labels and Tags Across Platforms: Both To Do and Planner support labels and tags, allowing you to categorize tasks. Consistent use of labels and tags across both platforms can help you maintain a cohesive task management system. For example, you can use a specific tag to indicate tasks related to a particular project, regardless of whether they are managed in To Do or Planner.

3. Collaborative Task Management

Collaboration is at the heart of integrating Microsoft To Do with Teams and Planner. Here's how you can enhance your collaborative efforts through this integration:

- Sharing Lists with Teams: In Microsoft To Do, you can share task lists with others, making it easier to collaborate on shared responsibilities. By sharing a list with your team, everyone can contribute to the task list, add new tasks, and update existing ones. This is particularly useful for smaller teams or projects that don't require the full functionality of Planner.

- Assigning Tasks in Planner and Viewing in To Do: When tasks are assigned in Planner, they automatically appear in the assignee's To Do app. This ensures that team members are always aware of their responsibilities, even if they primarily manage their tasks in To

Do. This seamless integration helps in maintaining accountability and ensures that team members are notified of their tasks without needing to monitor multiple apps.

- Tracking Team Progress: While Microsoft To Do is great for individual task management, Planner's visual tools like boards and charts are more suited for tracking team progress. By integrating the two, team members can manage their tasks in To Do while project managers can track overall progress in Planner. This dual approach leverages the strengths of both tools—personal productivity and team collaboration.

4. Workflow Automation with Power Automate

One of the key advantages of using Microsoft To Do with Teams and Planner is the ability to automate workflows using Power Automate. Power Automate allows you to create automated workflows between your favorite apps and services to synchronize files, get notifications, collect data, and more.

- Automating Task Creation: You can create automated workflows that trigger task creation in Microsoft To Do or Planner based on specific conditions. For example, you can set up a flow that creates a new task in Microsoft To Do whenever a new task is assigned to you in Planner. This ensures that your personal task list is always up to date with your team assignments.

- Syncing Tasks Across Platforms: If you frequently move tasks between To Do and Planner, Power Automate can help streamline this process. For instance, you can create a workflow that automatically syncs tasks between To Do and Planner, ensuring that changes made in one app are reflected in the other.

- Automating Notifications and Reminders: Power Automate can also be used to set up customized notifications and reminders. For example, you can create a workflow that sends a Teams message or email reminder whenever a task's due date is approaching. This helps ensure that deadlines are met, and tasks are completed on time.

5. Best Practices for Using Microsoft To Do with Teams and Planner

To maximize the benefits of integrating Microsoft To Do with Teams and Planner, consider the following best practices:

- Consistent Task Management: Maintain consistency in how you manage tasks across To Do, Teams, and Planner. For example, use similar naming conventions, tags, and labels across all platforms. This consistency will make it easier to track and manage tasks regardless of where they originate.

- Regular Reviews: Make it a habit to review your tasks regularly, both in Microsoft To Do and Planner. Use the Weekly Review process (as part of the GTD methodology) to ensure that all tasks are up to date and that nothing has been overlooked.

- Leverage Automation: Use Power Automate to reduce manual work and improve efficiency. Automating routine tasks and workflows can save you time and help prevent errors.

- Effective Communication: Use Microsoft Teams to communicate about tasks and projects. Whenever possible, link tasks in To Do or Planner to your conversations in Teams. This contextual linking helps team members understand the task's relevance and any discussions that have taken place around it.

- Training and Support: Ensure that all team members are familiar with how to use Microsoft To Do, Teams, and Planner effectively. Provide training sessions or resources to help them understand how these tools work together.

6. Case Study: Practical Application of Integration

To illustrate the effectiveness of integrating Microsoft To Do with Teams and Planner, consider the following case study of a project team managing a product launch:

- Scenario: A marketing team is planning the launch of a new product. The project manager creates a comprehensive plan in Microsoft Planner, outlining tasks such as market research, content creation, advertising, and event planning. Each task is assigned to different team members.

- Integration: Team members use Microsoft To Do to manage their personal tasks, including the tasks assigned to them in Planner. They view and prioritize their tasks in To Do, ensuring that product launch-related tasks are included in their daily and weekly plans.

- Collaboration: The team communicates primarily through Microsoft Teams, where they discuss progress, share files, and provide updates on their tasks. The project manager uses Planner's charts to track overall progress and identify any bottlenecks.

- Automation: The project manager sets up Power Automate workflows to send reminders to team members as task deadlines approach. They also automate the creation of new tasks in To Do whenever new tasks are added to Planner.

- Outcome: The integration of Microsoft To Do, Teams, and Planner allows the team to work efficiently, stay organized, and ensure that all aspects of the product launch are managed effectively. The project is completed on time, and the product launch is successful.

Conclusion

Integrating Microsoft To Do with Teams and Planner offers a powerful way to manage both personal and team tasks within the Microsoft 365 ecosystem. By leveraging the strengths of each tool—personal task management in To Do, team collaboration in Teams, and project management in Planner—you can create a cohesive, efficient workflow that supports productivity at all levels.

This integration not only enhances individual productivity but also fosters better teamwork, communication, and project management. Whether you're working on small daily tasks or managing complex projects, the combination of Microsoft To Do, Teams, and Planner can help you get things done more effectively.

As you continue to explore the possibilities of these tools, remember to experiment with different workflows, automation, and collaboration techniques. The more you tailor the integration to your specific needs, the more value you'll derive from it, ultimately helping you and your team achieve your goals.

4.2.3 Automating Workflows with Power Automate

In today's fast-paced world, automation is key to enhancing productivity and reducing the manual effort required to complete repetitive tasks. Microsoft To Do, while powerful on its own, can be further optimized when integrated with Microsoft Power Automate. Power Automate, formerly known as Microsoft Flow, is a cloud-based service that allows you to create automated workflows between various apps and services to synchronize files, get notifications, collect data, and much more.

Understanding Power Automate

Power Automate is a versatile tool that empowers users to create automated workflows—known as "flows"—that perform a series of actions triggered by specific events. These flows can range from simple automations, like sending an email notification when a task is completed, to more complex workflows that involve multiple steps and applications. Power Automate connects to a wide range of Microsoft and third-party services, making it an ideal tool for enhancing your Microsoft To Do experience.

By integrating Power Automate with Microsoft To Do, you can streamline your task management process, ensure timely updates, and automate routine operations, allowing you to focus on more strategic work.

Getting Started with Power Automate

Before diving into specific workflows, it's important to familiarize yourself with the basics of Power Automate. Here's a quick overview to get you started:

1. Creating a Power Automate Account: If you haven't already, sign up for a Microsoft account and navigate to the Power Automate portal (https://flow.microsoft.com). You can use your existing Microsoft 365 credentials to log in.

2. Navigating the Interface: The Power Automate interface consists of several key components:

   - My Flows: Where you manage your created flows.

   - Create: Start creating new flows from scratch or using templates.

   - Templates: Pre-built workflows that can be customized to your needs.

   - Connectors: Integrate with various Microsoft and third-party apps.

3. Creating Your First Flow: Power Automate offers a variety of flow types:

   - Automated Flow: Triggered by an event, such as when a task is added in Microsoft To Do.

   - Instant Flow: Triggered manually, such as by pressing a button.

   - Scheduled Flow: Runs at specific times, like a daily task summary.

   - Business Process Flow: Guides users through a set of steps in a business process.

Building Custom Workflows for Microsoft To Do

Now that you have a basic understanding of Power Automate, let's explore how you can build custom workflows specifically for Microsoft To Do. Here are some examples of how automation can be applied to enhance your task management:

1. Automatically Add Tasks from Emails

One of the most common use cases is converting emails into tasks. With Power Automate, you can create a flow that automatically adds a new task in Microsoft To Do whenever you flag an email in Outlook.

- Step 1: In Power Automate, select "Create" and then choose "Automated Flow."

- Step 2: Set the trigger to "When an email is flagged" from the Outlook connector.

- Step 3: Add an action to "Create a task" in Microsoft To Do.

- Step 4: Customize the task details, such as setting the subject line as the task name and the email body as the task description.

- Step 5: Save and test the flow to ensure it works as expected.

This flow ensures that important emails never slip through the cracks and are tracked within your task management system.

2. Sync Tasks Across Microsoft To Do and Planner

For users who work extensively in both Microsoft To Do and Microsoft Planner, automating task synchronization can save a significant amount of time. With Power Automate, you can create a flow that automatically adds tasks created in Planner to a specific list in Microsoft To Do.

- Step 1: Create an automated flow with the trigger "When a task is created" in Planner.

- Step 2: Add an action to "Create a task" in Microsoft To Do.

- Step 3: Map the fields from Planner to To Do, such as using the Planner task title for the To Do task name and the Planner task due date for the To Do due date.

- Step 4: Save and test your flow to ensure that new tasks in Planner are accurately reflected in Microsoft To Do.

This flow ensures that all your tasks are consolidated in one place, making it easier to manage your workload.

3. Create Recurring Tasks Automatically

For tasks that you need to complete regularly, such as daily reports or weekly meetings, Power Automate can help you automate the creation of recurring tasks in Microsoft To Do.

- Step 1: Start by creating a "Scheduled Flow" in Power Automate.

- Step 2: Set the trigger to run at your desired interval, such as daily or weekly.

- Step 3: Add an action to "Create a task" in Microsoft To Do.

- Step 4: Customize the task details, including the task name, due date, and any relevant notes.

- Step 5: Save the flow, and your recurring tasks will be automatically generated according to the schedule you've set.

This automation is particularly useful for ensuring that routine tasks are consistently tracked and completed without the need for manual entry.

4. Send Notifications for Overdue Tasks

Keeping track of overdue tasks is crucial to staying on top of your responsibilities. With Power Automate, you can create a flow that sends a notification—via email or Teams—whenever a task in Microsoft To Do becomes overdue.

- Step 1: Create an automated flow with the trigger "When a task is overdue" using the Microsoft To Do connector.

- Step 2: Add an action to "Send an email" or "Post a message in Teams" to notify you of the overdue task.

- Step 3: Customize the notification to include the task details, such as the task name and due date.

- Step 4: Save and test the flow to ensure you receive timely notifications for overdue tasks.

This flow helps you stay informed and take action on overdue tasks before they become critical issues.

5. Automate Task Creation from Forms or Surveys

If you collect data through forms or surveys (e.g., Microsoft Forms), Power Automate can be used to automatically create tasks in Microsoft To Do based on the responses received.

- Step 1: Create an automated flow with the trigger "When a new response is submitted" using the Microsoft Forms connector.

- Step 2: Add an action to "Get response details" to capture the form data.

- Step 3: Add another action to "Create a task" in Microsoft To Do, mapping the form fields to the task details.

- Step 4: Save and test the flow to ensure that tasks are created correctly based on form responses.

This automation is particularly useful for managing follow-ups or actions that need to be taken based on survey responses, ensuring that nothing is missed.

Leveraging Pre-Built Templates

While creating custom flows allows for greater flexibility, Power Automate also offers a wide range of pre-built templates that can be easily adapted to suit your needs. Here are a few templates that can enhance your Microsoft To Do experience:

- "Create a task in Microsoft To Do for important emails": This template automatically adds a task to Microsoft To Do for emails marked as important in Outlook.

- "Notify me when a new task is assigned to me in Planner": This template sends a notification whenever a new task is assigned to you in Planner, ensuring you never miss an important task.

- "Add a task to Microsoft To Do when a new file is added to OneDrive": This template creates a task in Microsoft To Do whenever a new file is added to a specified OneDrive folder, helping you keep track of new files that require your attention.

To use these templates, simply search for them in the Power Automate portal, customize them as needed, and activate them to start automating your workflows.

Best Practices for Automating Workflows

When integrating Power Automate with Microsoft To Do, it's important to follow best practices to ensure your workflows are efficient and reliable:

1. Start Simple: Begin with simple workflows to familiarize yourself with Power Automate and how it interacts with Microsoft To Do. As you gain confidence, you can create more complex automations.

2. Test Your Flows: Always test your flows thoroughly before deploying them to ensure they function as expected. This includes checking for any errors or unintended consequences.

3. Monitor and Optimize: After deploying a flow, monitor its performance and make adjustments as needed. Power Automate provides tools to track flow runs and troubleshoot issues.

4. Document Your Workflows: Keep a record of the flows you create, including their purpose and how they interact with other systems. This documentation can be invaluable when troubleshooting or updating workflows.

5. Be Mindful of Triggers: Consider the frequency and conditions of your triggers to avoid unnecessary flow runs, which can lead to performance issues or unexpected outcomes.

Expanding Automation Beyond Microsoft To Do

The potential of Power Automate goes beyond just integrating with Microsoft To Do. By connecting with other Microsoft 365 apps and third-party services, you can create sophisticated workflows that enhance productivity across your entire work environment.

- Integrate with SharePoint:

 Automate task creation based on changes in SharePoint lists or document libraries, ensuring that updates in SharePoint are reflected in your task management system.

- Connect with CRM Systems: Automatically create tasks in Microsoft To Do based on updates or actions in your CRM system, helping you stay on top of customer follow-ups and sales activities.

- Use AI Builder: Incorporate AI-driven actions into your workflows, such as extracting data from documents or predicting outcomes, to further enhance your automation capabilities.

By leveraging the full potential of Power Automate, you can transform Microsoft To Do into a central hub for task management, seamlessly connected to the rest of your digital workspace.

Conclusion

Automating workflows with Power Automate is a powerful way to enhance the functionality of Microsoft To Do, enabling you to manage tasks more efficiently and effectively. Whether you're automating simple tasks or creating complex workflows that span multiple applications, Power Automate offers the tools you need to streamline your processes and focus on getting things done.

As you continue to explore and experiment with automation, you'll discover new ways to integrate Power Automate into your daily routines, making Microsoft To Do an even more indispensable tool in your productivity toolkit.

4.3 Using Microsoft To Do for Team Collaboration

Microsoft To Do isn't just a personal task management tool—it's also a powerful resource for teams who need to collaborate on tasks and projects efficiently. In this section, we will explore how to leverage Microsoft To Do's features to facilitate teamwork, ensuring that everyone on your team is aligned, productive, and moving towards shared goals. We'll start with the process of sharing lists with team members, which is a fundamental aspect of collaboration within Microsoft To Do.

4.3.1 Sharing Lists with Team Members

Introduction to List Sharing

Sharing lists is a key feature in Microsoft To Do that allows team members to collaborate on tasks seamlessly. Whether you're working on a small project with a few colleagues or managing a large team with multiple ongoing tasks, sharing lists ensures that everyone has access to the same information, can contribute to the workload, and stays updated on progress.

When you share a list in Microsoft To Do, you enable a collaborative environment where tasks can be assigned, tracked, and completed by multiple people. This feature is especially useful for teams that need to divide responsibilities, coordinate efforts, and ensure that all tasks are accounted for and completed on time.

How to Share a List

Sharing a list in Microsoft To Do is straightforward. Here's how you can do it:

1. Create a List: Start by creating a list if you haven't already. Navigate to the Microsoft To Do interface and click on the "+ New List" button. Give your list a descriptive name that clearly indicates its purpose, such as "Marketing Campaign Tasks" or "Product Development To-Dos."

2. Invite Team Members: Once your list is created, look for the sharing icon (usually a silhouette of a person with a plus sign) near the list's title. Click on this icon to open the

sharing options. You will have the option to invite team members by entering their email addresses. Microsoft To Do will send them an invitation to join the list.

3. Set Permissions: After inviting team members, you can manage permissions to control what they can do within the list. For most collaborative tasks, you'll want to give members full access, allowing them to add, edit, and complete tasks. However, in some cases, you might prefer to restrict editing permissions while allowing members to view tasks and mark them as completed.

4. Accepting the Invitation: Invited team members will receive an email with a link to the shared list. By clicking the link, they will be redirected to Microsoft To Do (or prompted to sign in if they haven't already) where they can accept the invitation and gain access to the list.

5. Collaborate in Real-Time: Once the list is shared, all members can start collaborating in real time. They can add new tasks, assign tasks to themselves or others, set due dates, and add notes or comments to tasks. Any changes made by one member will be instantly visible to all others, ensuring that everyone stays on the same page.

Best Practices for List Sharing

To maximize the benefits of list sharing in Microsoft To Do, consider the following best practices:

1. Clear and Descriptive Task Names: When collaborating with a team, it's important to use clear and descriptive task names. This helps team members understand what needs to be done without needing additional clarification. For example, instead of naming a task "Write report," use "Write quarterly financial report."

2. Use Tags for Categorization: Utilize tags to categorize tasks within a shared list. Tags can be used to indicate priority levels (e.g., High Priority), departments (e.g., Marketing), or status (e.g., In Progress). This makes it easier for team members to filter and find tasks relevant to them.

3. Assign Tasks Appropriately: Microsoft To Do allows you to assign tasks to specific team members. This ensures accountability, as each task has a designated owner. When assigning tasks, consider each member's strengths, workload, and deadlines to optimize efficiency.

4. Regularly Update Task Status: Encourage team members to regularly update the status of their tasks. This could involve marking tasks as "In Progress," "Blocked," or "Completed." Frequent updates help the entire team stay informed about the progress and any potential delays.

5. Use Comments for Communication: The comment feature within tasks allows for in-context communication. Team members can leave notes, ask questions, or provide updates directly within the task. This minimizes the need for lengthy email threads or separate chat conversations, keeping all communication tied to the relevant task.

6. Regularly Review and Clean Up Lists: Over time, lists can become cluttered with completed tasks or outdated information. Schedule regular reviews of your shared lists to archive completed tasks and reorganize or delete items that are no longer relevant. This keeps the list manageable and easy to navigate.

Use Cases for List Sharing

To illustrate the versatility of list sharing in Microsoft To Do, let's explore some real-world use cases:

1. Project Management: A project manager can create a shared list for a specific project, such as "Website Redesign." Tasks can be categorized into phases (e.g., Design, Development, Testing) and assigned to different team members. As each member completes their tasks, the project manager can track overall progress and adjust timelines as needed.

2. Event Planning: When organizing an event, such as a corporate conference, the event coordinator can share a list with all team members involved in the planning process. Tasks such as "Book Venue," "Send Invitations," and "Prepare Agenda" can be assigned to appropriate individuals, ensuring that all aspects of the event are covered.

3. Marketing Campaigns: In a marketing team, a shared list can be used to manage tasks related to an ongoing campaign. For example, tasks like "Create Social Media Content," "Launch Email Campaign," and "Monitor Analytics" can be tracked and assigned within the list. This ensures that the campaign runs smoothly and all deliverables are met.

4. Personal Task Sharing: Even outside of professional environments, list sharing can be useful. For example, a couple planning a vacation can create a shared list to manage tasks such as "Book Flights," "Reserve Hotel," and "Create Itinerary." Both individuals can contribute to the planning process and ensure nothing is overlooked.

Advanced Features for Shared Lists

Microsoft To Do offers several advanced features that can enhance the experience of using shared lists:

1. Subtasks for Detailed Tracking: Break down larger tasks into subtasks within a shared list. This is particularly useful for complex tasks that require multiple steps to complete. Subtasks can be assigned individually and tracked separately, ensuring that every detail is accounted for.

2. Task Reminders for Deadlines: Set reminders for critical tasks within shared lists to ensure deadlines are met. Reminders can be scheduled for specific dates and times, and they will notify all relevant team members, helping to prevent tasks from slipping through the cracks.

3. Recurring Tasks for Regular Activities: For tasks that need to be completed on a regular basis, such as "Weekly Team Meeting" or "Monthly Report," set them as recurring tasks. This eliminates the need to manually recreate tasks each time and ensures that regular activities are consistently tracked.

4. Using To Do with Microsoft Planner: For teams already using Microsoft Planner for project management, shared lists in Microsoft To Do can complement this tool. Tasks from Planner can be synced with To Do, allowing team members to manage their tasks in the environment they prefer, whether it's the more detailed Planner or the simpler To Do interface.

5. Real-Time Notifications: Team members can opt to receive real-time notifications for updates made to shared lists. This ensures that everyone is immediately informed of changes, such as new tasks being added, assignments being updated, or tasks being completed.

Common Challenges and How to Overcome Them

While sharing lists in Microsoft To Do offers numerous benefits, teams may encounter some challenges. Here's how to address them:

1. Overloaded Lists: In larger teams or projects, lists can become overloaded with too many tasks, making it difficult to manage. To overcome this, consider breaking down large projects into smaller, more focused lists. You can also use the grouping feature to organize related tasks together.

2. Lack of Engagement: Sometimes, team members may not actively engage with shared lists, leading to tasks being overlooked or delayed. To address this, encourage regular check-ins and establish a routine for updating the list. Setting up automated reminders can also help keep the team engaged.

3. Confusion Over Task Ownership: If tasks are not clearly assigned, it can lead to confusion over who is responsible for what. To avoid this, make sure every task is assigned to a specific team member, and use the comment feature to clarify any questions about responsibilities.

4. Version Control Issues: In some cases, multiple team members may try to edit the same task simultaneously, leading to version control issues. While Microsoft To Do generally handles this well, it's important to communicate within the team to avoid conflicting changes. Consider using the comment section to discuss major updates before making them.

Conclusion

Sharing lists in Microsoft To Do is a powerful way to enhance collaboration within your team. By leveraging this feature, you can ensure that everyone is aligned, accountable, and productive, no matter the size or scope of your project. From setting up shared lists to managing tasks in real-time, Microsoft To Do provides the tools you need to keep your team on track and working efficiently.

In the next section, we'll explore more advanced collaboration features within Microsoft To Do, focusing on how to effectively collaborate on tasks and track team progress.

4.3.2 Collaborating on Tasks

In today's collaborative work environments, efficient communication and task management are crucial for team success. Microsoft To Do offers powerful features that enable teams to work together seamlessly, ensuring that tasks are completed on time, and goals are achieved. Collaborating on tasks within Microsoft To Do is more than just assigning responsibilities—it's about creating a shared vision, fostering teamwork, and ensuring everyone is aligned and informed.

Understanding Task Collaboration in Microsoft To Do

Task collaboration in Microsoft To Do is designed to support teamwork by allowing multiple users to view, edit, and manage tasks within a shared list. This feature is particularly useful for projects where responsibilities are distributed among team members, and continuous communication is necessary to keep the project moving forward.

When collaborating on tasks in Microsoft To Do, team members can:

- Assign tasks: Assign specific tasks to individual team members, making it clear who is responsible for what.

- Set deadlines: Establish clear deadlines for each task to ensure timely completion.

- Share progress: Update task statuses to keep everyone informed of what has been completed and what remains to be done.

- Communicate within tasks: Use the notes section to add comments, instructions, or updates related to the task, ensuring that all relevant information is easily accessible.

By leveraging these features, teams can improve their efficiency and ensure that tasks are completed in a coordinated manner.

Creating Shared Lists for Team Collaboration

The foundation of task collaboration in Microsoft To Do is the shared list. A shared list is a collection of tasks that can be accessed and managed by multiple users. Creating a shared list is simple and can be done in a few steps:

1. Create a new list: Start by creating a new list in Microsoft To Do. This list will serve as the central hub for the tasks you want to collaborate on with your team.

2. Invite team members: Once the list is created, invite team members to join the list. You can do this by selecting the "Share" option and sending an invitation link to your colleagues.

3. Assign tasks: After the team members have joined the list, you can start assigning tasks to them. Each member will receive notifications about their assigned tasks and any updates made to the list.

Shared lists in Microsoft To Do are dynamic, meaning that any changes made to the list—such as adding new tasks, updating task details, or marking tasks as complete—are immediately visible to all team members. This ensures that everyone is on the same page and can stay updated on the progress of the project.

Best Practices for Task Assignment

Effective task assignment is key to successful collaboration. When assigning tasks in Microsoft To Do, consider the following best practices:

- Clear roles and responsibilities: Ensure that each team member knows their role in the project and understands what tasks they are responsible for. This clarity helps avoid confusion and ensures that tasks are completed efficiently.

- Use task descriptions: Provide detailed descriptions for each task, outlining the specific actions that need to be taken. This helps prevent misunderstandings and ensures that tasks are completed correctly.

- Set realistic deadlines: Assign realistic deadlines that consider the workload and availability of each team member. Overly aggressive deadlines can lead to stress and burnout, while overly lenient deadlines can lead to procrastination.

- Encourage communication: Encourage team members to communicate openly about their tasks. If someone is facing challenges or needs assistance, they should feel comfortable reaching out for help.

By following these best practices, you can ensure that tasks are assigned effectively, and that your team can work together smoothly.

Tracking Task Progress

One of the key benefits of using Microsoft To Do for task collaboration is the ability to track task progress in real-time. This feature allows team members to stay informed about the status of each task and ensures that everyone is aware of the overall progress of the project.

To track task progress in Microsoft To Do:

1. Mark tasks as complete: When a task is completed, it should be marked as such in Microsoft To Do. This immediately updates the task status for all team members, providing a clear view of what has been accomplished.

2. Update task details: If a task's details change—such as a change in priority or deadline— update the task in Microsoft To Do to reflect these changes. This ensures that all team members are working with the most up-to-date information.

3. Use task notes for updates: The notes section of each task can be used to provide updates on the task's progress. For example, if a task is partially completed, a team member can add a note to indicate what has been done and what remains to be done.

Tracking task progress in Microsoft To Do not only keeps the team informed but also helps identify potential bottlenecks or issues that need to be addressed. If a task is delayed or if a team member is struggling with their workload, this can be quickly identified, and steps can be taken to resolve the issue.

Collaborative Task Management with Subtasks

Subtasks are a powerful feature in Microsoft To Do that can enhance task collaboration. Subtasks allow you to break down a larger task into smaller, more manageable components. This is particularly useful for complex tasks that require multiple steps or the involvement of several team members.

To create and manage subtasks:

1. Add subtasks to a main task: When creating a task, you can add subtasks by selecting the "Add a step" option. Each subtask can be assigned to a different team member, or all subtasks can be handled by one person.

2. Assign subtasks: Just like main tasks, subtasks can be assigned to specific team members. This allows for a more granular distribution of work, ensuring that each aspect of a task is handled by the appropriate person.

3. Track subtask completion: As with main tasks, subtasks can be marked as complete once they are finished. This provides visibility into the progress of each step of the task.

Using subtasks is an effective way to manage complex tasks and ensure that all components are completed on time. It also allows for greater collaboration, as team members can work together on different aspects of the same task.

Collaborative Task Prioritization

Prioritizing tasks is a crucial aspect of project management, especially when collaborating with a team. In Microsoft To Do, tasks can be prioritized to help team members focus on the most important and urgent tasks first. When collaborating on tasks, it's essential to align on task priorities to ensure that everyone is working towards the same goals.

To prioritize tasks collaboratively:

1. Set task importance: Microsoft To Do allows you to mark tasks as "Important." Use this feature to highlight tasks that require immediate attention or are critical to the project's success.

2. Order tasks by priority: Organize tasks in your shared list by dragging and dropping them into the desired order. This helps team members quickly identify which tasks should be tackled first.

3. Discuss priorities in meetings: Regularly discuss task priorities in team meetings to ensure that everyone is aligned. If priorities change, update the task list in Microsoft To Do accordingly.

Collaborative task prioritization helps the team stay focused and ensures that the most critical tasks are completed on time.

Effective Communication within Microsoft To Do

Communication is the cornerstone of successful collaboration. Microsoft To Do provides several features that facilitate communication within tasks, helping team members stay connected and informed.

1. Task notes: The notes section of each task is an ideal place for team members to communicate about the task. Notes can be used to provide instructions, share updates, or ask questions.

2. Notifications: Microsoft To Do sends notifications to team members when they are assigned a task, when a task is due, or when a task is updated. This keeps everyone informed and ensures that no important updates are missed.

3. Integrate with communication tools: For more in-depth discussions, Microsoft To Do can be integrated with communication tools like Microsoft Teams. This allows for real-time chat and video calls, providing a more robust platform for collaboration.

By using these communication features effectively, teams can reduce misunderstandings and ensure that everyone is on the same page.

Automating Collaboration with Power Automate

Automation can significantly enhance collaboration by reducing the time spent on repetitive tasks and ensuring that key actions are taken automatically. Microsoft To Do can be integrated with Power Automate, a powerful automation tool that allows you to create workflows between Microsoft To Do and other apps.

Here are some examples of how automation can be used to enhance collaboration:

1. Automatic task creation: Create workflows that automatically generate tasks in Microsoft To Do based on triggers, such as receiving an email in Outlook or completing a task in another app.

2. Task reminders: Set up automated reminders for upcoming deadlines or tasks that need immediate attention. These reminders can be sent via email, SMS, or as notifications within Microsoft To Do.

3. Team notifications: Automate notifications to team members when tasks are assigned, updated, or completed. This ensures that everyone is kept in the loop without the need for manual updates.

By leveraging automation, teams can work more efficiently and ensure that critical tasks and updates are never overlooked.

Collaborating Across Multiple Projects

In many organizations, team members are often involved in multiple projects simultaneously. Microsoft To Do makes it easy to collaborate across multiple projects by allowing you to manage multiple shared lists, each dedicated to a different project.

To effectively manage collaboration across multiple projects:

1. Create separate lists for each project: Organize your tasks by creating separate lists for each project. This helps keep tasks organized and ensures that team members can focus on the tasks related to their specific projects.

2. Assign tasks to the appropriate list: When assigning tasks, make sure they are added to the correct project list. This prevents tasks from getting mixed up and ensures that each project remains organized.

3. Use tags and categories: Use tags and categories to further organize tasks within each project list. This can help team members quickly find the tasks they need to work on, especially in projects with a large number of tasks.

By organizing tasks and projects in this way, teams can collaborate more effectively, even when working on multiple projects simultaneously.

Overcoming Collaboration Challenges

While Microsoft To Do provides powerful tools for collaboration, teams may still face challenges when working together. Common collaboration challenges include miscommunication, overlapping responsibilities, and inconsistent task management practices.

To overcome these challenges:

1. Establish clear communication channels: Ensure that all team members know how and where to communicate about tasks. Whether it's through task notes, email, or a chat tool like Microsoft Teams, having a clear communication protocol is essential.

2. Regularly review tasks and responsibilities: Hold regular meetings to review tasks and ensure that responsibilities are clearly defined. This helps prevent overlapping responsibilities and ensures that everyone knows what they need to do.

3. Provide training and support: Ensure that all team members are comfortable using Microsoft To Do and understand how to collaborate effectively within the platform. Provide training sessions or resources if necessary.

By addressing these challenges proactively, teams can collaborate more effectively and ensure that their projects are successful.

Case Studies: Successful Task Collaboration with Microsoft To Do

To illustrate the effectiveness of task collaboration in Microsoft To Do, let's look at a few case studies of organizations that have successfully used the platform to improve their teamwork and productivity.

Case Study 1: Marketing Agency

A marketing agency used Microsoft To Do to manage their client projects, which involved multiple team members working on tasks such as content creation, design, and social media management. By creating shared lists for each client, they were able to assign tasks to the appropriate team members, track progress, and ensure that deadlines were met. The team also used the notes feature to provide updates and feedback, which reduced the need for constant email communication and improved overall efficiency.

Case Study 2: Non-Profit Organization

A non-profit organization used Microsoft To Do to manage their fundraising campaigns. They created shared lists for each campaign, with tasks assigned to different volunteers. The organization used Microsoft To Do's integration with Outlook to ensure that all tasks were synced with their calendars, making it easier to manage deadlines and schedules. The collaboration features in Microsoft To Do allowed the team to work together effectively, even when volunteers were spread across different locations.

Case Study 3: Software Development Team

A software development team used Microsoft To Do to manage their sprint tasks. By creating shared lists for each sprint, they were able to assign tasks to developers, track progress, and ensure that all tasks were completed before the end of the sprint. The team also used subtasks to break down larger development tasks into smaller, more manageable components. This approach improved the team's ability to collaborate and ensured that their software releases were completed on time.

These case studies highlight how Microsoft To Do can be used to enhance collaboration in a variety of contexts, from marketing and non-profit work to software development.

In conclusion, collaborating on tasks with Microsoft To Do offers a streamlined and efficient way for teams to work together. By leveraging shared lists, effective task assignment, real-time progress tracking, and robust communication features, teams can achieve their goals and complete projects successfully. Whether you're working on a small project or managing a large team, Microsoft To Do provides the tools you need to collaborate effectively and get things done.

4.3.3 Tracking Team Progress

Tracking team progress is a crucial aspect of collaboration and project management. With Microsoft To Do, you can effectively monitor how tasks are progressing within your team, ensuring that everyone is aligned and moving toward common goals. This section delves into various strategies and features that can help you keep track of progress, identify potential bottlenecks, and maintain momentum in your projects.

1. The Importance of Tracking Progress

Before diving into the technical aspects, it's essential to understand why tracking progress is important. For any team, the ability to monitor progress ensures that:

- Accountability: Team members know that their work is being observed, which encourages them to meet deadlines and fulfill their responsibilities.

- Transparency: Everyone on the team has a clear view of how tasks are moving forward, which fosters an environment of trust and openness.

- Early Detection of Issues: By tracking progress, you can quickly identify tasks that are falling behind or not moving as expected, allowing you to address problems before they escalate.

- Resource Management: Understanding where the team stands in terms of progress allows for better allocation of resources, such as time, personnel, and tools.

- Motivation: Visual representations of progress, such as completed tasks and milestones, can serve as motivation for team members to continue their work with enthusiasm.

Microsoft To Do provides several built-in tools and techniques to help you effectively track your team's progress. Let's explore these in detail.

2. Using Task Statuses to Monitor Progress

One of the simplest yet most effective ways to track progress in Microsoft To Do is by using task statuses. Task statuses indicate whether a task is in progress, completed, or yet to be started. Here's how to utilize them:

- Setting Task Statuses: When you create a task in Microsoft To Do, you can set its status based on its current state. For example, when a task is started, you can mark it as "In Progress," and once it's completed, you can mark it as "Completed." This simple tracking method allows you to quickly glance at a list and see which tasks are moving forward.

- Filtering by Status: Microsoft To Do allows you to filter tasks based on their status. This can be particularly useful in team meetings, where you need to focus on tasks that are still pending or in progress.

- Updating Task Statuses: It's essential to keep task statuses updated. Encourage team members to regularly update their task statuses in Microsoft To Do. This ensures that the team's progress is accurately reflected and everyone is on the same page.

3. Leveraging My Day and Planned Views

Microsoft To Do's "My Day" and "Planned" views can be powerful tools for tracking team progress. These views provide a snapshot of tasks that are due today or in the future, helping you stay on top of what's coming up.

- My Day View: The "My Day" view is a personalized daily planner that shows tasks due today. For team leaders, reviewing the "My Day" view for each team member (if shared) can provide insights into their daily priorities and workloads. You can use this information to ensure that everyone is focused on the right tasks and to reassign tasks if necessary.

- Planned View: The "Planned" view shows all tasks that have due dates, giving you a longer-term perspective on what's ahead. This view is especially useful for project managers who need to keep track of deadlines and ensure that the team is on schedule. By regularly reviewing the "Planned" view, you can identify tasks that are at risk of falling behind and take corrective action.

4. Using Labels and Tags for Progress Tracking

Labels and tags are powerful tools in Microsoft To Do for categorizing and organizing tasks. They can also be used to track the progress of tasks across different categories, projects, or team members.

- Creating Custom Labels: You can create custom labels to represent different stages of progress or to categorize tasks by team members or projects. For example, labels like "Urgent," "Review Required," or "Pending Approval" can help you quickly identify the status and priority of tasks.

- Applying Tags: Tags can be used similarly to labels but are often more flexible. You can tag tasks with specific keywords that represent their current status or the team member responsible for them. For example, tags like "Design Phase," "Client Feedback," or "Assigned to John" can provide additional context to tasks, making it easier to track progress.

- Filtering by Labels and Tags: Once you've applied labels and tags to tasks, you can filter your task lists to focus on specific categories. This can be particularly useful during progress reviews, where you may want to focus on tasks that are in a particular phase or assigned to a specific team member.

5. Utilizing Smart Lists for Automated Tracking

Smart Lists in Microsoft To Do are dynamic lists that automatically organize tasks based on specific criteria. These lists are a powerful feature for tracking team progress without manually sorting tasks.

- Customizing Smart Lists: By customizing Smart Lists, you can create views that automatically show tasks that are due soon, have high priority, or are assigned to specific team members. For example, a Smart List that shows all "Overdue Tasks" can help you quickly identify where the team is falling behind.

- Smart Lists for Project Phases: You can create Smart Lists that group tasks by project phases or milestones. This allows you to see how tasks within a particular phase are progressing, making it easier to manage complex projects with multiple stages.

- Monitoring with Smart Lists: Regularly review your Smart Lists to monitor progress and make adjustments as needed. These lists provide real-time updates, ensuring that you're always aware of the current status of your team's tasks.

6. Collaborating Through Shared Lists

One of the key features of Microsoft To Do is the ability to share lists with team members. Shared lists are an excellent way to track progress collaboratively, as everyone on the team can contribute to and update the list.

- Creating Shared Lists: Start by creating shared lists for each project or team initiative. Invite team members to the list, allowing them to add, edit, and complete tasks. This shared ownership fosters collaboration and ensures that everyone is engaged in tracking progress.

- Using Comments for Updates: Microsoft To Do allows you to add comments to tasks within shared lists. Use this feature to provide updates on task progress, ask questions, or leave notes for other team members. Comments keep the conversation about each task organized and in one place.

- Tracking Changes in Shared Lists: As tasks in shared lists are updated or completed, Microsoft To Do logs these changes. This change log provides a history of task updates, allowing you to track who completed what and when. This transparency is crucial for accountability and progress tracking.

7. Integrating Microsoft To Do with Power BI for Advanced Tracking

For teams and organizations that require more advanced progress tracking, integrating Microsoft To Do with Power BI can provide deeper insights. Power BI is a business analytics service that allows you to visualize data and generate reports.

- Connecting Microsoft To Do with Power BI: You can connect Microsoft To Do with Power BI to create custom dashboards that visualize task progress across your team. These dashboards can show key metrics like the number of tasks completed, tasks in progress, overdue tasks, and more.

- Creating Custom Reports: With Power BI, you can create custom reports that provide detailed insights into team performance. For example, you might create a report that breaks down progress by team member, project, or task category. These reports can be shared with stakeholders to keep them informed about the team's progress.

- Automating Reporting: Power BI allows you to automate the generation and distribution of reports. This means you can set up daily, weekly, or monthly reports that automatically pull data from Microsoft To Do and distribute it to team members, managers, or clients.

Automated reporting ensures that everyone stays informed without the need for manual updates.

8. Analyzing Team Performance with Metrics and KPIs

In addition to tracking progress on individual tasks, it's important to analyze overall team performance using key performance indicators (KPIs) and metrics. Microsoft To Do, combined with other Microsoft 365 tools, provides the data you need to measure and improve team performance.

- Defining KPIs for Progress Tracking: Start by defining the KPIs that are most relevant to your team's goals. Common KPIs might include the percentage of tasks completed on time, average task completion time, or the number of overdue tasks. These KPIs provide a clear benchmark for evaluating team performance.

- Using Microsoft To Do Data for Analysis: Microsoft To Do logs various data points, such as task creation dates, due dates, and completion dates. You can export this data for analysis or use it within Power BI to create performance dashboards. Analyzing this data allows you to identify trends, such as which team members are completing tasks most efficiently or which projects are consistently running behind schedule.

- Making Data-Driven Decisions: Use the insights gained from your analysis to make data-driven decisions. For example, if you notice that certain types of tasks are consistently overdue, you might allocate more resources to those tasks or provide additional training to team members. Data-driven decisions help you optimize team performance and improve overall progress tracking.

9. Addressing Common Challenges in Progress Tracking

While tracking progress in Microsoft To Do is generally straightforward, there are some common challenges that teams may encounter. Being aware of these challenges and knowing how to address them can help you maintain accurate and effective progress tracking.

- Inconsistent Task Updates: One of the most common challenges is inconsistent updating of tasks by team members. To address this, establish clear expectations for how and when tasks should be updated. Regularly remind team members to update their task statuses, and consider setting up periodic check-ins to review progress.

- Overwhelming Number of Tasks: In large projects, the sheer number of tasks can become overwhelming, making it difficult to track progress. To manage this, break down tasks into smaller, more manageable sub-tasks, and use Smart Lists or labels to categorize and filter tasks. This makes it easier to focus on specific areas of progress without getting lost in the details.

- Lack of Engagement in Shared Lists: Sometimes, team members may not fully engage with shared lists, leading to incomplete or outdated progress information. Encourage active participation by making shared lists central to team meetings and discussions. Highlight the importance of these lists in achieving team goals, and recognize team members who consistently contribute.

10. Best Practices for Maintaining Accurate Progress Tracking

Finally, let's explore some best practices for maintaining accurate and reliable progress tracking in Microsoft To Do.

- Regular Reviews and Updates: Schedule regular reviews of your task lists, Smart Lists, and reports. These reviews ensure that progress is being tracked accurately and allow you to make necessary adjustments.

- Encourage Team Collaboration: Foster a collaborative environment where team members feel comfortable sharing updates, asking for help, and providing feedback. Collaboration is key to accurate progress tracking.

- Automate Where Possible: Take advantage of automation features in Microsoft To Do, Power Automate, and Power BI to reduce manual work and ensure that progress data is always up-to-date.

- Provide Training and Support: Ensure that all team members are comfortable using Microsoft To Do and understand the importance of progress tracking. Provide training and support as needed to help them make the most of the tool.

- Celebrate Successes: Recognize and celebrate milestones and completed tasks. Celebrating successes not only motivates the team but also reinforces the importance of tracking progress.

By effectively using the features and strategies outlined in this section, you can ensure that your team's progress is consistently tracked, enabling you to achieve your goals with Microsoft To Do. Progress tracking is more than just monitoring tasks; it's about fostering a collaborative environment, making informed decisions, and driving your team toward success.

CHAPTER V
Best Practices for Getting Things Done

5.1 Optimizing Your Task Management System

5.1.1 Keeping Your Lists Organized

Effective task management is crucial to achieving your goals, and the foundation of any productive system lies in how well you organize your tasks. With Microsoft To Do, you have a powerful tool at your disposal that offers a range of features to help you keep your lists structured, clear, and manageable. This section will guide you through best practices for keeping your task lists organized in Microsoft To Do, ensuring that you can stay on top of your responsibilities and work efficiently.

Why Organization Matters

Before diving into the specifics, it's important to understand why organization is key to successful task management. An organized list is more than just a neat collection of tasks; it represents a clear roadmap to achieving your goals. When your lists are well-organized:

- Prioritization becomes easier: You can quickly identify what needs to be done first, reducing the likelihood of missing important deadlines.

- Clarity is maintained: Clear lists help you understand the scope of your work at a glance, avoiding the feeling of being overwhelmed.

- Efficiency is improved: With an organized list, you spend less time searching for tasks and more time getting things done.

- Motivation is boosted: There's a psychological benefit to checking off tasks from a well-structured list, as it provides a sense of progress and accomplishment.

Now, let's explore how to apply these principles using Microsoft To Do.

Structuring Your Lists

The first step in keeping your tasks organized is structuring your lists in a way that aligns with your workflow and goals. Microsoft To Do allows you to create multiple lists, each dedicated to different areas of your life or work. Here's how to effectively structure your lists:

1. Create Dedicated Lists for Different Projects or Areas of Responsibility

Start by identifying the key areas of your life or work that require regular attention. For example, you might have separate lists for:

- Work Projects: Tasks related to specific projects, client work, or internal responsibilities.

- Personal Tasks: Daily chores, appointments, or personal development goals.

- Long-Term Goals: Larger objectives that require consistent effort over time, such as learning a new skill or planning a major event.

By creating dedicated lists for each area, you can easily compartmentalize your tasks and avoid the clutter that comes with mixing different types of tasks together. This separation also helps in maintaining focus, as you can direct your attention to one area at a time without being distracted by unrelated tasks.

2. Use Groups to Cluster Related Lists

Microsoft To Do's Groups feature allows you to cluster related lists under a single umbrella. For instance, if you're managing multiple projects at work, you can group all your project-related lists under a "Work Projects" group. Similarly, you can create a "Personal" group for lists related to home, family, and personal development.

Groups not only help in keeping your sidebar tidy but also make it easier to navigate between related tasks. When you open a group, you can quickly access any list within it, providing a streamlined experience. This is particularly useful if you have numerous lists, as it reduces visual clutter and helps you maintain focus on specific areas.

3. Name Your Lists Clearly and Consistently

The way you name your lists has a significant impact on how easily you can navigate them. Use clear, descriptive names that immediately convey the purpose of each list. For example:

- Instead of a vague name like "To Do," use "Client Project A" or "Marketing Campaign Tasks."

- For personal lists, consider names like "Home Maintenance" or "Fitness Goals."

Consistency in naming conventions is also crucial. If you have multiple projects, consider a naming pattern that makes them easy to distinguish, such as "Project A - Tasks," "Project B - Milestones," etc. This consistency not only helps in quickly locating lists but also reinforces the structured approach to your work.

4. Prioritize Lists Based on Importance and Urgency

While Microsoft To Do doesn't natively support the direct prioritization of lists, you can manually arrange them in the sidebar. Place your most important or time-sensitive lists at the top, ensuring they are the first thing you see when you open the app. For example:

- Place lists related to immediate deadlines or high-priority projects at the top.

- Move less urgent or long-term lists further down.

By arranging your lists in this way, you create a natural workflow where your focus automatically shifts to the most critical tasks first.

Organizing Tasks Within Lists

Once your lists are structured, the next step is to organize the tasks within each list. Microsoft To Do offers several features to help you maintain order within your lists, ensuring that each task is easy to locate and manage.

1. Break Down Large Tasks into Subtasks

Large tasks can be overwhelming and difficult to approach. Microsoft To Do allows you to break down these tasks into subtasks, which can be individually managed and checked off. For instance, if you have a task like "Prepare Quarterly Report," you can break it down into subtasks such as:

- Gather financial data

- Analyze performance metrics

- Draft report sections

- Review and edit the report

By breaking down tasks in this way, you make them more manageable and ensure that each step is clearly defined. This not only helps in organizing your tasks but also provides a clear path to completion.

2. Use Tags to Categorize and Filter Tasks

Tags are a powerful feature in Microsoft To Do that allows you to categorize tasks within a list. You can create custom tags based on different criteria, such as:

- Priority: Tags like "High Priority," "Medium Priority," or "Low Priority."

- Type of Task: Tags like "Research," "Writing," "Meeting," etc.

- Context: Tags like "@Work," "@Home," "@Errands."

Tags make it easy to filter and view tasks based on specific criteria. For example, if you're at home and want to focus on tasks that can be done there, you can filter your list by the "@Home" tag. This level of categorization helps in maintaining order within lists and ensures that you can quickly find the tasks that are relevant to your current context.

3. Utilize Due Dates and Reminders

Assigning due dates and setting reminders are essential for keeping your tasks organized and ensuring that nothing falls through the cracks. In Microsoft To Do, you can set specific due dates for each task, which will then appear in the Planned list. This feature is particularly useful for managing deadlines and prioritizing tasks that need to be completed within a certain timeframe.

In addition to due dates, setting reminders ensures that you're notified about tasks at the right time. For instance, if you have a task like "Submit Expense Report" due by Friday, setting a reminder for Thursday morning will give you enough time to complete it without rushing. Reminders can be set for specific times, allowing you to schedule tasks around your daily routine.

4. Leverage the "My Day" Feature for Daily Planning

The My Day feature in Microsoft To Do is designed to help you focus on what needs to be done today. Each morning, you can review your lists and select tasks to add to My Day, creating a daily agenda that keeps you on track.

The beauty of My Day is its flexibility—it resets every day, allowing you to start fresh each morning. This encourages you to be intentional about what you plan to accomplish each day, rather than being overwhelmed by a long list of tasks. By selecting only the most important or urgent tasks for My Day, you create a focused, manageable to-do list that aligns with your daily goals.

5. Archive or Delete Completed Tasks

Over time, your lists can become cluttered with completed tasks, making it harder to focus on what still needs to be done. To keep your lists clean and organized, regularly archive or delete completed tasks. Microsoft To Do automatically hides completed tasks, but you can choose to view them if needed.

Archiving or deleting completed tasks not only declutters your lists but also provides a psychological boost—seeing a list with fewer tasks can make you feel more in control and less overwhelmed.

Regularly Reviewing and Updating Your Lists

Keeping your lists organized isn't a one-time effort—it requires regular review and maintenance. Microsoft To Do's features make this process straightforward, allowing you to keep your lists aligned with your current priorities and goals.

1. Conduct Weekly Reviews

A weekly review is a crucial part of the GTD methodology and is equally important in Microsoft To Do. Set aside time each week to:

- Review each list and ensure that tasks are still relevant.

- Update due dates and reminders based on your current schedule.

- Reorganize tasks or lists as needed to reflect changes in your priorities.

This weekly review helps you stay on top of your tasks and ensures that your lists remain a true reflection of your responsibilities and goals.

2. Adjust Lists Based on Changing Priorities

As projects progress and circumstances change, your priorities will shift. Microsoft To Do allows you to easily adjust your lists and tasks to reflect these changes. For example:

- If a project's deadline is moved up, you can reorganize tasks to prioritize those that need to be completed sooner.

- If new tasks emerge, add them to the appropriate list and adjust your workflow accordingly.

Being flexible and adjusting your lists regularly ensures that you stay aligned with your current goals and avoid falling behind.

3. Keep Your Lists Focused and Minimal

While it's tempting to add every possible task to your lists, doing so can lead to overwhelm. Aim to keep your lists focused and minimal by:

- Limiting the number of tasks in each list to those that are truly actionable.

- Avoiding the inclusion of tasks that are vague or undefined.

By maintaining focused and minimal lists, you create a more streamlined workflow that's easier to manage and less stressful to navigate.

Conclusion

Keeping your lists organized is a foundational practice in effective task management. By structuring your lists thoughtfully, organizing tasks within them, and regularly reviewing and updating your system, you can ensure that Microsoft To Do serves as a powerful tool for getting things done. Remember, an organized list isn't just about neatness—it's about creating a clear, actionable plan that guides you towards achieving your goals efficiently and effectively.

5.1.2 Using Recurring Tasks for Routine Actions

Introduction to Recurring Tasks in Microsoft To Do

Routine actions and recurring tasks are essential elements of both personal and professional productivity. These are the tasks you perform regularly—whether daily, weekly, monthly, or at any other interval. Managing recurring tasks effectively ensures that these important yet repetitive duties don't slip through the cracks. Microsoft To Do offers a robust feature for setting up recurring tasks, allowing users to automate the process of re-adding tasks to their lists, thereby freeing up mental space for more creative or strategic thinking.

Recurring tasks are the backbone of an organized task management system. They help to maintain consistency in your workflow, ensuring that no crucial steps are missed, and that your routine remains intact. Whether it's a weekly team meeting, a daily exercise routine, or a monthly report, having these tasks set to recur can significantly enhance your productivity by reducing the cognitive load of remembering to add them manually each time.

In this section, we will explore the importance of recurring tasks, how to set them up in Microsoft To Do, and best practices for managing them efficiently. By the end of this chapter, you will have a comprehensive understanding of how to leverage recurring tasks to optimize your task management system.

The Importance of Recurring Tasks

Recurring tasks are foundational for establishing and maintaining a productive routine. These tasks ensure that important activities are consistently completed without the need for constant manual input. Here are a few reasons why recurring tasks are vital:

1. Consistency and Reliability: Recurring tasks ensure that routine actions are performed consistently. Whether it's a daily review of your task list or a monthly audit, these tasks help maintain the rhythm of your workflow.

2. Reducing Mental Load: By automating the scheduling of recurring tasks, you free up cognitive resources that would otherwise be spent remembering and re-entering these tasks manually.

3. Time Management: Recurring tasks help you allocate specific times for routine activities, allowing you to plan your day, week, or month more effectively.

4. Accountability: Regularly scheduled tasks create a sense of accountability. By setting them to recur, you commit to completing these tasks on a consistent basis.

5. Tracking Progress: Recurring tasks allow you to track your progress over time. By completing these tasks regularly, you can measure your consistency and identify areas where you might need to improve.

Setting Up Recurring Tasks in Microsoft To Do

Microsoft To Do makes it simple to set up recurring tasks, giving you the flexibility to tailor these tasks to your specific needs. Here's a step-by-step guide on how to create and manage recurring tasks in Microsoft To Do:

1. Creating a New Task:

  - Start by creating a new task as you normally would. Enter the task's name and any other relevant details.

  - For example, you might create a task titled "Weekly Team Meeting."

2. Setting the Recurrence:

  - After creating the task, click on the task to open its details.

  - Look for the option labeled "Repeat" or "Recurring." This option allows you to set how often the task should repeat.

- Microsoft To Do offers various recurrence options, including daily, weekly, monthly, yearly, and custom intervals. You can choose from these options based on the frequency of the task.

3. Customizing the Recurrence:

- If the predefined options don't fit your needs, you can create a custom recurrence pattern.

- For example, you might need a task to recur every two weeks or on specific days of the week. To do this, select the "Custom" option and specify the desired recurrence pattern.

- For a task like "Review Monthly Budget," you might set it to recur on the last day of every month.

4. Setting End Dates (Optional):

- You can also set an end date for the recurrence if the task is only needed for a certain period.

- For example, if you have a recurring task to "Submit Quarterly Report" and you know you'll only be doing this for the next year, you can set an end date to stop the recurrence after a specific time.

5. Saving the Task:

- Once you've set the recurrence, save the task. It will now appear in your task list with the recurrence pattern indicated.

- Microsoft To Do will automatically generate the next occurrence of the task once the current one is marked as complete.

6. Managing Recurring Tasks:

- Recurring tasks are managed just like regular tasks. You can add subtasks, set priorities, and assign reminders.

- However, it's important to note that when you complete a recurring task, it will reappear in your list according to the recurrence pattern you've set.

Best Practices for Using Recurring Tasks

While setting up recurring tasks is straightforward, there are best practices you can follow to ensure they contribute effectively to your overall productivity:

1. Be Selective with Recurring Tasks:

  - Not every task needs to be recurring. Reserve this feature for tasks that genuinely benefit from regular repetition. Overloading your task list with too many recurring tasks can lead to clutter and reduce focus.

  - Prioritize the recurring tasks that are essential to your workflow, such as "Daily Check-In," "Weekly Report," or "Monthly Client Meeting."

2. Review and Adjust Regularly:

  - Periodically review your recurring tasks to ensure they still align with your goals and responsibilities. As your projects and priorities evolve, your recurring tasks should adapt accordingly.

  - For example, if a recurring task becomes obsolete, either modify the recurrence pattern or remove it from your list.

3. Set Clear and Specific Tasks:

  - Make your recurring tasks as specific as possible to avoid ambiguity. A clear, actionable task is more likely to be completed than a vague one.

  - Instead of setting a recurring task like "Work on Project," specify the action, such as "Update Project Timeline."

4. Leverage Reminders for Important Tasks:

  - For crucial recurring tasks, use reminders to ensure you don't overlook them. Microsoft To Do allows you to set reminders at specific times, helping you stay on track.

  - For instance, set a reminder for your recurring task "Prepare for Weekly Meeting" a day before the meeting occurs.

5. Use Categories and Tags:

  - Organize your recurring tasks by applying categories or tags. This makes it easier to filter and manage tasks within specific contexts.

- For example, you can tag tasks related to "Finance," "Meetings," or "Personal Development" to quickly access them when needed.

6. Combine with My Day Feature:

- Microsoft To Do's "My Day" feature can be a powerful tool when combined with recurring tasks. Each morning, review your recurring tasks and add the most relevant ones to your "My Day" list to keep them top of mind.

- For example, if you have a recurring task like "Daily Exercise," add it to your "My Day" list to ensure it gets done.

7. Sync with Calendar for Time-Sensitive Tasks:

- For recurring tasks that are time-sensitive, consider syncing them with your calendar. This ensures that you allocate the necessary time to complete them.

- Tasks like "Submit Weekly Report" can be scheduled on your calendar to remind you of the time commitment required.

8. Plan for Recurrence Gaps:

- If there's a possibility that a recurring task might not need to be completed during certain periods (e.g., holidays, vacations), plan accordingly. You can either skip the recurrence for that period or adjust the recurrence pattern temporarily.

- For example, if you have a recurring task like "Weekly Inventory Check," and you know you'll be on vacation, adjust the recurrence to skip that week.

9. Use Recurrence for Habit Building:

- Recurring tasks are an excellent tool for habit building. By setting tasks to recur daily or weekly, you can reinforce positive habits and track your consistency.

- For instance, create a recurring task like "Read for 30 Minutes" to establish a daily reading habit.

10. Evaluate Completion Metrics:

- Periodically assess how often you complete your recurring tasks on time. This can give you insights into your productivity patterns and highlight areas for improvement.

- If you notice a recurring task like "Weekly Reflection" often gets delayed, it may indicate the need to adjust your schedule or approach.

Avoiding Common Pitfalls

While recurring tasks are incredibly useful, they can sometimes lead to challenges if not managed properly. Here are some common pitfalls to avoid:

1. Overloading Your Task List:

  - Too many recurring tasks can overwhelm your task list, making it difficult to focus on what's important. Be mindful of the number of recurring tasks you create and ensure they serve a clear purpose.

2. Ignoring Task Completion:

  - It's easy to become complacent with recurring tasks, especially if they seem routine. However, neglecting to complete them regularly can lead to a backlog and disrupt your workflow.

3. Setting Inflexible Recurrence Patterns:

  - While consistency is key, it's important to allow some flexibility in your recurrence patterns. Life is unpredictable, and your task management system should be able to accommodate changes in your schedule.

4. Forgetting to Review and Adjust:

  - Recurring tasks are not "set it and forget it." Regularly review and adjust them to ensure they continue to align with your current priorities and goals.

Conclusion

Using recurring tasks in Microsoft To Do can significantly enhance your task management system, making it more efficient, reliable, and aligned with your goals. By automating routine actions, you free up valuable mental space and ensure that essential tasks are consistently completed. Remember to follow best practices such as being selective with recurring tasks, regularly reviewing and adjusting them, and using reminders and tags for better organization. By leveraging recurring tasks effectively, you can optimize your productivity, maintain consistency in your workflow, and ultimately achieve your goals with greater ease.

5.1.3 Breaking Down Large Tasks into Manageable Steps

Breaking down large tasks into manageable steps is a critical aspect of effective task management and a core principle of the Getting Things Done (GTD) methodology. This practice not only makes daunting tasks more approachable but also provides a clear roadmap for completion, reducing stress and increasing productivity. Microsoft To Do offers several features that can help you deconstruct and manage large tasks efficiently.

Understanding the Importance of Task Breakdown

Large tasks, often referred to as projects, can be overwhelming due to their complexity and the time required to complete them. Breaking these tasks down into smaller, manageable steps has several advantages:

- Enhanced Focus: Smaller tasks are easier to focus on and complete. This reduces the cognitive load and prevents procrastination.

- Progress Tracking: It becomes easier to monitor progress and stay motivated as you can see tangible progress through the completion of each subtask.

- Improved Planning: Smaller tasks can be scheduled and prioritized more effectively, allowing for better time management.

- Reduced Stress: Breaking down tasks can alleviate the anxiety associated with large, ambiguous projects by providing a clear action plan.

Step-by-Step Process to Break Down Large Tasks

1. Define the End Goal:

   - Clearly articulate what you aim to achieve with the large task. Understanding the end goal provides a sense of direction and purpose.

   - Example: If the large task is "Organize a conference," the end goal would be "Host a successful conference."

2. Identify Key Milestones:

- Break the task into major milestones or phases. These are significant steps that mark the progress towards the completion of the task.

- Example: For organizing a conference, milestones could include "Finalize the venue," "Secure speakers," "Send out invitations," and "Prepare conference materials."

3. Create Subtasks for Each Milestone:

- For each milestone, identify the specific actions needed to achieve it. These actions become your subtasks.

- Example: For the milestone "Finalize the venue," subtasks could include "Research potential venues," "Visit shortlisted venues," "Negotiate terms and conditions," and "Sign the contract."

4. Prioritize and Sequence the Subtasks:

- Determine the order in which the subtasks should be completed. Some tasks may be dependent on the completion of others.

- Example: You cannot "Visit shortlisted venues" before "Research potential venues."

5. Set Deadlines and Assign Responsibilities:

- Assign realistic deadlines to each subtask to ensure steady progress. If working in a team, assign tasks to specific team members.

- Example: Set a deadline for "Research potential venues" by the end of the week and assign it to a team member responsible for logistics.

Using Microsoft To Do to Manage Large Tasks

Microsoft To Do provides a user-friendly interface to help you break down and manage large tasks effectively. Here's how you can utilize its features:

1. Creating Lists for Projects:

- Create a new list for each large task or project. This list will house all related subtasks and milestones.

- Example: Create a list named "Organize Conference."

2. Adding Tasks and Subtasks:

   - Within the project list, add tasks for each milestone. For each task, use the "Add step" feature to create subtasks.

   - Example: Add a task named "Finalize the venue" and use the "Add step" feature to include "Research potential venues," "Visit shortlisted venues," etc.

3. Setting Due Dates and Reminders:

   - Assign due dates to each subtask to ensure timely completion. Use reminders to stay on track.

   - Example: Set a due date for "Research potential venues" and add a reminder to review progress mid-week.

4. Prioritizing Tasks:

   - Use the priority feature to mark critical tasks. This helps in focusing on what's important and urgent.

   - Example: Mark "Sign the contract" as a high-priority task.

5. Using My Day:

   - Each day, add relevant subtasks to "My Day" to stay focused on daily objectives.

   - Example: On a specific day, add "Visit shortlisted venues" to "My Day" to ensure it gets done.

6. Tracking Progress:

   - Check off subtasks as you complete them. This visual progress tracker keeps you motivated and on track.

   - Example: Once you've researched potential venues, check off that subtask in the app.

Best Practices for Breaking Down Tasks

1. Be Specific and Action-Oriented:

   - Subtasks should be clear and specific. Each subtask should represent a single action.

- Example: Instead of "Plan event logistics," use "Create event schedule" and "Book catering services."

2. Avoid Overcomplicating:

  - Break tasks down to a level that is manageable but not overly detailed. Aim for balance.

  - Example: If a task can be completed in one sitting without much effort, it may not need further breakdown.

3. Regularly Review and Adjust:

  - Periodically review your task lists to ensure they remain relevant and adjust as needed.

  - Example: During your weekly review, update tasks based on new information or changes in priorities.

4. Use Visual Aids:

  - Visual tools like Gantt charts or flow diagrams can help in planning and visualizing tasks.

  - Example: A simple flowchart showing the steps to "Finalize the venue" can provide a clear visual guide.

5. Delegate When Possible:

  - If working in a team, delegate subtasks to distribute workload and leverage individual strengths.

  - Example: Assign the task "Visit shortlisted venues" to a team member with experience in event planning.

Examples of Task Breakdown

Example 1: Writing a Research Paper

- Large Task: Write a Research Paper

- Milestones and Subtasks:

  - Topic Selection:

   - Brainstorm ideas

   - Conduct preliminary research

- Select a topic

- Research:

  - Gather sources

  - Review literature

  - Take notes

- Writing:

  - Create an outline

  - Write the introduction

  - Write the body

  - Write the conclusion

- Editing:

  - Proofread the paper

  - Revise for clarity

  - Format the paper

Example 2: Planning a Vacation

- Large Task: Plan a Vacation

- Milestones and Subtasks:

  - Destination Selection:

    - Research potential destinations

    - Compare travel costs

    - Choose a destination

  - Travel Arrangements:

    - Book flights

- Reserve accommodations

- Arrange transportation

- Itinerary Planning:

  - Research attractions

  - Create a daily itinerary

  - Make reservations for activities

- Packing and Preparation:

  - Create a packing list

  - Purchase necessary items

  - Pack luggage

Conclusion

Breaking down large tasks into manageable steps is a powerful technique to enhance productivity and ensure successful task completion. By dividing complex tasks into smaller, actionable steps, you can approach your work with clarity and confidence. Microsoft To Do's features are perfectly suited to support this process, helping you to organize, prioritize, and track your tasks effectively.

Remember, the goal is to make each step simple enough to be manageable yet comprehensive enough to keep the big picture in focus. Regularly review and adjust your tasks as needed to stay on track and maintain progress. With these strategies in place, you'll find it easier to manage large projects, reduce stress, and achieve your goals efficiently.

5.2 Time Management and Productivity Techniques

5.2.1 Prioritizing Tasks Effectively

In the pursuit of productivity, not all tasks are created equal. Understanding how to prioritize your tasks effectively is crucial to maximizing efficiency and ensuring that your most important work gets done. This section will guide you through the principles and techniques for prioritizing tasks using Microsoft To Do, ensuring that your focus aligns with your goals and that you make the best use of your time.

Understanding Task Prioritization

Task prioritization is the process of determining the order in which tasks should be tackled based on their importance, urgency, and impact. In an environment where multiple tasks are competing for your attention, knowing which tasks to prioritize can prevent overwhelm and ensure that critical deadlines are met.

The Eisenhower Matrix, also known as the Urgent-Important Matrix, is a well-known framework for prioritizing tasks. It categorizes tasks into four quadrants:

1. Urgent and Important: Tasks that require immediate attention and contribute significantly to your goals.

2. Important but Not Urgent: Tasks that are critical to your long-term success but do not require immediate action.

3. Urgent but Not Important: Tasks that demand immediate attention but do not significantly impact your long-term objectives.

4. Not Urgent and Not Important: Tasks that have little value and do not require immediate or even any action.

Using this matrix within Microsoft To Do can help you identify which tasks to tackle first and which to delegate or eliminate.

Implementing Prioritization in Microsoft To Do

Microsoft To Do offers several features that can help you prioritize tasks effectively. These features, combined with your understanding of task importance and urgency, allow you to create a system that ensures you're always working on the right tasks at the right time.

1. Using the Importance Flag

The Importance flag in Microsoft To Do is a simple yet powerful tool for marking high-priority tasks. By clicking the star icon next to a task, you can highlight tasks that need your immediate attention. These tasks will then appear in the Important smart list, giving you a quick overview of your most pressing work.

Best Practice: Reserve the Importance flag for tasks that are both urgent and important. This ensures that the Important list remains focused and only contains tasks that truly require your attention.

2. Utilizing Due Dates and Reminders

Due dates and reminders are essential for managing deadlines and ensuring that tasks are completed on time. In Microsoft To Do, you can assign a specific due date to each task, which will then appear in the Planned list. Additionally, you can set reminders to notify you when a task is approaching its due date, helping you stay on top of your schedule.

Best Practice: Assign due dates to all tasks that have a clear deadline, and use reminders for tasks that need to be started or completed at a specific time. This will help you manage your time effectively and prevent tasks from slipping through the cracks.

3. Organizing Tasks by Categories and Tags

Microsoft To Do allows you to categorize tasks using lists and tags. By grouping related tasks together, you can focus on specific areas of your work at a time, making it easier to manage your priorities.

Best Practice: Create separate lists for different projects or areas of your life (e.g., Work, Personal, Health). Within each list, use tags to further categorize tasks by their priority level (e.g., High Priority, Low Priority). This allows you to quickly identify the most important tasks in each area.

4. Prioritizing with the My Day Feature

The My Day feature in Microsoft To Do is designed to help you focus on what needs to be done today. Each morning, you can review your tasks and add the most important ones to My Day. This feature allows you to create a daily to-do list that keeps you focused on your immediate priorities.

Best Practice: At the start of each day, review your tasks and select the top 3-5 tasks that you must complete by the end of the day. Add these tasks to My Day and commit to completing them before moving on to less critical work.

Advanced Prioritization Techniques

While the basic prioritization tools in Microsoft To Do are highly effective, there are also more advanced techniques that can help you take your productivity to the next level.

1. The ABCDE Method

The ABCDE Method is a prioritization technique that categorizes tasks based on their relative importance. In this system:

- A tasks are very important and must be done first.

- B tasks are important but not as critical as A tasks.

- C tasks are nice to do but have no serious consequences if not done.

- D tasks are tasks that can be delegated to others.

- E tasks are tasks that should be eliminated.

Implementation in Microsoft To Do: You can use tags in Microsoft To Do to label tasks with their respective ABCDE categories. Then, focus on completing all A tasks before moving on to B tasks, and so on.

2. The Pareto Principle (80/20 Rule)

The Pareto Principle states that 80% of your results come from 20% of your efforts. In the context of task prioritization, this means that a small number of high-priority tasks will have the greatest impact on your goals.

Implementation in Microsoft To Do: Identify the top 20% of tasks that will produce the most significant results and prioritize them. These tasks should be flagged as Important and added to your daily focus in My Day.

3. The 1-3-5 Rule

The 1-3-5 Rule is a simple method for structuring your day. According to this rule, each day you should aim to complete:

- 1 big task (high priority)

- 3 medium tasks (important but less urgent)

- 5 small tasks (minor tasks or quick wins)

Implementation in Microsoft To Do: At the start of the day, use the My Day feature to add one big task, three medium tasks, and five small tasks. This structured approach helps you manage your workload and ensures that you're making consistent progress on both large and small tasks.

Avoiding Common Pitfalls in Task Prioritization

Prioritizing tasks effectively requires not only the right techniques but also an awareness of common pitfalls that can derail your productivity. Here are some common challenges and how to avoid them:

1. Overloading Your To-Do List

It's easy to fall into the trap of adding too many tasks to your to-do list, leading to overwhelm and decreased productivity. When your list becomes too long, it's challenging to identify and focus on the most important tasks.

Solution: Limit the number of tasks you add to your My Day list. Stick to a manageable number of high-priority tasks, and resist the urge to add more unless you've completed the most critical ones.

2. Failing to Review and Adjust Priorities

Priorities can change quickly based on new information, shifting goals, or unexpected tasks. If you don't regularly review and adjust your priorities, you risk focusing on outdated or less important tasks.

Solution: Conduct a daily or weekly review of your tasks in Microsoft To Do. Reassess your priorities and adjust your to-do list accordingly. This ensures that you're always working on the most relevant and impactful tasks.

3. Confusing Urgency with Importance

Not all urgent tasks are important. It's easy to get caught up in tasks that demand immediate attention but don't contribute to your long-term goals.

Solution: Use the Eisenhower Matrix to differentiate between urgent and important tasks. Focus on completing important tasks first, even if they're not immediately urgent, to ensure that you're making meaningful progress toward your goals.

4. Procrastination on High-Priority Tasks

High-priority tasks are often the most challenging, leading to procrastination. Delaying these tasks can result in missed deadlines and increased stress.

Solution: Break down large, intimidating tasks into smaller, more manageable steps. Use the My Day feature to focus on one step at a time, making it easier to start and maintain momentum.

Integrating Prioritization into Your Daily Workflow

Prioritizing tasks effectively is not just a one-time activity—it's a daily practice that should be integrated into your workflow. Here's how you can make task prioritization a seamless part of your day-to-day routine:

1. Start Your Day with Prioritization

Begin each day by reviewing your tasks in Microsoft To Do. Use the My Day feature to select your top priorities and create a focused to-do list for the day. This ensures that you start your day with clarity and purpose.

2. End Your Day with Reflection

At the end of each day, review what you've accomplished and assess whether your priorities were met. Reflect on any tasks that were left incomplete and consider whether they should be carried over to the next day's My Day list.

3. Use Weekly Reviews to Reassess Priorities

In addition to daily prioritization, conduct a weekly review to reassess your overall priorities. This review allows you to adjust your to-do lists based on your progress, upcoming deadlines, and any new tasks that have arisen.

4. Stay Flexible and Adaptable

Finally, remember that prioritization is not set in stone. Stay flexible and be willing to adjust your priorities as new information and tasks come in. Microsoft To Do's dynamic lists and tagging features make it easy to reorganize your tasks as needed.

5.2.2 Combining GTD with Other Productivity Methods

The Getting Things Done (GTD) methodology is a powerful system designed to help individuals manage their tasks, projects, and commitments in a structured and organized manner. However, it's not the only productivity method available. Many other systems, such as the Pomodoro Technique, Eisenhower Matrix, and Bullet Journaling, offer unique approaches to time management and task prioritization. By combining GTD with these other methods, you can create a personalized productivity system that maximizes your efficiency and helps you achieve your goals.

Understanding the Synergy Between GTD and Other Methods

Before diving into the specifics of how GTD can be combined with other productivity methods, it's essential to understand why these combinations can be beneficial. Each productivity method has its strengths and weaknesses, and no single method is perfect for every situation. GTD is excellent for capturing and organizing tasks, but it may not always address specific needs such as time management, decision-making, or motivation. By integrating elements from other productivity systems into your GTD workflow, you can address these gaps and create a more holistic approach to managing your work and life.

Example: Imagine you're using GTD to manage a large project at work. While GTD helps you capture all the tasks and organize them into actionable steps, you may still struggle with time management or prioritization. By incorporating techniques like the Pomodoro Technique or the Eisenhower Matrix, you can enhance your productivity and ensure that you're working on the right tasks at the right time.

Combining GTD with the Pomodoro Technique

The Pomodoro Technique is a time management method developed by Francesco Cirillo in the late 1980s. It involves breaking your work into intervals, typically 25 minutes long, separated by short breaks. These intervals are called "Pomodoros." The Pomodoro Technique is designed to improve focus and prevent burnout by encouraging regular breaks and reducing the likelihood of multitasking.

Integration with GTD: GTD helps you identify and organize tasks, but it doesn't dictate how you should manage your time while working on those tasks. The Pomodoro Technique can be seamlessly integrated into your GTD system by using it to tackle tasks on your Next Actions list. Here's how:

- Step 1: Choose a Task from Your Next Actions List: Start by selecting a task from your GTD Next Actions list that you want to work on. Ensure the task is well-defined and actionable.

- Step 2: Set a Timer for 25 Minutes: Set a timer for 25 minutes (one Pomodoro) and focus solely on the chosen task during this time. Avoid distractions and stay committed to the task until the timer goes off.

- Step 3: Take a Short Break: Once the Pomodoro is complete, take a 5-minute break. Use this time to relax, stretch, or do something enjoyable.

- Step 4: Repeat the Process: After your break, start a new Pomodoro with the same task or choose a new one from your Next Actions list. After completing four Pomodoros, take a more extended break of 15-30 minutes.

Benefits: The Pomodoro Technique complements GTD by helping you manage your time more effectively and maintain focus on specific tasks. It can be particularly useful for tasks that require deep concentration or when you're struggling with procrastination. Additionally, the regular breaks help prevent burnout and keep your energy levels high throughout the day.

Integrating the Eisenhower Matrix with GTD

The Eisenhower Matrix, also known as the Urgent-Important Matrix, is a decision-making tool that helps you prioritize tasks based on their urgency and importance. The matrix divides tasks into four quadrants:

- Quadrant I: Urgent and Important (Tasks that need to be done immediately)

- Quadrant II: Not Urgent but Important (Tasks that are important but can be scheduled for later)

- Quadrant III: Urgent but Not Important (Tasks that are urgent but not crucial to your goals)

- Quadrant IV: Not Urgent and Not Important (Tasks that are neither urgent nor important)

Integration with GTD: GTD is excellent at capturing tasks, but it doesn't inherently prioritize them. By incorporating the Eisenhower Matrix into your GTD workflow, you can prioritize tasks more effectively and ensure that you're focusing on what truly matters. Here's how:

- Step 1: Capture Tasks in GTD: Start by capturing all your tasks, projects, and commitments in your GTD system. This step ensures that nothing is overlooked and that you have a comprehensive view of everything that needs to be done.

- Step 2: Classify Tasks Using the Eisenhower Matrix: Once you've captured your tasks, use the Eisenhower Matrix to classify each task based on its urgency and importance. Assign tasks to the appropriate quadrant:

  - Quadrant I: These tasks should be your top priority. Schedule them for immediate action or complete them as soon as possible.

  - Quadrant II: These tasks are important for your long-term goals but don't require immediate attention. Schedule them in your calendar to ensure they get done.

  - Quadrant III: These tasks may seem urgent, but they don't contribute significantly to your goals. Consider delegating or minimizing time spent on them.

  - Quadrant IV: These tasks are neither urgent nor important. Eliminate them if possible or limit the time you spend on them.

- Step 3: Align Your Next Actions List with the Matrix: Once you've classified your tasks, update your GTD Next Actions list to reflect your priorities. Focus on completing Quadrant I tasks first, followed by Quadrant II tasks.

Benefits: The Eisenhower Matrix enhances your GTD system by adding a prioritization layer. It helps you make informed decisions about where to focus your time and energy, ensuring that you're working on tasks that align with your goals. By regularly reviewing your tasks through the lens of the Eisenhower Matrix, you can avoid getting caught up in unimportant or low-priority activities.

Combining GTD with Bullet Journaling

Bullet Journaling is a customizable organizational system developed by Ryder Carroll. It combines elements of task management, goal setting, and journaling into a single, flexible system. The Bullet Journal, or "BuJo," allows users to track their daily tasks, set goals, and reflect on their progress in a visually appealing and personalized format.

Integration with GTD: While GTD is a structured system for managing tasks and projects, Bullet Journaling offers a creative and reflective approach to productivity. By combining the two, you can create a system that is both organized and adaptable to your personal preferences. Here's how:

- Step 1: Set Up Your Bullet Journal: Start by setting up your Bullet Journal with key elements such as the Index, Future Log, Monthly Log, Daily Log, and Collections. These elements provide a framework for tracking tasks, events, and notes.

- Step 2: Capture Tasks and Ideas: Use your Bullet Journal to capture tasks, ideas, and notes as they come to mind. This step aligns with the GTD principle of capturing everything in a trusted system.

- Step 3: Migrate Tasks to Your GTD System: At the end of each day or week, review the tasks and notes in your Bullet Journal and migrate them to your GTD system. Organize tasks into the appropriate lists, such as Next Actions, Projects, or Waiting For.

- Step 4: Use Collections for Project Planning: Use the Collections feature in your Bullet Journal to plan and track specific projects. This feature allows you to break down projects into actionable steps, set deadlines, and monitor progress.

- Step 5: Reflect and Review: Regularly review your Bullet Journal to reflect on your progress, identify areas for improvement, and make adjustments to your GTD system. This reflective practice helps you stay aligned with your goals and maintain a sense of purpose.

Benefits: The combination of GTD and Bullet Journaling offers the best of both worlds: the structure and efficiency of GTD with the flexibility and creativity of Bullet Journaling. This approach allows you to customize your productivity system to suit your unique style and preferences. Additionally, the reflective aspect of Bullet Journaling helps you stay mindful of your progress and fosters a deeper connection to your goals.

Integrating GTD with the Time Blocking Method

Time Blocking is a time management technique that involves dividing your day into blocks of time dedicated to specific tasks or activities. By allocating time blocks for different tasks, you can minimize distractions, enhance focus, and ensure that you're making progress on your most important tasks.

Integration with GTD: While GTD focuses on organizing tasks, it doesn't prescribe when you should work on them. Time Blocking adds this temporal dimension, allowing you to schedule tasks from your Next Actions list into your calendar. Here's how:

- Step 1: Identify Your Most Important Tasks: Start by reviewing your GTD system and identifying the tasks that are most important for the day or week. Prioritize tasks that align with your goals and have deadlines.

- Step 2: Create Time Blocks in Your Calendar: Allocate specific blocks of time in your calendar for each task. For example, you might schedule a two-hour block in the morning for deep work on a critical project and a one-hour block in the afternoon for meetings or administrative tasks.

- Step 3: Focus on One Task During Each Time Block: When it's time to work on a task, focus exclusively on that task during the designated time block. Avoid multitasking and minimize distractions to make the most of your time.

- Step 4: Review and Adjust Your Time Blocks: At the end of each day or week, review how well you adhered to your time blocks and make adjustments as needed. If certain tasks took longer than expected, consider allocating more time for similar tasks in the future.

Benefits: Time Blocking enhances your GTD system by providing a structured schedule for completing tasks. It helps you stay focused and productive throughout the day, ensuring that you're making steady progress on your most important tasks. Additionally, Time Blocking can help you achieve a better work-life balance by setting clear boundaries between work and personal time.

Combining GTD with the Ivy Lee Method

The Ivy Lee Method is a simple productivity technique that involves creating a daily to-do list with a maximum of six tasks, prioritized by importance. The method encourages you to focus on completing one task at a time, starting with the most important task and moving down the list.

Integration with GTD: The Ivy Lee Method can be used to streamline your daily GTD workflow by helping you focus on the most critical tasks. Here's how:

- Step 1: Review Your Next Actions List: At the end of each day, review your GTD Next Actions list and identify the six most important tasks that you need to complete the next day.

- Step 2: Prioritize Your Tasks: Rank the six tasks in order of importance, with the most important task at the top of the list.

- Step 3: Focus on One Task at a Time: On the following day, start with the first task on your list and work on it until it's completed. Then move on to the next task, and so on.

- Step 4: Carry Over Unfinished Tasks: If you don't complete all six tasks, carry over the remaining tasks to the next day's list and repeat the process.

Benefits: The Ivy Lee Method adds a layer of simplicity and focus to your GTD system. By limiting your daily task list to six items, you can avoid feeling overwhelmed and ensure that you're making progress on your most important tasks. This method also encourages you to work on one task at a time, reducing the tendency to multitask and improving your overall productivity.

Conclusion

Combining GTD with other productivity methods can create a more comprehensive and personalized approach to task management. Whether you're using the Pomodoro Technique to manage your time, the Eisenhower Matrix to prioritize tasks, Bullet Journaling to reflect on your progress, Time Blocking to schedule your day, or the Ivy Lee Method to streamline your workflow, these integrations can enhance the effectiveness of your GTD system. The key is to experiment with different combinations and find the methods that work best for your unique needs and preferences. By doing so, you'll be better equipped to manage your tasks, achieve your goals, and ultimately get more things done.

5.2.3 Avoiding Common Productivity Pitfalls

In the pursuit of getting things done, even the most organized individuals can fall into productivity traps that hinder their efficiency. Avoiding these pitfalls is essential for maintaining momentum and ensuring that your task management system continues to work for you, rather than against you. Below, we explore some common productivity pitfalls and provide strategies for steering clear of them, with a particular focus on how Microsoft To Do can be leveraged to enhance your productivity and keep you on track.

Procrastination: The Silent Productivity Killer

Understanding Procrastination:

Procrastination is a well-known enemy of productivity. It manifests when you delay tasks, even when you know they need to be done. Often, this delay comes from a place of fear—fear of failure, fear of making mistakes, or even fear of the unknown. The result is that important tasks are pushed aside for less critical or easier activities, leading to a pile-up of work and increased stress.

Strategies to Combat Procrastination:

- Use Microsoft To Do's "My Day" Feature: Start your day by selecting tasks that are achievable and align with your priorities. This helps create a focused to-do list for the day, reducing the temptation to procrastinate.

- Break Tasks into Smaller Steps: Large tasks can feel overwhelming, which can lead to procrastination. Microsoft To Do allows you to break tasks into subtasks. By focusing on completing these smaller steps, you can reduce the mental barrier that contributes to procrastination.

- Set Specific Deadlines: Tasks without deadlines can easily be postponed. Assign specific due dates to your tasks in Microsoft To Do. This creates a sense of urgency and encourages you to act sooner rather than later.

- Prioritize Tasks with the Eisenhower Matrix: The Eisenhower Matrix is a time-management technique that categorizes tasks into four quadrants: urgent and important, important but not urgent, urgent but not important, and neither urgent nor important. Use tags or lists in Microsoft To Do to categorize tasks according to this matrix, ensuring you focus on what truly matters.

Multitasking: The Illusion of Productivity

Understanding Multitasking:

Multitasking is often hailed as a sign of efficiency, but in reality, it can significantly reduce productivity. The human brain is not designed to handle multiple complex tasks simultaneously. When you multitask, you're not actually doing several things at once; rather, you're rapidly switching your focus between tasks, which can lead to mistakes, slower progress, and burnout.

Strategies to Avoid Multitasking:

- Focus on One Task at a Time: Use Microsoft To Do to prioritize your tasks and tackle them one by one. The "My Day" feature can be particularly useful here, allowing you to plan a sequence of tasks rather than trying to juggle multiple at once.

- Set Time Blocks: Allocate specific blocks of time to each task and stick to them. For example, you can set aside 30 minutes to work on a report, then move on to the next task. Use reminders in Microsoft To Do to signal the start and end of each time block.

- Turn Off Notifications: Notifications from various apps can disrupt your focus and tempt you to multitask. Customize your Microsoft To Do settings to minimize distractions, and consider putting your phone on "Do Not Disturb" mode during work sessions.

- Review and Reflect: At the end of the day, review what you've accomplished. Microsoft To Do's completed tasks view can help you see what you've finished and give you a sense of accomplishment, which can reinforce the habit of focusing on one task at a time.

Overcommitting: The Path to Burnout

Understanding Overcommitment:

In an effort to be productive, it's easy to overcommit—taking on more tasks and responsibilities than you can reasonably handle. Overcommitment often leads to stress, reduced quality of work, and eventually burnout. It's crucial to recognize your limits and prioritize your well-being alongside your productivity.

Strategies to Manage Overcommitment:

- Evaluate Your Capacity: Before agreeing to new tasks or projects, assess your current workload using Microsoft To Do. Create a list of your ongoing tasks and deadlines, and be realistic about what you can handle. This helps you make informed decisions about whether to take on additional work.

- Learn to Say No: It's okay to decline tasks that would stretch you too thin. Microsoft To Do can help you maintain a clear view of your priorities, making it easier to explain why you can't take on new commitments.

- Delegate When Possible: If you're in a position to delegate, use Microsoft To Do's task-sharing feature to assign tasks to others. This not only lightens your load but also empowers your team or colleagues to take on more responsibility.

- Set Boundaries: Protect your personal time by setting boundaries around work. Use Microsoft To Do to schedule breaks and personal activities, ensuring that you don't overextend yourself in your professional life.

Lack of Prioritization: Focusing on the Wrong Tasks

Understanding the Consequences of Poor Prioritization:

Without proper prioritization, you may find yourself working hard but not necessarily making progress on what matters most. It's easy to get caught up in busywork—tasks that keep you occupied but don't contribute to your larger goals. Effective prioritization ensures that your efforts are aligned with your most important objectives.

Strategies for Effective Prioritization:

- Use Microsoft To Do's "Important" Tag: Tagging tasks as "Important" helps you quickly identify which tasks require your immediate attention. Review this list regularly to ensure that you're focusing on high-priority items.

- Adopt the Pareto Principle: Also known as the 80/20 rule, the Pareto Principle suggests that 80% of your results come from 20% of your efforts. Identify the tasks that have the greatest impact on your goals, and prioritize them using Microsoft To Do.

- Regularly Reevaluate Priorities: Your priorities can change over time, so it's important to reassess them regularly. Microsoft To Do allows you to easily rearrange tasks and adjust deadlines, keeping your to-do list aligned with your current priorities.

- Balance Short-Term and Long-Term Goals: It's easy to focus on urgent tasks at the expense of long-term objectives. Create separate lists in Microsoft To Do for short-term and long-term goals, ensuring that you dedicate time to both.

Inadequate Planning: Setting Yourself Up for Failure

Understanding the Importance of Planning:

Without a clear plan, it's easy to lose track of what needs to be done and when. Inadequate planning can lead to missed deadlines, incomplete tasks, and a general sense of overwhelm. Proper planning, on the other hand, gives you a roadmap to follow, making it easier to stay on track and achieve your goals.

Strategies for Effective Planning:

- Use Microsoft To Do to Plan Your Week: At the start of each week, create a plan that outlines your key tasks and objectives. Break down larger projects into manageable steps, and distribute these tasks across the week using Microsoft To Do.

- Set Realistic Goals: Overly ambitious plans can set you up for failure. Use Microsoft To Do to set achievable goals, ensuring that your plans are realistic and aligned with your capacity.

- Incorporate Buffer Time: Unexpected tasks and delays are inevitable, so it's important to build buffer time into your schedule. Microsoft To Do allows you to adjust deadlines easily, helping you accommodate these disruptions without derailing your entire plan.

- Review and Adjust: Your plan is not set in stone—it's a living document that should evolve as your circumstances change. Use Microsoft To Do's flexibility to update your plan as needed, ensuring that it remains relevant and effective.

Neglecting Self-Care: The Cost of Continuous Productivity

Understanding the Impact of Neglecting Self-Care:

While productivity is important, it's crucial to remember that you're not a machine. Continuous focus on work without taking care of your physical and mental well-being can lead to burnout, decreased productivity, and even serious health issues. Maintaining a balance between work and self-care is essential for sustained productivity and overall well-being.

Strategies to Incorporate Self-Care:

- Schedule Breaks in Microsoft To Do: Use the task scheduling feature to plan regular breaks throughout your day. Short breaks can refresh your mind and improve your focus when you return to work.

- Prioritize Sleep and Nutrition: Your productivity is directly linked to your physical health. Use Microsoft To Do to set reminders for important self-care activities, such as getting enough sleep, eating healthy meals, and exercising regularly.

- Practice Mindfulness: Incorporating mindfulness practices, such as meditation or deep breathing exercises, can help reduce stress and improve concentration. Consider adding a daily mindfulness reminder to your to-do list.

- Set Boundaries Between Work and Personal Time: It's easy to let work spill over into your personal life, especially if you're working from home. Use Microsoft To Do to schedule clear start and end times for your workday, and stick to them.

Perfectionism: The Trap of Over-Refining Tasks

Understanding Perfectionism:

Perfectionism, while often seen as a positive trait, can be a significant hindrance to productivity. The pursuit of perfection can lead to excessive time spent on minor details, procrastination due to fear of not meeting high standards, and ultimately, delays in completing tasks. Perfectionism often results in diminishing returns, where the extra time spent refining something does not significantly improve the final outcome.

Strategies to Manage Perfectionism:

- Set Time Limits for Tasks: Assign specific time limits to tasks using Microsoft To Do. By setting a deadline, you force yourself to complete the task within a reasonable timeframe, reducing the tendency to over-refine.

- Focus on Progress, Not Perfection: Shift your mindset from achieving perfection to making consistent progress. Use Microsoft To Do's tracking features to monitor your progress and celebrate milestones, even if the work isn't perfect.

- Accept Imperfection: Recognize that not every task requires perfection. Use Microsoft To Do to differentiate between tasks that need to be perfect and those that simply need to be completed. This can help you allocate your time and energy more effectively.

- Review and Move On: Once a task is complete, review it briefly and then move on to the next one. Microsoft To Do allows you to archive completed tasks, helping you mentally close the chapter on that task and focus on what's next.

By addressing these common productivity pitfalls and implementing the strategies outlined above, you can significantly enhance your efficiency and effectiveness in managing your tasks with Microsoft To Do. The key is to remain mindful of these potential challenges and to continuously refine your approach to task management. Microsoft To Do provides the tools and flexibility needed to avoid these traps and maintain a high level of productivity, enabling you to achieve your goals without unnecessary stress or burnout.

5.3 Maintaining Balance and Focus

5.3.1 Setting Realistic Goals

In the pursuit of productivity, setting realistic goals is crucial. Goals are the driving force behind our actions and serve as the blueprint for what we wish to accomplish. However, unrealistic goals can lead to frustration, burnout, and ultimately failure, which is why it's essential to ensure that the goals you set are achievable and aligned with your capabilities and resources.

This section will explore the importance of setting realistic goals and how Microsoft To Do can be an invaluable tool in helping you achieve them.

The Importance of Setting Realistic Goals

Realistic goals are the cornerstone of effective productivity. They provide direction and motivation, ensuring that your efforts are focused and intentional. When goals are realistic, they are more likely to be achieved, leading to a sense of accomplishment that fuels further productivity.

Setting unrealistic goals, on the other hand, can have the opposite effect. It can lead to discouragement, stress, and a sense of inadequacy when the goals are not met. This can create a vicious cycle where the fear of failure prevents you from setting new goals, ultimately stalling your progress.

Realistic goals are specific, measurable, achievable, relevant, and time-bound (SMART). The SMART criteria are a widely used framework for goal-setting, helping individuals and teams create goals that are both challenging and attainable. Let's break down each component:

- Specific: Goals should be clear and specific, outlining exactly what you want to achieve. A specific goal has a much greater chance of being accomplished than a general one. For example, rather than setting a goal to "improve productivity," you might set a goal to "reduce time spent on emails by 30% using Microsoft To Do."

- Measurable: A goal should have measurable outcomes so that you can track your progress and know when it has been achieved. This might involve setting a specific number, percentage, or other quantifiable metrics.

- Achievable: Goals need to be realistic and attainable. While it's important to challenge yourself, setting goals that are too far out of reach can lead to failure. Consider your current resources, constraints, and time available when setting a goal.

- Relevant: Your goals should align with your broader objectives, whether personal or professional. If a goal does not contribute to your long-term plans, it may not be worth pursuing.

- Time-bound: Every goal should have a deadline or time frame. This creates a sense of urgency and helps prevent procrastination.

Using Microsoft To Do to Set and Track Realistic Goals

Microsoft To Do is a versatile tool that can assist you in setting, organizing, and tracking your goals. With features that allow you to create tasks, set due dates, prioritize, and review your progress, Microsoft To Do is perfectly suited to help you stay on top of your goals.

Here's how you can use Microsoft To Do to set realistic goals:

1. Breaking Down Goals into Tasks

One of the key aspects of setting realistic goals is breaking them down into smaller, manageable tasks. Large goals can seem daunting, and without a clear plan, you may struggle to know where to start. Microsoft To Do allows you to break down your goals into individual tasks that are easier to manage and complete.

- Create a New List: Start by creating a new list in Microsoft To Do for each of your major goals. For example, if your goal is to complete a project, you can create a list specifically for that project.

- Add Tasks: Under each list, add tasks that represent the individual steps needed to achieve the goal. These should be actionable items that move you closer to your goal. For instance, if your goal is to write a book, your tasks might include "outline the chapters," "write the first draft of chapter 1," "revise chapter 1," and so on.

- Prioritize Tasks: Microsoft To Do allows you to prioritize tasks by marking them as "Important" or "My Day." Use these features to identify which tasks are most critical and need to be addressed first.

2. Setting Deadlines and Reminders

Deadlines are a crucial part of the goal-setting process. They provide a timeframe within which you aim to complete a task, helping you to stay focused and avoid procrastination.

- Assign Due Dates: For each task, assign a due date that reflects when you intend to complete it. This not only keeps you on track but also helps you to evenly distribute your workload over time, preventing last-minute rushes.

- Use Reminders: Microsoft To Do allows you to set reminders for your tasks. This feature ensures that you don't forget important deadlines and can help you to allocate time to work on tasks well in advance of their due dates.

- Schedule Tasks for "My Day": The "My Day" feature in Microsoft To Do lets you plan your daily tasks. Each morning, you can review your tasks and decide which ones you will focus on that day. This keeps your daily workload manageable and aligned with your longer-term goals.

3. Reviewing and Adjusting Goals

It's important to regularly review your goals to assess your progress and make adjustments if necessary. A goal that seemed realistic at the outset might need to be adjusted due to changes in circumstances, priorities, or new information.

- Weekly Reviews: Set aside time each week to review your progress. In Microsoft To Do, you can view all tasks within a specific list or across all lists, making it easy to see what has been accomplished and what still needs to be done.

- Adjust Deadlines and Priorities: If you find that certain tasks are taking longer than expected, or if new tasks have arisen, don't hesitate to adjust your deadlines and priorities. Microsoft To Do's flexible interface allows you to easily change due dates, reorder tasks, and update priorities as needed.

- Reflect on Achievements: Take time to celebrate your successes, no matter how small. Completing tasks and making progress towards your goals is an accomplishment that should be recognized. Use the "Completed" tasks view in Microsoft To Do to see all that you've achieved, which can be a great motivator to keep going.

4. Keeping Goals Aligned with Your Values

Goals should not only be realistic in terms of achievability but should also align with your personal values and long-term aspirations. Misalignment can lead to a lack of motivation and satisfaction, even if the goals are technically achieved.

- Reflect on Your Values: Before setting goals, take some time to reflect on your personal and professional values. What is most important to you? What do you want to achieve in the long run? Use these reflections to guide your goal-setting process.

- Evaluate Goals Regularly: As you work towards your goals, periodically evaluate whether they still align with your values and overall objectives. If you find that a goal no longer serves you, it may be time to adjust it or let it go. Microsoft To Do allows you to archive or delete lists and tasks that are no longer relevant, helping you to stay focused on what truly matters.

- Set Meaningful Goals: Ensure that the goals you set are meaningful and contribute to your long-term happiness and success. This will keep you motivated and engaged in the process of achieving them.

5. Using the Power of Small Wins

Achieving smaller, intermediate goals can provide a sense of accomplishment and motivation that fuels your progress towards larger goals. Microsoft To Do can help you to harness the power of these small wins.

- Track Progress Incrementally: Break down larger tasks into smaller, more manageable sub-tasks. For example, if your goal is to complete a course, your sub-tasks might include "complete module 1," "take quiz for module 1," and so on. As you complete each sub-task, check it off in Microsoft To Do. This creates a sense of momentum and progress.

- Celebrate Small Wins: Use the "Completed Tasks" view to see all that you've accomplished, no matter how small. This can be a powerful motivator and a reminder of how far you've come.

- Set Short-Term Goals: In addition to long-term goals, set short-term goals that can be achieved within a week or a month. Microsoft To Do's interface is perfect for managing both short-term and long-term goals simultaneously.

6. Balancing Ambition with Realism

While it's important to be realistic, it's also important to remain ambitious. Striking the right balance between ambition and realism is key to setting goals that challenge you without overwhelming you.

- Start Small, Aim High: Begin with goals that are easily achievable to build confidence and momentum. As you gain experience and success, gradually increase the difficulty and ambition of your goals.

- Use Microsoft To Do to Track Both Short and Long-Term Goals: Use separate lists for short-term and long-term goals, or combine them within a single list. Microsoft To Do's flexibility allows you to tailor your task management system to your specific needs.

- Review and Revise: Ambitious goals may require frequent review and revision. As you progress, you may find that you need to adjust your goals to reflect new opportunities or challenges. Microsoft To Do makes it easy to update tasks, due dates, and priorities as your situation changes.

Conclusion

Setting realistic goals is a fundamental aspect of effective productivity and task management. By ensuring that your goals are specific, measurable, achievable, relevant, and time-bound, you set yourself up for success. Microsoft To Do is an excellent tool to help you in this process, offering features that make it easy to break down goals, set deadlines, track progress, and stay aligned with your values.

Remember, the journey to achieving your goals is just as important as the destination. By setting realistic goals and using tools like Microsoft To Do, you can maintain balance, focus, and motivation, ultimately leading to greater productivity and satisfaction.

5.3.2 Managing Work-Life Balance with Microsoft To Do

In today's fast-paced world, maintaining a healthy work-life balance can be challenging. With the increasing demands of work, personal responsibilities, and social obligations, it can be easy to feel overwhelmed and stretched too thin. However, by leveraging Microsoft To Do, you can create a system that helps you manage both your professional and personal life, ensuring that you give adequate attention to both areas. This section will explore how

Microsoft To Do can be a powerful tool for achieving and maintaining a healthy work-life balance.

Understanding Work-Life Balance

Before diving into specific strategies, it's important to understand what work-life balance really means. Work-life balance is the equilibrium between your professional duties and personal activities. It's not about splitting your time equally between work and personal life but rather about managing your time effectively so that you can fulfill your work responsibilities while also enjoying your personal time. Achieving this balance is crucial for your overall well-being, as it can lead to reduced stress, increased productivity, and improved mental and physical health.

Incorporating Microsoft To Do into your daily routine can help you manage your time better, ensuring that you can focus on both your professional and personal priorities without feeling overwhelmed.

Using Microsoft To Do for Work-Life Balance

1. Creating Separate Lists for Work and Personal Tasks

One of the first steps to achieving work-life balance with Microsoft To Do is to create separate lists for your work and personal tasks. By doing this, you can clearly distinguish between your professional responsibilities and your personal obligations. This separation helps you focus on one area at a time, reducing the mental load of constantly switching between work and personal tasks.

   - Work List: This list should include all your work-related tasks, such as project deadlines, meetings, follow-ups, and other professional duties. It's important to keep this list organized by priority and due dates, so you can focus on what needs to be done first.

   - Personal List: Your personal list should include tasks such as household chores, errands, personal appointments, and activities related to your hobbies or self-care. Just like your work list, organizing this list by priority can help you focus on what's most important.

   Having separate lists allows you to mentally switch off from work when you're focusing on personal tasks and vice versa. This distinction is crucial for maintaining a healthy boundary between work and personal life.

2. Scheduling Downtime and Personal Time

It's easy to get caught up in work and forget to take breaks or spend time on personal activities. Microsoft To Do can help you schedule downtime and personal time, ensuring that you allocate time for relaxation, hobbies, and socializing.

- Adding Downtime to Your Schedule: Use Microsoft To Do to block out specific times for breaks throughout your day. For example, you can set reminders to take a short walk, meditate, or have a cup of tea. By scheduling these breaks, you're more likely to take them and avoid burnout.

- Planning Personal Activities: Just as you would schedule a meeting or deadline at work, use Microsoft To Do to plan personal activities such as spending time with family, pursuing a hobby, or exercising. By treating these activities as important as your work tasks, you ensure that you're making time for yourself.

Remember, personal time is essential for recharging your energy and maintaining your overall well-being. Don't be afraid to prioritize it in your daily schedule.

3. Setting Boundaries with Microsoft To Do

Boundaries are a key component of maintaining a work-life balance. With the rise of remote work and the blurring of lines between work and home, it's more important than ever to set clear boundaries.

- Defining Work Hours: Use Microsoft To Do to set reminders for the start and end of your workday. For example, you can create a task that reminds you to shut down your computer at 6 PM or to start winding down at 8 AM. This helps you stick to your designated work hours and prevents work from spilling over into your personal time.

- Turning Off Work Notifications After Hours: Once your workday is over, consider turning off notifications for your work-related lists. This helps you disconnect from work and focus on your personal life. Microsoft To Do allows you to customize your notification settings, so you can ensure that work-related tasks don't interrupt your personal time.

- Creating "Do Not Disturb" Times: Another way to set boundaries is by creating "do not disturb" times in your Microsoft To Do. During these times, focus solely on personal activities without the distraction of work tasks. For example, you could set a "do not disturb" time during dinner or when you're spending time with family.

Establishing these boundaries helps you protect your personal time and ensures that you're not constantly thinking about work, leading to a healthier work-life balance.

4. Prioritizing Self-Care

Self-care is an essential part of maintaining work-life balance, yet it's often the first thing to be neglected when life gets busy. Microsoft To Do can help you prioritize self-care by allowing you to schedule activities that promote your well-being.

- Scheduling Regular Exercise: Use Microsoft To Do to set reminders for regular exercise, whether it's a daily walk, a yoga session, or a trip to the gym. Exercise is crucial for both physical and mental health, and scheduling it in your to-do list ensures that it becomes a non-negotiable part of your routine.

- Planning Relaxation Activities: In addition to exercise, it's important to schedule activities that help you relax and unwind. This could be anything from reading a book, taking a bath, or practicing mindfulness. By adding these activities to your Microsoft To Do list, you're more likely to make time for them.

- Prioritizing Sleep: Don't forget to prioritize sleep as part of your self-care routine. Use Microsoft To Do to set reminders for winding down at night and going to bed at a reasonable hour. Getting enough sleep is essential for maintaining your energy levels and overall health.

By making self-care a priority in your Microsoft To Do list, you're taking proactive steps towards maintaining a healthy work-life balance.

5. Reviewing and Reflecting Regularly

Maintaining work-life balance is an ongoing process that requires regular reflection and adjustment. Microsoft To Do can help you review and reflect on your progress, allowing you to make necessary changes to your routine.

- Weekly Reviews: Set a weekly task in Microsoft To Do to review your work and personal lists. During this review, assess how well you're managing your time, whether you're sticking to your boundaries, and if you're making enough time for personal activities. If you find that work is taking up too much of your time, adjust your schedule to create more balance.

- Reflecting on Your Well-being: In addition to reviewing your tasks, take some time to reflect on your overall well-being. Are you feeling stressed or overwhelmed? Are you getting enough rest and relaxation? Use these reflections to make adjustments to your schedule and prioritize activities that support your well-being.

- Adjusting Your Goals: As part of your review, consider whether your goals are still aligned with your current priorities. If your work-life balance is off, you may need to adjust your goals to focus more on personal time or self-care. Use Microsoft To Do to update your goals and create tasks that support them.

Regularly reviewing and reflecting on your progress helps you stay on track with your work-life balance goals and ensures that you're continuously improving your approach.

6. Using Microsoft To Do with Other Productivity Tools

Microsoft To Do is a powerful tool on its own, but it can be even more effective when used in conjunction with other productivity tools. By integrating Microsoft To Do with other apps, you can create a seamless workflow that supports your work-life balance.

- Integrating with Microsoft Outlook: If you use Microsoft Outlook for email and calendar management, consider integrating it with Microsoft To Do. This integration allows you to view your tasks alongside your emails and appointments, helping you manage your time more effectively. For example, you can use Outlook to schedule meetings and use Microsoft To Do to track the tasks that come out of those meetings.

- Using Microsoft Teams: For those who work in a collaborative environment, integrating Microsoft To Do with Microsoft Teams can be beneficial. You can share tasks with colleagues, track team progress, and ensure that everyone is on the same page. This collaboration helps prevent work from becoming overwhelming and supports a more balanced workload.

- Automating with Microsoft Power Automate: Microsoft Power Automate allows you to create automated workflows between different apps. For example, you can set up a workflow that automatically adds a task to Microsoft To Do when you receive a specific type of email in Outlook. This automation saves time and ensures that nothing falls through the cracks.

By using Microsoft To Do in combination with other productivity tools, you can create a comprehensive system that supports your work-life balance and enhances your overall productivity.

7. Adapting to Life Changes with Microsoft To Do

Life is constantly changing, and your work-life balance needs to adapt accordingly. Whether you're starting a new job, moving to a new city, or experiencing a major life event, Microsoft To Do can help you manage these transitions smoothly.

- Adjusting Your Routines: When life changes, your routines may need to change as well. Use Microsoft To Do to update your daily routines and create new tasks that reflect your current priorities. For example, if you've just started a new job, you may need to create a new work list and adjust your personal tasks to accommodate your new schedule.

- Managing Major Life Events: During major life events, such as moving or having a baby, it's easy to become overwhelmed by the sheer number of tasks that need to be done. Microsoft To Do can help you break down these tasks into manageable steps and keep track of everything that needs to be done. By organizing your tasks in this way, you can reduce stress and focus on what's most important.

- Maintaining Flexibility: Life is unpredictable, and sometimes things don't go as planned. Microsoft To Do allows you to maintain flexibility by easily adjusting your tasks and priorities as needed. If something unexpected comes up, you can quickly re-prioritize your tasks and ensure that you're still maintaining a healthy work-life balance.

Adapting to life changes with Microsoft To Do ensures that you can maintain your work-life balance even during times of transition and uncertainty.

Conclusion

Achieving and maintaining work-life balance is a continuous process that requires intentional effort and regular reflection. By leveraging the features and capabilities of Microsoft To Do, you can create a system that helps you manage both your work and personal life effectively. Whether it's separating your work and personal tasks, setting boundaries, prioritizing self-care, or adapting to life changes, Microsoft To Do can support you in maintaining a healthy balance that promotes your overall well-being.

Remember, work-life balance is not a one-size-fits-all concept. It's about finding what works best for you and making adjustments as needed. With Microsoft To Do as your tool, you have the flexibility and control to create a balanced and fulfilling life that allows you to achieve your goals without sacrificing your personal happiness and well-being.

5.3.3 Staying Motivated and Avoiding Burnout

Motivation and energy are critical to sustaining productivity over time, but they can be easily depleted if not managed carefully. Burnout—a state of chronic physical and mental exhaustion—is a significant risk for anyone who is consistently pushing themselves to achieve more without adequate rest and recovery. In this section, we'll explore strategies for staying motivated and avoiding burnout while using Microsoft To Do as a tool to support these efforts.

Understanding Burnout

Burnout is more than just feeling tired; it's a condition that arises from prolonged stress and overwork, leading to emotional, mental, and physical exhaustion. It's characterized by feelings of cynicism, detachment, and a sense of ineffectiveness. When burnout sets in, it can be challenging to stay motivated, and your productivity can suffer as a result.

Several factors contribute to burnout, including:

- Work Overload: Taking on too many tasks or responsibilities without sufficient breaks can lead to exhaustion.

- Lack of Control: Feeling powerless to influence decisions or manage your workload can increase stress.

- Unclear Goals: Ambiguous or unrealistic goals can lead to frustration and a sense of futility.

- Poor Work-Life Balance: Neglecting personal time and self-care in favor of work can drain your energy and enthusiasm.

Understanding the signs of burnout is the first step toward preventing it. These signs include persistent fatigue, irritability, difficulty concentrating, and a lack of satisfaction in your achievements. If you recognize these symptoms, it's essential to take proactive steps to address them before they escalate.

Staying Motivated

Motivation is the driving force that propels you toward your goals. It's what keeps you going when tasks are challenging or when progress seems slow. However, motivation can fluctuate, and it's natural to experience periods of low energy or enthusiasm. The key is to develop strategies that help you maintain a steady level of motivation, even when external circumstances are challenging.

Here are some techniques to help you stay motivated:

1. Set Clear, Achievable Goals: Break down large, daunting goals into smaller, manageable tasks. Microsoft To Do allows you to create subtasks under a main task, helping you visualize the steps needed to achieve your objective. Celebrating small wins along the way can keep you motivated and provide a sense of accomplishment.

2. Use Positive Reinforcement: Reward yourself for completing tasks, especially those that are challenging or time-consuming. Rewards don't have to be extravagant; even small treats or breaks can provide the positive reinforcement needed to stay motivated.

3. Visualize Success: Use the "My Day" feature in Microsoft To Do to focus on what you want to accomplish today. Visualizing the successful completion of your tasks can boost your motivation and make your goals feel more attainable.

4. Stay Connected with Your Purpose: Remind yourself of the bigger picture and why your goals matter. Whether it's a personal ambition, a professional milestone, or a contribution to a larger cause, connecting your tasks to your overall purpose can reignite your motivation.

5. Maintain Variety in Your Tasks: Doing the same type of work for extended periods can lead to boredom and decreased motivation. Try to mix up your tasks by alternating between different types of activities—creative, analytical, physical, etc. Microsoft To Do's

flexible list system allows you to organize tasks by category, making it easier to vary your workload.

6. Seek Feedback and Support: Sharing your progress with others and receiving feedback can boost your motivation. Whether it's a colleague, mentor, or friend, having someone to share your journey with can provide encouragement and new perspectives. Consider sharing your lists or tasks within Microsoft To Do with trusted colleagues to foster collaboration and support.

7. Practice Self-Compassion: Motivation can wane when you're too hard on yourself. Recognize that setbacks are a natural part of the process, and treat yourself with kindness and understanding. If you miss a deadline or fall short of a goal, use it as a learning opportunity rather than a reason for self-criticism.

Avoiding Burnout

Avoiding burnout requires a proactive approach to managing stress, maintaining energy levels, and ensuring that you're taking care of your mental and physical health. Here's how you can use Microsoft To Do and other strategies to prevent burnout:

1. Prioritize Rest and Recovery: Schedule regular breaks and downtime in your calendar, just as you would for important meetings or tasks. Use Microsoft To Do to set reminders for these breaks, ensuring that you step away from work to recharge. Remember that rest is not a luxury—it's a necessity for sustained productivity.

2. Set Boundaries: Clearly define your work hours and stick to them. Microsoft To Do allows you to set deadlines and reminders, helping you manage your time effectively. However, it's equally important to recognize when to stop working and transition to personal time. Avoid the temptation to check work tasks during off-hours.

3. Delegate and Share the Load: If you're overwhelmed by your workload, consider delegating tasks to others. Microsoft To Do's sharing and collaboration features make it easy to assign tasks to team members. Delegation not only lightens your load but also empowers others to contribute and grow.

4. Focus on High-Impact Activities: Use the 80/20 rule (also known as the Pareto Principle) to focus on the 20% of tasks that will yield 80% of the results. By prioritizing high-impact activities, you can achieve more with less effort, reducing the risk of burnout. Microsoft To Do's prioritization tools, such as importance markers and task ordering, can help you identify and focus on these critical tasks.

5. Incorporate Relaxation Techniques: Incorporate relaxation techniques into your daily routine to manage stress. Whether it's deep breathing, meditation, or a short walk, these practices can help you stay calm and centered. Consider setting up a "Wellness" list in Microsoft To Do, where you can track and schedule activities that promote relaxation and well-being.

6. Regularly Review and Adjust Your Workload: Conduct weekly reviews to assess your workload and make necessary adjustments. During these reviews, ask yourself if you're taking on too much and whether you need to redistribute or postpone certain tasks. Microsoft To Do's list and task management features make it easy to review your responsibilities and make changes as needed.

7. Seek Professional Help When Needed: If you're feeling persistently overwhelmed or stressed, it may be helpful to seek professional support. This could be in the form of counseling, coaching, or therapy. Recognizing when you need help is a sign of strength, not weakness, and can be crucial in preventing burnout.

Using Microsoft To Do as a Support Tool

Microsoft To Do is not just a task management app; it can also be a valuable tool in your efforts to stay motivated and avoid burnout. Here's how you can leverage its features to support your well-being:

- Custom Lists for Well-Being: Create lists specifically dedicated to activities that nurture your well-being, such as exercise, hobbies, or relaxation. By giving these activities a place in your task management system, you're more likely to prioritize and make time for them.

- Use Due Dates and Reminders Wisely: While due dates and reminders are useful for staying on track, they can also create pressure if overused. Be mindful of setting realistic deadlines, and avoid overloading yourself with too many reminders. Strike a balance between keeping yourself accountable and allowing flexibility.

- Track Your Achievements: Microsoft To Do's "Completed" tasks view is a great way to reflect on your achievements. Take time at the end of each day or week to review what you've accomplished. This practice can boost your motivation and provide a sense of satisfaction, helping to counteract feelings of burnout.

- Plan for Flexibility: Life is unpredictable, and plans often need to change. Use Microsoft To Do's drag-and-drop feature to easily reschedule tasks or adjust your priorities.

Flexibility is key to managing stress and avoiding burnout, so don't hesitate to adapt your plans as needed.

- Incorporate Positive Affirmations: Add motivational quotes or affirmations to your task lists as a reminder to stay positive and focused. You can include these as notes within tasks or create a separate list dedicated to daily affirmations. These small boosts of positivity can help maintain your motivation throughout the day.

Conclusion: Sustaining Motivation and Preventing Burnout

Staying motivated and avoiding burnout is a continuous process that requires attention and effort. By setting clear goals, maintaining a balanced workload, and using Microsoft To Do strategically, you can support your productivity while also taking care of your well-being. Remember, the ultimate goal is not just to get things done, but to do so in a way that is sustainable, fulfilling, and aligned with your values.

As you continue your journey with Microsoft To Do, keep these principles in mind. Use the tools and strategies discussed in this chapter to stay motivated, manage your energy levels, and prevent burnout. By doing so, you'll be better equipped to achieve your goals and enjoy the process along the way.

CHAPTER VI
Troubleshooting and Support

6.1 Common Issues and How to Fix Them

6.1.1 Syncing Problems Across Devices

Microsoft To Do is designed to work seamlessly across various devices, providing users with the flexibility to manage tasks on the go. However, syncing issues can occasionally disrupt this smooth experience, leading to out-of-date task lists, missed reminders, or incomplete data. Understanding the common causes of syncing problems and knowing how to resolve them can ensure that your productivity remains uninterrupted.

Understanding Syncing in Microsoft To Do

Before delving into troubleshooting, it's essential to understand how syncing works in Microsoft To Do. The application syncs data through the cloud, utilizing your Microsoft account. When you create, update, or delete tasks, these changes are uploaded to Microsoft's servers and then downloaded to your other devices. This process should occur automatically in real-time, ensuring that your tasks are consistent across all platforms—whether you're using To Do on your smartphone, tablet, desktop, or the web.

Syncing issues generally fall into a few categories: problems with your Microsoft account, network connectivity issues, device-specific bugs, or server-side errors. By methodically addressing each of these areas, you can usually resolve any syncing issues that arise.

Common Causes of Syncing Issues

1. Connectivity Problems

The most common cause of syncing issues is network connectivity. Since Microsoft To Do relies on an active internet connection to sync data, any disruption in your connection can prevent the app from syncing tasks correctly. This can occur if you're connected to a weak Wi-Fi network, if there's a temporary outage, or if you're in an area with poor cellular coverage.

2. Account Authentication Errors

If Microsoft To Do is having trouble authenticating your Microsoft account, syncing can be disrupted. This could happen if there's an issue with your account credentials, or if the app is unable to verify your identity due to outdated or incorrect login information. It's also possible that your account is locked or there's a problem with the account settings.

3. Outdated App or Operating System

Running an outdated version of Microsoft To Do or your operating system can cause syncing problems. Updates often include bug fixes and improvements that are necessary for the app to function correctly. If you haven't updated the app or your device in a while, you may encounter compatibility issues that affect syncing.

4. Server-Side Issues

Occasionally, syncing issues may originate from Microsoft's servers. This is relatively rare but can happen if there's a temporary server outage or if Microsoft is performing maintenance. In these cases, syncing problems are typically widespread and affect many users at once.

5. Device-Specific Bugs

Certain devices may have unique issues that cause syncing problems with Microsoft To Do. This could be due to specific configurations, security settings, or conflicts with other apps. These bugs can be more challenging to identify and may require device-specific troubleshooting.

6. Conflicts with Other Apps

Sometimes, other applications on your device can interfere with Microsoft To Do's ability to sync. This might happen if another app is consuming too many system resources, or if there's a conflict with background processes. Security apps, VPNs, and firewalls are also known to sometimes block or delay syncing.

Troubleshooting Syncing Problems

Step 1: Check Your Internet Connection

The first step in troubleshooting syncing issues is to ensure that your device has a stable internet connection. Here's how you can check:

- Wi-Fi: Make sure you're connected to a reliable Wi-Fi network. If your connection is weak or unstable, try moving closer to the router or resetting your Wi-Fi connection.

- Mobile Data: If you're using mobile data, ensure that you have a strong signal. Consider switching to a different network if possible.

- Airplane Mode: Make sure that airplane mode is not enabled, as this will disable all wireless communications.

Once you've confirmed that your internet connection is stable, open Microsoft To Do and see if the app begins syncing. If it doesn't, proceed to the next step.

Step 2: Verify Account Authentication

Next, ensure that Microsoft To Do is properly authenticated with your Microsoft account. Follow these steps:

- Log Out and Log In Again: Sometimes, re-authenticating your account can resolve syncing issues. Go to the settings in Microsoft To Do, log out of your account, and then log back in. This can refresh the connection between your account and the app.

- Check Account Settings: Ensure that your Microsoft account is in good standing. Go to the Microsoft Account page on the web and verify that there are no issues with your account, such as payment problems or security alerts.

- Update Passwords: If you've recently changed your Microsoft account password, make sure that you've updated it in the To Do app on all your devices. An outdated password can prevent syncing.

After verifying your account, check if the syncing issue has been resolved. If not, proceed to the next step.

CHAPTER VI: TROUBLESHOOTING AND SUPPORT

Step 3: Update the App and Operating System

If your Microsoft To Do app or operating system is outdated, it might be causing syncing issues. Follow these steps:

- Update the App: Go to the app store on your device (e.g., Google Play Store for Android, App Store for iOS, Microsoft Store for Windows) and check if there's an update available for Microsoft To Do. If there is, install it.

- Update Your Operating System: Ensure that your device's operating system is up to date. Updates often include important fixes and improvements that enhance app performance and compatibility.

- Restart the Device: After updating, restart your device to ensure that all changes take effect.

Once your app and operating system are updated, check to see if the syncing issue persists.

Step 4: Clear App Cache and Data

Sometimes, clearing the app's cache and data can resolve syncing issues. This step will remove temporary files and reset the app, but it won't delete your tasks or lists since they're stored in the cloud. Here's how you can do it:

- On Android:

  - Go to Settings > Apps > Microsoft To Do.

  - Tap on Storage and then Clear Cache.

  - If the issue persists, you can also tap Clear Data. This will reset the app, and you'll need to log in again.

- On iOS:

  - Unfortunately, iOS doesn't provide a straightforward way to clear an app's cache. If you're experiencing issues, consider uninstalling and reinstalling the app.

- On Windows:

  - Go to Settings > Apps > Apps & Features > Microsoft To Do.

- Click on Advanced options, then scroll down and click Reset.

After clearing the cache or resetting the app, open Microsoft To Do and check if the syncing issue has been resolved.

Step 5: Check Microsoft Server Status

If none of the above steps work, the issue may be on Microsoft's end. Here's what you can do:

- Check the Microsoft Service Status Page: Visit the [Microsoft Service Status page](https://status.office.com/) to see if there are any known issues or outages affecting Microsoft To Do. If there is a widespread problem, you may need to wait until Microsoft resolves it.

- Follow Microsoft Support on Social Media: Microsoft often posts updates about service issues on their official social media channels. Following them on platforms like Twitter can provide real-time information.

If Microsoft is experiencing a service outage, your best course of action is to wait until service is restored. Syncing should resume automatically once the issue is resolved.

Step 6: Troubleshoot Device-Specific Issues

If syncing issues are isolated to a particular device, there may be a device-specific problem. Here's how to troubleshoot:

- Check Device Storage: Ensure that your device has enough storage space available. A lack of storage can prevent apps from functioning correctly, including syncing.

- Disable Background App Restrictions: Some devices have power-saving features that restrict background processes. Make sure that Microsoft To Do is not restricted. On Android, this is often found in Settings > Battery or Settings > Apps > Special Access. On iOS, check Settings > General > Background App Refresh.

- Uninstall and Reinstall the App: If the issue persists, uninstall Microsoft To Do from the affected device and reinstall it. This can often resolve deeper issues related to app installation or configuration.

After completing these steps, check if the syncing problem has been resolved.

Step 7: Report the Issue to Microsoft

If you've exhausted all troubleshooting steps and the syncing issue persists, it may be necessary to report the problem to Microsoft. Here's how you can do it:

- Use the In-App Support Feature: Open Microsoft To Do, go to Settings, and select Help & Feedback. Here, you can report the issue directly to Microsoft. Be sure to provide as much detail as possible, including the steps you've already taken to troubleshoot.

- Contact Microsoft Support: If you need more direct assistance, you can contact Microsoft Support via their website. They may be able to provide more specific guidance or escalate the issue if necessary.

Preventing Future Syncing Issues

While syncing issues can be frustrating, there are several steps you can take to minimize the likelihood of encountering them in the future:

- Regularly Update Your App and Device: Keeping your app and operating system up to date can prevent many common syncing problems.

- Maintain a Stable Internet Connection: Ensure that your devices are always connected to a reliable internet source. If you frequently move between networks, consider syncing manually before disconnecting.

- Monitor Microsoft Service Status: If you notice syncing issues, check Microsoft's service status before troubleshooting extensively. This can save you time if the problem is on their end.

- Use a Single Device When Making Major Changes: If you're making significant updates to your task lists, try to do so on a single device at a time. This can prevent conflicts that might arise from multiple devices attempting to sync simultaneously.

By following these steps, you can effectively diagnose and resolve syncing problems in Microsoft To Do, ensuring that your tasks remain up-to-date across all your devices. Maintaining a stable and efficient syncing process is essential for staying productive and getting things done.

6.1.2 Issues with Task Reminders

Task reminders are an essential feature in Microsoft To Do, designed to help you stay on top of your tasks and ensure nothing slips through the cracks. However, like any software, users may occasionally encounter issues with reminders not functioning as expected. These issues can range from reminders not appearing at the right time to reminders not working at all. In this section, we will explore the common problems users face with task reminders and provide solutions to ensure that your reminders work flawlessly, helping you stay productive and on track.

Understanding the Basics of Task Reminders in Microsoft To Do

Before diving into the troubleshooting process, it's important to understand how task reminders are designed to function within Microsoft To Do. Reminders in Microsoft To Do allow you to set a specific date and time when you want to be alerted about a task. This feature is particularly useful for time-sensitive tasks or deadlines that require immediate attention. Reminders can be set on individual tasks or on recurring tasks to ensure that you are notified regularly about ongoing responsibilities.

Microsoft To Do syncs across multiple devices, including desktops, tablets, and smartphones, so reminders should ideally notify you on all your connected devices. This synchronization is what makes the To Do app a powerful tool for task management, allowing you to stay organized no matter where you are.

However, when reminders fail to trigger as expected, it can lead to missed deadlines and disrupted schedules. Let's take a closer look at the common issues users encounter with task reminders and the steps you can take to resolve them.

Common Issues with Task Reminders

1. Reminders Not Triggering on Time

   - One of the most common issues users face is reminders not triggering at the specified time. This problem can be particularly frustrating, especially if the task is time-sensitive. There are several reasons why this might happen:

     - Incorrect Time Zone Settings: If your device's time zone is incorrect, the reminder might trigger at the wrong time or not trigger at all.

- Do Not Disturb Mode: If your device is in Do Not Disturb mode, notifications, including reminders, might be suppressed.

- Battery Optimization Settings: On some devices, battery optimization settings might prevent Microsoft To Do from running in the background, leading to missed reminders.

- App Not Running in the Background: If Microsoft To Do is not allowed to run in the background, reminders may not trigger.

2. Reminders Not Syncing Across Devices

- Microsoft To Do is designed to sync across multiple devices, ensuring that your reminders are consistent no matter which device you are using. However, some users experience issues where reminders set on one device do not sync to others. This can result in missing important reminders if you switch devices frequently.

- Sync Issues: If there is a problem with your account syncing between devices, reminders may not be updated across all your devices.

- Outdated App Version: Using an outdated version of Microsoft To Do on one of your devices might lead to syncing issues, including problems with reminders.

- Internet Connectivity: Poor or intermittent internet connectivity can disrupt the syncing process, causing delays or failures in reminders being shared across devices.

3. Duplicate Reminders

- Another issue that users sometimes encounter is duplicate reminders. This occurs when the same reminder is triggered multiple times for the same task. While this might not seem as problematic as a missed reminder, it can still be disruptive and cause unnecessary distractions.

- Multiple Tasks with the Same Reminder: If you have multiple tasks with identical due dates and times, it's possible to receive multiple reminders simultaneously, which can appear as duplicates.

- Syncing Delays: In some cases, syncing delays between devices can cause the same reminder to trigger more than once.

- App Glitches: Occasionally, app glitches or bugs may lead to duplicate reminders being triggered.

4. Reminders Not Clearing After Completing Tasks

- Users may also encounter an issue where reminders do not clear after completing a task. This can cause confusion and clutter your notification center, making it difficult to distinguish between tasks that are still pending and those that have already been completed.

- Syncing Issues: If the completion of a task is not properly synced across devices, the reminder may remain active even after the task has been marked as complete.

- App Glitches: Occasionally, the app might not properly register the completion of a task, leaving the reminder active.

- Delayed Notification Clearing: Some users have reported delays in the notification clearing process, where reminders remain visible for a short period after a task has been marked as complete.

Troubleshooting Steps for Task Reminder Issues

1. Ensuring Correct Time Zone Settings

- Check Your Device's Time Zone: Go to your device's settings and ensure that the time zone is set correctly. On most devices, this setting can be found under Date & Time settings. Make sure that the option to automatically set the time zone is enabled, or manually set it to your current location.

- Verify Time Zone in Microsoft To Do: Within the Microsoft To Do app, check if the app is reflecting the correct time zone. This can typically be found in the app's settings under the account or preferences section.

2. Managing Do Not Disturb Mode

- Disable Do Not Disturb: If you rely on reminders for time-sensitive tasks, make sure that Do Not Disturb mode is turned off or appropriately configured. On most devices, you can schedule Do Not Disturb mode to automatically turn off during certain hours, ensuring that reminders come through during your active hours.

- Customize Notification Settings: In the notification settings of your device, make sure that Microsoft To Do is allowed to send notifications even when Do Not Disturb mode is on.

3. Adjusting Battery Optimization Settings

- Exclude Microsoft To Do from Battery Optimization: On Android devices, battery optimization settings can prevent apps from running in the background. Go to your device's battery settings, find Microsoft To Do, and exclude it from battery optimization. This will allow the app to run in the background and ensure that reminders are triggered on time.

- Check Background App Refresh (iOS): On iOS devices, make sure that Background App Refresh is enabled for Microsoft To Do. This setting ensures that the app can refresh its data and trigger reminders even when not actively in use.

4. Resolving Sync Issues Across Devices

- Force Sync Your Account: If reminders are not syncing across devices, try manually syncing your Microsoft account. In the Microsoft To Do app, go to the settings and find the sync option. Force a sync to ensure that all devices are updated with the latest tasks and reminders.

- Log Out and Back In: Sometimes, logging out of your Microsoft account on all devices and then logging back in can resolve sync issues. This forces the app to re-establish a connection to the server and can resolve issues with reminders.

- Update Microsoft To Do: Make sure that you are using the latest version of Microsoft To Do on all your devices. App updates often include bug fixes and improvements that can resolve issues with reminders and syncing.

- Check Internet Connection: Ensure that all your devices have a stable internet connection. Without a proper connection, Microsoft To Do cannot sync your reminders and tasks, leading to inconsistencies across devices.

5. Addressing Duplicate Reminders

- Identify Duplicate Tasks: If you are receiving duplicate reminders, check if you have accidentally created multiple tasks with the same due date and time. If so, delete or merge these tasks to prevent duplicate reminders.

- Restart Your Device: In some cases, restarting your device can clear out any temporary glitches that might be causing duplicate reminders.

- Clear Cache (Android): On Android devices, clearing the app cache can sometimes resolve issues with duplicate reminders. Go to your device's settings, find the Microsoft To Do app, and clear the cache. This will remove any temporary files that might be causing the problem.

6. Ensuring Reminders Clear After Completing Tasks

- Sync Your Completed Tasks: If reminders are not clearing after completing a task, manually sync your account to ensure that the task completion is updated across all devices. This should remove the reminder from your notification center.

- Restart Microsoft To Do: Closing and reopening the Microsoft To Do app can sometimes resolve issues where reminders do not clear. This forces the app to refresh its data and can remove stale reminders.

- Report the Issue: If reminders continue to persist after completing tasks, it may be a bug that needs to be reported to Microsoft. Use the in-app feedback option to report the issue and provide details about the problem.

Preventive Measures to Avoid Reminder Issues

To minimize the risk of encountering issues with task reminders in the future, consider the following preventive measures:

1. Regularly Update Microsoft To Do

- Ensure that you are always using the latest version of Microsoft To Do. Regular updates often include important bug fixes and performance improvements that can resolve issues with reminders and other features.

2. Keep Your Devices Synced

- Regularly check that your Microsoft To Do account is synced across all your devices. Doing so will ensure that reminders are consistent and accurate no matter which device you are using.

3. Organize Your Task Lists

- Keep your task lists organized and avoid creating multiple tasks with the same due dates and times. This will reduce the likelihood of receiving duplicate reminders.

4. Test Reminders Before Critical Tasks

- If you have an important task coming up, set a test reminder in advance to ensure that your reminders are functioning properly. This can give you peace of mind and allow you to troubleshoot any issues before the actual task reminder is due.

5. Backup Important Data

   - Consider backing up your task data regularly, especially if you use Microsoft To Do for critical tasks. This can help you recover your tasks and reminders in case of an unexpected issue.

When to Contact Support

If you've tried all the troubleshooting steps and are still experiencing issues with task reminders in Microsoft To Do, it may be time to contact Microsoft support. Microsoft offers a variety of support options, including in-app support, community forums, and direct customer service. Be sure to provide detailed information about your issue, including the steps you've already taken to try to resolve it. This will help the support team assist you more efficiently.

6.1.3 Handling Duplicated Tasks

One of the most common and frustrating issues users encounter with Microsoft To Do is the occurrence of duplicated tasks. These duplicates can clutter your task lists, cause confusion, and make it challenging to manage your workload effectively. Fortunately, there are several strategies and solutions to address and prevent this issue.

Understanding the Causes of Duplicated Tasks

Before diving into the solutions, it's essential to understand the root causes of duplicated tasks. Duplicates can occur due to several reasons, including:

1. Syncing Issues Across Devices: When using Microsoft To Do across multiple devices, sync conflicts can sometimes lead to duplicated tasks. This is especially true if you have unstable internet connections or if you're making changes on different devices simultaneously.

2. Integration with Other Apps: If you've integrated Microsoft To Do with other apps, such as Microsoft Outlook, Microsoft Planner, or third-party task management tools, these integrations can sometimes lead to task duplication. This is often caused by different platforms not recognizing updates made in one app, resulting in a task being added again when the apps sync.

3. Manual Task Creation: Users often inadvertently create duplicates by manually adding the same task more than once. This can happen if you're working on different lists or projects and accidentally re-enter a task without realizing it's already been added.

4. Importing Tasks: When you import tasks from other platforms, particularly when switching from a different task management tool to Microsoft To Do, you might end up with duplicates if the import process is not handled carefully.

5. Recurring Tasks: Issues with recurring tasks can also lead to duplicates. If a recurring task is not marked as complete properly or if there's a syncing delay, the task might appear multiple times.

Steps to Identify Duplicated Tasks

To effectively handle duplicated tasks, the first step is identifying them. Here's how you can quickly spot duplicates in your Microsoft To Do lists:

1. Use the Search Feature: Microsoft To Do has a built-in search function that allows you to search for tasks by name. By entering the task name or a keyword, you can quickly see if the task appears more than once.

2. Review Recent Activity: In the "Planned" and "My Day" sections, review recent additions to your lists. This can help you spot any duplicates that were recently created.

3. Check Task Details: Sometimes, duplicates may not be immediately noticeable if tasks have slightly different names or details. Open the task details to compare due dates, notes, and attachments, which can help identify duplicates that might not be obvious at first glance.

4. Sort and Filter Tasks: Sorting tasks by due date, creation date, or priority can help bring duplicates closer together, making them easier to spot.

Strategies to Handle Duplicated Tasks

Once you've identified duplicated tasks, it's important to handle them in a way that minimizes disruption to your workflow. Here are several strategies you can use:

1. Manually Delete Duplicates: The simplest way to handle duplicates is to manually delete them. This is feasible if you only have a few duplicates. However, make sure to verify that

you're deleting the correct duplicate by checking task details such as due dates, notes, and any attached files.

2. Merge Task Information: If the duplicated tasks have slightly different details (e.g., one version has an attached file while the other does not), you might want to merge the information before deleting the duplicate. For example, copy the missing details from one task to the other and then delete the redundant task.

3. Use Task Management Rules: If you consistently face issues with duplicated tasks due to specific workflows or integrations, consider establishing rules for task management. For example, you could decide to only create tasks in Microsoft To Do and avoid creating tasks in integrated apps like Outlook or Planner to reduce the chance of duplicates.

4. Leverage Microsoft To Do's Built-in Features: Microsoft To Do has features that can help manage and prevent duplicated tasks. For example, you can utilize the "My Day" feature to focus on a curated list of tasks for the day, reducing the likelihood of overlooking or duplicating tasks.

5. Use Third-Party Tools: There are third-party tools and scripts available that can help identify and manage duplicated tasks in Microsoft To Do. These tools can automatically detect duplicates based on certain criteria and prompt you to take action.

Preventing Duplicated Tasks in the Future

While handling existing duplicates is important, preventing them from occurring in the future is equally crucial. Here are some preventative measures you can implement:

1. Ensure Proper Syncing Across Devices: To avoid sync-related duplicates, make sure that all your devices are properly synced. Avoid making simultaneous changes on different devices, and give Microsoft To Do enough time to sync changes before switching devices. If you notice a device isn't syncing correctly, troubleshoot it immediately to prevent duplication issues.

2. Optimize Integrations: If you use Microsoft To Do with other apps, review the settings of these integrations to ensure they're configured correctly. For example, in Outlook, you can choose to sync only specific lists or folders with Microsoft To Do to avoid unnecessary duplication. Regularly monitor how tasks are being imported or synced between apps.

3. Regular Reviews: Regularly review your tasks and lists to catch any duplicates early. Weekly or bi-weekly reviews can help you spot duplicates before they become a significant

issue. During these reviews, also look for patterns that might indicate why duplicates are being created, and take corrective action as needed.

4. Avoid Duplicate Task Creation: When creating new tasks, double-check your existing lists to ensure you're not duplicating a task that's already been added. This is especially important if you manage multiple projects or work on different lists within Microsoft To Do.

5. Manage Recurring Tasks Carefully: Pay special attention to recurring tasks. Make sure you mark them as complete promptly to prevent the system from generating a duplicate. If you notice recurring tasks duplicating, check the settings for these tasks to ensure they're configured correctly.

6. Backup and Restore: Consider periodically backing up your tasks. This way, if duplicates occur due to syncing or import issues, you can restore your lists to a previous state without the duplicates. Microsoft To Do itself doesn't have a direct backup feature, but you can export your tasks or use third-party tools that integrate with Microsoft 365 for this purpose.

Common Scenarios of Task Duplication and How to Address Them

Below are some common scenarios where task duplication occurs and specific solutions for each:

1. Duplicate Tasks After Syncing Multiple Devices: If you frequently switch between a desktop, laptop, and mobile device, and notice duplicated tasks after syncing:

   - Ensure that all devices have a stable internet connection before syncing.

   - Sync one device at a time, and allow each device to fully sync before making changes on another.

   - If duplicates occur, manually delete them, and review your sync settings.

2. Duplicated Tasks Due to Integration with Outlook: When tasks created in Outlook appear as duplicates in Microsoft To Do:

   - Check Outlook's sync settings with Microsoft To Do, and ensure that only specific lists or tasks are being synced.

   - Review your task creation process to avoid creating tasks in both Outlook and To Do unless necessary.

- Use Microsoft To Do's "Planned" section to track tasks, ensuring that duplicates are spotted and removed promptly.

3. Recurring Tasks Duplicating After Being Marked Complete: If you notice recurring tasks appearing multiple times after marking them complete:

  - Review the recurrence settings in Microsoft To Do to ensure they're set up correctly.

  - Avoid marking tasks as complete on multiple devices simultaneously.

  - Monitor the recurrence pattern, and adjust if you notice inconsistencies.

4. Duplicates After Importing Tasks from Another App: When migrating tasks from another app or platform results in duplicates:

  - Before importing, clean up tasks in the original app to reduce the chance of importing duplicates.

  - If possible, import tasks in smaller batches, and review them after each batch to catch any duplicates early.

  - Use sorting and filtering options in Microsoft To Do to group and identify duplicates post-import.

Conclusion

Handling duplicated tasks in Microsoft To Do is essential for maintaining a clean, organized, and efficient task management system. By understanding the causes of duplicates, utilizing effective strategies for identifying and removing them, and implementing preventative measures, you can significantly reduce the occurrence of this issue.

While Microsoft To Do is a powerful tool for task management, like any software, it's prone to certain challenges. However, with the right approach, you can manage and prevent duplicates, ensuring that your focus remains on getting things done rather than managing repetitive tasks. Remember to regularly review your lists, optimize your integrations, and be mindful of how you create and manage tasks across devices to keep your workflow smooth and productive.

6.2 Accessing Help and Support

When working with Microsoft To Do, you may occasionally encounter challenges that require additional assistance or guidance. Fortunately, Microsoft provides a variety of support resources to help you troubleshoot issues, find answers to your questions, and optimize your use of the software. This section will guide you through the key support options available, starting with official Microsoft resources.

6.2.1 Accessing Microsoft Support

Microsoft To Do is a part of the broader Microsoft 365 ecosystem, which means you have access to a comprehensive support network designed to assist users with any questions or issues they may encounter. Whether you need help with a specific feature, troubleshooting an issue, or exploring advanced functionalities, Microsoft Support Resources are a valuable tool. Let's explore these resources in more detail.

Understanding Microsoft Support

Microsoft Support is the official customer service platform provided by Microsoft. It offers a wide range of services, from self-help articles and tutorials to live support from Microsoft representatives. The goal of Microsoft Support is to ensure that all users, regardless of their technical expertise, can effectively use Microsoft products, including Microsoft To Do.

Here's a breakdown of the main types of support available:

1. Help Articles and Documentation

   - Microsoft offers a robust library of help articles and documentation tailored to various products and services, including Microsoft To Do. These resources cover a wide range of topics, from basic setup instructions to detailed guides on specific features.

- Where to Find Help Articles:

The easiest way to access Microsoft To Do help articles is through the official Microsoft Support website or directly within the Microsoft To Do app. To access these resources, simply go to the Help & Feedback section in the app, where you'll find links to relevant articles. Alternatively, visit the [Microsoft Support website](https://support.microsoft.com/) and search for "Microsoft To Do" to access the full library of articles.

- Using Help Articles Effectively:

When searching for help articles, use specific keywords related to your issue or question. For example, if you're having trouble syncing tasks across devices, search for "sync issues Microsoft To Do." Microsoft's search algorithm will provide you with the most relevant articles, helping you find a solution quickly.

2. User Guides and Tutorials

- In addition to help articles, Microsoft provides comprehensive user guides and tutorials that offer step-by-step instructions on using Microsoft To Do. These guides are particularly useful for new users or those looking to expand their knowledge of the app's features.

- Types of User Guides:

Microsoft offers both written and video tutorials, catering to different learning styles. Written guides are typically more detailed and allow users to follow along at their own pace, while video tutorials provide a visual demonstration of how to use the app.

- Finding the Right Guide:

To find the most relevant guide for your needs, visit the Microsoft Support website or the [Microsoft 365 Learning Pathways](https://support.microsoft.com/en-us/office/microsoft-365-learning-pathways-a2da357e-9a6e-4a7f-99d1-05d1e50d3bd8). Here, you'll find curated learning paths for different Microsoft products, including Microsoft To Do.

3. Community Forums

- The Microsoft Community is an online forum where users can ask questions, share tips, and discuss their experiences with Microsoft products. The community is active and includes contributions from both users and Microsoft experts.

- Engaging with the Community:

To participate in the Microsoft Community, create a Microsoft account if you don't already have one. Once logged in, you can browse existing threads or start your own by posting a question. Be sure to provide as much detail as possible about your issue to receive accurate and helpful responses.

- Benefits of the Community:

The community forum is a great resource for discovering tips and tricks that may not be covered in official documentation. Users often share innovative ways to use Microsoft To Do, as well as workarounds for common issues.

4. Contacting Microsoft Support

- If you're unable to resolve an issue using the self-help resources, Microsoft offers direct support through various channels, including live chat, phone support, and email.

- When to Contact Support:

Direct support is recommended for more complex issues that require personalized assistance, such as technical glitches, account problems, or in-depth troubleshooting. It's also useful if you need immediate help and can't wait for a community forum response.

- How to Contact Support:

To contact Microsoft Support, visit the Microsoft Support website and select the "Contact Support" option. From there, you'll be prompted to describe your issue and choose your preferred contact method. Microsoft provides a virtual assistant for quick issues, but you can also request to speak with a human representative.

5. Microsoft Virtual Agent

- The Microsoft Virtual Agent is an AI-powered tool that provides instant support for common questions and issues. It can help you find articles, guide you through troubleshooting steps, or connect you to a live support agent if needed.

- Using the Virtual Agent:

The Virtual Agent is accessible directly from the Microsoft Support website. Simply start a chat, and the agent will guide you through a series of questions to diagnose your issue. The Virtual Agent is ideal for quick queries or when you're unsure of where to start.

6. Microsoft Tech Support

- For users who encounter technical issues that go beyond the scope of basic support, Microsoft offers specialized tech support services. This includes assistance with software bugs, performance issues, and compatibility problems.

- Accessing Tech Support:

Tech support is typically accessed through the standard Microsoft Support channels. However, depending on your issue, you may be referred to a specialized technician. Keep in mind that tech support may be subject to additional fees, especially for non-warranty services or issues that require in-depth technical assistance.

7. Microsoft To Do Blog and Updates

- Microsoft regularly publishes updates, tips, and news about Microsoft To Do on their official blog. This is a great resource for staying informed about new features, upcoming changes, and best practices.

- Following the Blog:

You can access the Microsoft To Do blog through the official Microsoft 365 blog platform. Consider subscribing to updates or following Microsoft on social media to receive the latest information directly.

Maximizing the Value of Microsoft Support

While Microsoft provides a wealth of support resources, knowing how to use these resources effectively is key to resolving issues quickly and improving your overall experience with Microsoft To Do.

1. Be Specific When Searching

  - The more specific you are when searching for help articles or contacting support, the more likely you are to find a relevant solution. Use precise language and include as much detail as possible about your issue, such as error messages, the steps you've already taken, and your system configuration.

2. Document Your Issue

  - Before reaching out for help, take the time to document your issue. This includes noting down when the issue started, any changes you made to your system or app, and any troubleshooting steps you've already attempted. Providing this information upfront can help support staff diagnose the problem more efficiently.

3. Stay Patient and Persistent

  - Resolving complex issues can sometimes take time, especially if they require multiple rounds of troubleshooting or escalation to specialized support. Stay patient, follow the guidance provided, and don't hesitate to seek further help if your issue isn't resolved on the first attempt.

4. Leverage Community Knowledge

  - Don't underestimate the value of the Microsoft Community. Often, users have encountered and solved issues similar to yours, and their insights can save you time and frustration. Engage with the community regularly, and consider contributing your own tips and solutions once you've gained experience with Microsoft To Do.

5. Stay Informed About Updates

  - Regularly check for updates to Microsoft To Do and read the release notes provided by Microsoft. Staying informed about new features and bug fixes can help you avoid issues and take full advantage of the app's capabilities.

By utilizing these Microsoft Support resources effectively, you can ensure that your experience with Microsoft To Do is as smooth and productive as possible. Whether you're troubleshooting an issue, learning a new feature, or seeking advice from the community, the support network is there to help you get the most out of your task management system.

6.2.2 Using the To Do Community Forums

One of the most valuable resources available to Microsoft To Do users is the Community Forums. These forums are a hub where users from around the world gather to share experiences, ask questions, and offer solutions related to Microsoft To Do and other Microsoft 365 products. Whether you're troubleshooting an issue, seeking advice on best practices, or exploring new ways to use the tool, the Community Forums provide a rich environment for learning and collaboration.

What Are the To Do Community Forums?

The Microsoft To Do Community Forums are part of the larger Microsoft Community, an online platform that connects users of various Microsoft products. These forums are designed to facilitate discussions among users, as well as between users and Microsoft representatives. The To Do forums specifically focus on all aspects of the Microsoft To Do app, including how to use its features, integrate it with other apps, and resolve technical issues.

The forums are organized into different sections, typically based on topics or specific features of the tool. This organization makes it easy for users to find the right place to post their questions or browse existing discussions that may already address their concerns. For example, there might be separate sections for general questions, troubleshooting, feature requests, and integration tips.

Benefits of Participating in the Community Forums

There are several advantages to actively participating in the To Do Community Forums:

- Access to Collective Knowledge: The forums are populated by a diverse group of users, ranging from beginners to advanced users and even Microsoft employees. This diversity means that you're likely to find a wide range of perspectives and solutions that can help you overcome challenges and discover new ways to use Microsoft To Do.

- Real-Time Problem Solving: When you post a question or issue on the forums, you can often expect a prompt response from other users who have faced similar challenges. This real-time interaction can be particularly valuable when you're dealing with urgent problems that need immediate attention.

- Learning from Others: By browsing through existing threads, you can learn from the experiences of other users. You may discover new features, alternative methods for completing tasks, or creative solutions that you hadn't considered. The forums are a great place to expand your understanding of Microsoft To Do and improve your productivity.

- Contributing to the Community: As you become more familiar with Microsoft To Do, you may find yourself in a position to help others. Contributing answers, tips, and solutions not only benefits the community but also reinforces your own knowledge and expertise. It can be a rewarding experience to give back to a community that has helped you in the past.

- Direct Interaction with Microsoft Employees: Microsoft employees often participate in the forums, offering official advice, sharing updates, and addressing concerns directly. This level of interaction provides users with authoritative answers and ensures that feedback reaches the development team, potentially influencing future updates and features.

Navigating the To Do Community Forums

Getting started with the To Do Community Forums is straightforward, but there are a few tips that can help you navigate the platform more effectively:

- Creating a Microsoft Account: Before you can participate in the forums, you'll need to sign in with your Microsoft account. If you don't have one, you can easily create an account during the sign-up process. Your Microsoft account will also give you access to other Microsoft services, such as Outlook, OneDrive, and Office Online.

- Finding the Right Section: As mentioned earlier, the forums are organized into different sections based on topics. Spend some time familiarizing yourself with the layout of the forums to ensure that you're posting your questions in the appropriate section. This will increase the likelihood of receiving relevant and timely responses.

- Using the Search Function: Before posting a new question, it's a good idea to use the search function to see if your issue has already been addressed. Many common problems and questions have been discussed in detail, and you might find a solution without needing to start a new thread. The search function allows you to filter results by relevance, date, and other criteria, making it easier to find what you're looking for.

- Posting Your Questions: When posting a question, be as clear and detailed as possible. Provide relevant context, such as the version of Microsoft To Do you're using, the device you're on, and the specific issue you're encountering. The more information you provide, the easier it will be for others to assist you. Additionally, use descriptive titles for your posts to attract the right audience and increase the chances of getting helpful responses.

- Engaging with Responses: After posting a question, check back regularly to see if anyone has responded. Engage with those who reply by thanking them, asking follow-up questions, or clarifying details. If a response resolves your issue, consider marking it as the "Best Answer" to help other users who may have the same question. Engaging positively with the community encourages continued support and fosters a collaborative atmosphere.

- Following Threads: If you come across a discussion that interests you or addresses an issue you might face in the future, you can choose to follow the thread. This will notify you of any new replies, allowing you to stay updated on the conversation without needing to search for it again.

- Reporting Issues: If you encounter inappropriate content or behavior on the forums, you can report it to the moderators. The community forums are intended to be a safe and supportive environment, and reporting violations helps maintain this standard.

Common Topics and Discussions

The To Do Community Forums cover a wide range of topics, reflecting the diverse needs and interests of its users. Some of the most common discussions include:

- Troubleshooting: Users frequently turn to the forums for help with technical issues, such as syncing problems, bugs, or features not working as expected. These discussions often include step-by-step solutions, links to helpful resources, and advice on how to escalate unresolved issues to Microsoft support.

- Feature Requests: Many users use the forums to suggest new features or improvements to existing ones. These threads can gain significant attention, with other users chiming in to support the ideas or add their own suggestions. Microsoft employees often monitor these discussions, and popular requests may influence future updates.

- Best Practices: Users share tips and strategies for getting the most out of Microsoft To Do, such as how to organize tasks effectively, integrate To Do with other tools, or use specific features like My Day and Smart Lists. These discussions are invaluable for both new and experienced users looking to enhance their productivity.

- Integration Tips: Since Microsoft To Do is part of the Microsoft 365 suite, many users seek advice on how to integrate it with other apps like Outlook, Teams, and Planner. These threads often include practical examples and step-by-step instructions for setting up integrations that streamline workflows.

- Updates and New Features: Whenever Microsoft releases a new update or feature for To Do, users flock to the forums to discuss the changes. These discussions typically cover the impact of the updates, how to use the new features, and any bugs or issues that may have arisen. Microsoft employees may also participate in these threads to provide official explanations and guidance.

- Success Stories and Case Studies: Some users share their personal success stories and case studies on how Microsoft To Do has improved their productivity, organized their work, or helped them achieve specific goals. These posts can be inspiring and provide practical insights into how others are using the tool in various contexts.

Tips for Getting the Most Out of the Forums

To maximize the benefits of participating in the To Do Community Forums, consider the following tips:

- Stay Active: Regular participation in the forums will keep you informed about the latest discussions, updates, and trends related to Microsoft To Do. It also helps you build connections with other users who can offer ongoing support and advice.

- Be Respectful: The forums are a community space where users from diverse backgrounds come together. Always approach discussions with respect and kindness, even if you disagree with someone's opinion or approach. Constructive dialogue is key to maintaining a positive environment.

- Share Your Knowledge: If you've gained experience or discovered effective solutions while using Microsoft To Do, don't hesitate to share your insights with others. Your contributions can make a significant difference in helping other users resolve issues or improve their productivity.

- Stay Updated: Microsoft To Do is continuously evolving, with new features and updates being released regularly. Stay informed about these changes by following relevant threads and participating in discussions about new updates. This will ensure that you're always using the latest features and best practices.

- Build Relationships: The forums are a great place to connect with other users who share similar interests or work in similar fields. Building relationships within the community can lead to long-term support, collaboration, and the exchange of ideas.

- Give Feedback: If you have suggestions for improving the forums themselves, don't hesitate to share your thoughts. Microsoft values user feedback, and your input could lead to enhancements that benefit the entire community.

Examples of Community Forum Interactions

To illustrate the value of the To Do Community Forums, here are a few examples of how users might interact within the platform:

- Example 1: Syncing Issue Resolution

   User A: "I'm having trouble getting my tasks to sync between my phone and my desktop. The tasks I create on my phone don't appear on my desktop version of To Do. Has anyone else experienced this?"

User B: "I've had a similar issue before. Make sure you're signed in with the same Microsoft account on both devices. Also, try force-syncing by pulling down the task list on your phone. If that doesn't work, try logging out and back in on both devices."

User A: "Thanks, User B! Logging out and back in did the trick. Everything's syncing perfectly now."

Example 2: Feature Request Discussion

User C: "I think it would be really useful if To Do had a calendar view option, so we could see tasks spread out over a week or month. Does anyone else agree?"

User D: "That would be awesome! I rely on calendar views in other apps, and having it in To Do would make planning so much easier."

Microsoft Employee: "Thanks for the suggestion! We've noted this feature request and will pass it along to the development team. Keep an eye on future updates!"

- Example 3: Best Practices Sharing

User E: "I've found that using tags for contexts (like @Work, @Home, @Errands) has really helped me stay organized. It makes it so much easier to focus on specific tasks depending on where I am."

User F: "That's a great idea! I hadn't thought of using tags that way. I'll definitely give it a try."

User E: "Glad you found it useful! It's made a big difference in how I manage my tasks."

Conclusion

The Microsoft To Do Community Forums are an invaluable resource for users at all levels of expertise. Whether you're troubleshooting an issue, seeking advice on best practices, or simply looking to connect with other users, the forums provide a supportive and knowledgeable environment. By actively participating in the community, you can enhance your experience with Microsoft To Do, stay informed about the latest developments, and contribute to the collective knowledge of the community.

6.2.3 Finding Online Tutorials and Guides

In today's digital age, a wealth of information is available online to help you master Microsoft To Do and troubleshoot any issues you might encounter. Online tutorials and guides can be invaluable resources, providing step-by-step instructions, video demonstrations, and expert tips that can enhance your experience with the application. Here's a comprehensive guide to finding and utilizing these resources effectively:

1. Exploring Microsoft's Official Resources

1.1 Microsoft Support Website

The first place to start when looking for help with Microsoft To Do is the official Microsoft Support website. This site offers a range of resources, including:

- Help Articles: Detailed articles covering various aspects of Microsoft To Do, including setup, troubleshooting, and advanced features. These articles are updated regularly to reflect the latest changes and fixes.

- FAQs: Frequently Asked Questions that address common issues users face. The FAQ section can provide quick answers to common problems and might help you resolve issues without needing to contact support.

- Guided Walkthroughs: Step-by-step guides designed to walk you through common tasks and issues. These walkthroughs are especially useful for new users who need help understanding the basics.

1.2 Microsoft Learn

Microsoft Learn offers interactive learning modules and hands-on labs that can deepen your understanding of Microsoft To Do. Key features include:

- Learning Paths: Curated courses that cover different aspects of Microsoft To Do, from basic usage to advanced integration with other Microsoft 365 tools.

- Interactive Labs: Practice environments where you can try out features and tasks in a simulated setting. These labs allow you to gain practical experience without affecting your actual data.

1.3 Microsoft Community Forums

The Microsoft Community Forums are a great place to ask questions, share experiences, and seek advice from other users. You can:

- Search Existing Threads: Many common issues and questions have already been discussed in the forums. Searching for your issue might yield solutions from other users who have faced similar problems.

- Post New Questions: If you can't find an answer, you can post your question and receive responses from the community. Engaging with other users can provide new perspectives and solutions.

2. Leveraging Online Video Tutorials

2.1 YouTube Tutorials

YouTube is a treasure trove of video tutorials that can help you with Microsoft To Do. Here's how to find and use these resources:

- Search for Specific Topics: Use search terms like "Microsoft To Do tutorial," "Microsoft To Do troubleshooting," or "Microsoft To Do tips" to find relevant videos. Look for videos with high view counts and positive ratings, as these are often produced by experienced creators.

- Follow Step-by-Step Guides: Many YouTube tutorials are structured as step-by-step guides, making it easy to follow along and replicate the actions on your own device. This format is particularly useful for visual learners.

- Subscribe to Channels: Some channels specialize in productivity tools and software tutorials. Subscribing to these channels can provide ongoing tips and updates about Microsoft To Do and other related tools.

2.2 Online Course Platforms

Platforms like Udemy, Coursera, and LinkedIn Learning offer comprehensive courses on Microsoft To Do. These courses often include:

- Video Lessons: High-quality video lessons that cover everything from the basics to advanced features. Many courses are taught by experts who provide detailed explanations and practical demonstrations.

- Quizzes and Assignments: To reinforce learning, some courses include quizzes and practical assignments. Completing these can help you test your understanding and apply what you've learned in real-world scenarios.

- Certificates: Some platforms offer certificates upon completion of courses, which can be a valuable addition to your professional credentials.

3. Utilizing Blogs and Written Guides

3.1 Tech Blogs and Websites

Many tech blogs and websites offer in-depth reviews and how-to guides for Microsoft To Do. These resources often provide:

- Detailed Reviews: Comprehensive reviews of Microsoft To Do's features, pros, and cons. These reviews can help you understand how the tool compares to others and how to leverage its features effectively.

- How-To Articles: Step-by-step guides written by experts that cover various aspects of using Microsoft To Do. These articles can be a great way to learn new tips and tricks.

- Troubleshooting Tips: Articles specifically focused on troubleshooting common issues. These can provide solutions to problems you may encounter and offer advice on how to prevent them in the future.

3.2 User-Generated Content

Many users and productivity enthusiasts create their own guides and share them on personal blogs or forums. These guides can provide:

- Personal Insights: Tips and strategies based on real-world use. These guides often reflect practical experiences and can offer unique solutions and shortcuts.

- Customized Advice: Solutions tailored to specific use cases, such as managing personal tasks or coordinating team projects. User-generated content can be particularly useful for finding creative ways to use Microsoft To Do.

4. Engaging with Online Communities

4.1 Social Media Groups

Social media platforms like Facebook, Reddit, and LinkedIn host groups and communities focused on Microsoft To Do and productivity. Engaging with these groups can provide:

- Peer Support: Connect with other users who have similar interests and challenges. Sharing experiences and advice within these communities can help you solve problems and learn new techniques.

- Updates and News: Stay informed about the latest updates, features, and changes to Microsoft To Do. Many groups and forums share news and discuss new developments as they occur.

4.2 Professional Networks

Professional networks such as LinkedIn can provide access to industry experts and productivity coaches who offer advice and resources. Engaging with these professionals can help you:

- Get Expert Advice: Receive guidance from experienced users and professionals who specialize in productivity and task management.

- Join Webinars and Workshops: Many professionals offer webinars and workshops that cover various aspects of Microsoft To Do. Participating in these events can provide additional insights and hands-on experience.

5. Combining Resources for Maximum Effectiveness

To make the most of online tutorials and guides, consider combining different types of resources:

- Start with Official Resources: Use Microsoft's official support website and Microsoft Learn to build a solid foundation of knowledge.

- Supplement with Video Tutorials: Enhance your understanding by watching video tutorials that offer visual demonstrations and practical tips.

- Read Blogs and Guides: Use written guides and blogs to gain deeper insights and discover advanced tips.

- Engage with Communities: Participate in forums and social media groups to ask questions, share experiences, and stay updated on new developments.

By leveraging these online resources, you can effectively troubleshoot issues, enhance your productivity, and get the most out of Microsoft To Do. Whether you prefer visual learning, hands-on practice, or expert advice, there's a wealth of information available to support you on your journey to mastering Microsoft To Do.

6.3 Keeping Microsoft To Do Updated

Keeping your task management system updated is crucial for leveraging the latest improvements, features, and security enhancements. Microsoft To Do frequently receives updates to enhance functionality, improve user experience, and integrate new technologies. Understanding and adapting to these changes can significantly impact how effectively you use the application. In this section, we will explore the importance of staying updated, how to understand new features and updates, and the best practices for managing these changes.

6.3.1 Understanding New Features and Updates

Microsoft To Do is continually evolving, with Microsoft frequently rolling out updates that introduce new features, improve existing ones, and address any issues identified by users. Staying informed about these updates is essential for making the most of the application and ensuring that you are taking advantage of its full capabilities.

1. How Updates Are Communicated

Microsoft typically communicates updates to Microsoft To Do through several channels:

- Official Release Notes: Microsoft provides detailed release notes for each update, outlining the new features, improvements, and bug fixes included in the latest version. These notes are often available on the Microsoft 365 blog or the Microsoft To Do support page.

- In-App Notifications: Sometimes, when you open Microsoft To Do after an update has been applied, you may receive an in-app notification highlighting the new features and changes. This notification helps users quickly become aware of what has been added or modified.

- Microsoft 365 Admin Center: For organizations using Microsoft 365, updates and new features may also be communicated through the Microsoft 365 Admin Center. Admins can access detailed information about updates and manage the deployment of new features across their organization.

2. Key Types of Updates

Microsoft To Do updates generally fall into several categories:

- Feature Enhancements: These updates introduce new functionalities or improve existing ones. Examples might include new ways to organize tasks, additional integration options, or enhanced customization features.

- Performance Improvements: Updates in this category focus on making the application faster and more efficient. These improvements may involve optimizing the user interface, reducing loading times, or improving synchronization.

- Bug Fixes: Bug fix updates address specific issues reported by users. These can range from minor glitches to more significant problems that affect the application's stability or functionality.

- Security Updates: Security updates are crucial for protecting your data and ensuring that the application remains secure against potential threats. These updates might include patches for vulnerabilities or enhancements to data encryption.

3. Examples of Recent Updates

To give you an idea of what to expect, here are some examples of recent updates that Microsoft To Do has received:

- Enhanced Task Management: Recent updates have introduced features like new ways to categorize and prioritize tasks. For instance, the addition of custom tags allows users to better organize their tasks and filter them according to specific criteria.

- Improved Integration with Microsoft 365: Updates have strengthened the integration between Microsoft To Do and other Microsoft 365 applications, such as Outlook and Teams. This includes the ability to sync tasks with Outlook and view tasks from different apps within a single interface.

- User Interface (UI) Improvements: Microsoft has made several UI improvements to make the application more intuitive and user-friendly. These changes may involve redesigning elements of the interface or adding new features that enhance usability.

4. Staying Informed About Updates

To ensure you are always aware of the latest updates and features, consider the following practices:

- Subscribe to Microsoft 365 Blogs: Following Microsoft's official blogs and newsletters can help you stay informed about new updates and features. These resources often provide detailed information and insights about recent changes.

- Check the Microsoft To Do Help Center: Regularly visiting the Microsoft To Do Help Center can keep you updated on new features, improvements, and troubleshooting tips. The Help Center often includes articles and guides related to recent updates.

- Participate in User Forums: Engaging with the Microsoft To Do community forums can provide valuable insights into how other users are experiencing and utilizing new features. User discussions can offer tips and tricks for making the most of recent updates.

5. Adapting to New Features

When new features are introduced, it is essential to adapt and integrate them into your workflow effectively:

- Explore New Features: Take the time to explore and familiarize yourself with new features as soon as they are available. Microsoft often provides tutorials or guides on how to use new functionalities.

- Update Your Workflow: Assess how the new features align with your existing workflow and make adjustments as needed. For example, if a new task management feature is introduced, consider how it can improve your task organization and productivity.

- Provide Feedback: If you encounter issues or have suggestions regarding new features, providing feedback to Microsoft can help improve future updates. Microsoft values user feedback and often incorporates it into subsequent updates.

6. Troubleshooting Update Issues

Sometimes, updates can lead to unexpected issues. Here's how to address common problems:

- Check for Known Issues: If you experience issues after an update, check the release notes and Microsoft support forums for information about known problems and solutions.

- Reinstall the Application: If problems persist, try reinstalling Microsoft To Do. This can resolve issues related to corrupted files or incomplete updates.

- Contact Support: For persistent or critical issues, contact Microsoft support for assistance. They can provide guidance and solutions specific to your situation.

7. Best Practices for Managing Updates

To effectively manage updates and ensure a smooth experience with Microsoft To Do:

- Regularly Update the Application: Ensure that you keep Microsoft To Do updated to benefit from the latest features, improvements, and security patches. Enable automatic updates if available.

- Backup Your Data: Before applying major updates, consider backing up your data to avoid potential data loss. Microsoft To Do generally syncs your data with the cloud, but having an additional backup can provide peace of mind.

- Review Update Impact: Assess how updates might impact your workflow and make necessary adjustments. Understanding the implications of new features can help you integrate them seamlessly into your daily routine.

By staying informed and adapting to updates, you can maximize the benefits of Microsoft To Do and maintain an efficient and productive task management system.

6.3.2 Preparing for Major Changes

As Microsoft To Do evolves, it's essential to stay informed and prepare for major updates and changes to ensure that you can continue to use the application efficiently and effectively. Major changes often bring new features, enhancements, or shifts in functionality that can impact how you use the tool. Here's how you can prepare for and adapt to these changes:

Understanding Major Updates

1. Release Notes and Announcements

Microsoft frequently publishes release notes and announcements about upcoming features and updates for To Do. These documents provide detailed information on what changes are coming, how they will affect the user experience, and any new features that will be introduced.

 - Stay Updated: Regularly check the official Microsoft To Do blog, the Microsoft 365 admin center, or the Microsoft Tech Community for the latest updates and announcements.

 - Review Release Notes: When a new update is announced, take the time to read the release notes thoroughly. This will help you understand what's changing, how it might affect your workflow, and what new functionalities you can expect.

2. Beta Testing and Insider Programs

Microsoft often offers beta testing programs or insider previews for upcoming features. Participating in these programs can provide you with early access to new features and give you a chance to provide feedback before the updates are rolled out to the general public.

 - Join the Insider Program: Look for opportunities to join the Microsoft Office Insider program, which allows you to test new features and provide feedback.

 - Provide Feedback: Actively participating in feedback programs helps Microsoft improve the features and functionality based on user experience and needs.

3. Training and Documentation

Major updates can sometimes change the way features are accessed or used. Microsoft typically provides updated training materials and documentation to help users adapt to these changes.

- Access Training Resources: Utilize online training resources, including video tutorials, webinars, and documentation, to familiarize yourself with the new features and changes.

- Read Updated Documentation: Ensure you review any updated user guides or documentation provided by Microsoft to understand the changes and how to use the new features effectively.

Preparing for Functional Changes

1. Assessing Impact on Current Workflows

Major changes can impact your current workflows and task management processes. It's crucial to assess how these changes might affect your existing setup and plan accordingly.

- Evaluate Workflow Adjustments: Identify which workflows and processes might be impacted by the changes. Determine if you need to adjust your task management approach or retrain your team.

- Plan for Transition: Develop a transition plan to incorporate the new features or changes smoothly into your existing workflow.

2. Communicating Changes with Your Team

If you're using Microsoft To Do in a team setting, it's essential to communicate upcoming changes and updates to your team members. This ensures that everyone is aware of the changes and can adapt accordingly.

- Share Information: Use team meetings, emails, or collaboration tools to inform your team about the upcoming changes and how they will affect their tasks and processes.

- Provide Training: Offer training sessions or resources to help your team understand and utilize the new features effectively.

3. Updating Internal Documentation

If you have internal documentation or guides for using Microsoft To Do, update these documents to reflect the new features and changes. This helps ensure that everyone in your organization has access to the latest information.

- Revise Guides and Manuals: Update any internal user guides, process documentation, or training materials to include information about the new features and changes.

- Distribute Updated Documentation: Make sure the revised documentation is easily accessible to all users who need it.

Ensuring Compatibility and Integration

1. Checking Compatibility with Other Tools

Major updates to Microsoft To Do might affect its compatibility with other tools and applications you use. Ensure that any integrations or third-party tools you rely on remain compatible with the new version.

- Test Integrations: Before fully transitioning to the new version, test any integrations with other Microsoft 365 apps or third-party tools to ensure they continue to work as expected.

- Update Integration Settings: Adjust any integration settings or configurations as needed to accommodate the changes in Microsoft To Do.

2. Updating Customizations and Automations

If you've customized Microsoft To Do or created automations using Power Automate or other tools, verify that these customizations continue to work with the new updates.

- Review Customizations: Check your customizations and automations to ensure they are still functioning correctly after the update.

- Adjust Automations: Modify any automation workflows or custom scripts to align with the new features or changes in Microsoft To Do.

Staying Informed and Adapting

1. Participating in User Communities

Engaging with the Microsoft To Do user community can provide valuable insights and tips on how others are adapting to major changes. It also offers a platform to share your experiences and learn from others.

- Join Online Forums: Participate in online forums, discussion groups, or social media communities focused on Microsoft To Do.

- Share Feedback and Tips: Contribute to discussions by sharing your experiences with the new features and offering tips to others.

2. Continuous Learning

As Microsoft To Do continues to evolve, maintaining a mindset of continuous learning will help you stay ahead of changes and make the most of the new features.

- Attend Webinars and Training: Regularly attend webinars, training sessions, and workshops to keep up with the latest developments and best practices.

- Explore New Features: Actively explore and experiment with new features to understand their functionality and potential applications in your task management processes.

3. Adapting to Future Changes

The technology landscape is constantly evolving, and Microsoft To Do will continue to receive updates and enhancements. Being adaptable and proactive will help you leverage new features and maintain an efficient task management system.

- Stay Proactive: Keep an eye on upcoming changes and plan for future updates in advance.

- Embrace Change: Approach updates with an open mind and be willing to adjust your processes and workflows to incorporate new features and improvements.

Conclusion

Preparing for major changes in Microsoft To Do requires staying informed, assessing impacts, communicating with your team, and adapting your workflows and integrations. By proactively managing these updates and leveraging the resources available, you can ensure a smooth transition and continue to use Microsoft To Do effectively to manage your tasks and achieve your goals.

6.3.3 Reporting Bugs and Requesting Features

As a user of Microsoft To Do, you might encounter issues or have ideas for improvements that could enhance your productivity experience. Reporting bugs and requesting features are essential ways to contribute to the continuous improvement of the application. This section will guide you through the process of reporting bugs, requesting new features, and ensuring that your feedback reaches the appropriate channels effectively.

1. Understanding the Importance of Reporting Bugs and Requesting Features

1.1 The Role of User Feedback

User feedback plays a critical role in the development and refinement of software applications. When users report bugs or request features, they provide developers with valuable insights into how the application performs in real-world scenarios. This feedback helps identify issues that might not be evident during initial testing and allows the development team to prioritize enhancements that align with users' needs.

1.2 How Feedback Drives Improvements

Microsoft To Do, like any software, evolves over time. The continuous updates and feature additions are often driven by user feedback. By reporting bugs and suggesting features, you contribute to the creation of a more effective and user-friendly tool. Your input helps developers understand the strengths and weaknesses of the application and ensures that the tool evolves to meet the changing demands of its users.

2. Reporting Bugs in Microsoft To Do

2.1 Identifying the Issue

Before reporting a bug, it's crucial to thoroughly identify and document the issue. Make sure to:

- Replicate the Problem: Try to reproduce the issue consistently. Note the steps that lead to the problem to provide a clear context.

- Check for Known Issues: Look through Microsoft's support pages or forums to see if the issue is already known and if there are any existing solutions or workarounds.

- Document Details: Gather as much information as possible, including error messages, screenshots, and the version of Microsoft To Do you are using. This information will help the support team diagnose and address the issue more efficiently.

2.2 Submitting a Bug Report

There are several ways to report a bug in Microsoft To Do:

- In-App Feedback Tool:

  - Open Microsoft To Do.

  - Click on the profile icon or settings menu.

  - Select "Help & Feedback" or a similar option.

  - Choose "Send Feedback" or "Report a Problem."

  - Provide a detailed description of the issue, including the steps to reproduce it, and attach any relevant screenshots or error codes.

- Microsoft Support Website:

  - Visit the Microsoft Support website.

  - Navigate to the support section for Microsoft To Do.

  - Find the option for reporting bugs or issues and follow the instructions to submit your report.

- Microsoft Community Forums:

  - Go to the Microsoft Community forums related to Microsoft To Do.

  - Search for existing threads about similar issues or start a new thread detailing your problem.

  - Engage with other users and support staff who may offer solutions or workarounds.

2.3 Providing Useful Feedback

To ensure that your bug report is as helpful as possible:

- Be Specific: Provide clear and concise details about the problem, including the context and frequency of the issue.

- Include Reproduction Steps: Outline the exact steps needed to reproduce the problem.

- Attach Evidence: Use screenshots or screen recordings to illustrate the issue visually.

- Describe Your Environment: Mention your operating system, device, and Microsoft To Do version.

3. Requesting New Features in Microsoft To Do

3.1 Identifying the Need for New Features

When considering new features, think about how they could improve your workflow or solve existing problems. Reflect on:

- Current Limitations: What functionalities are missing or could be enhanced?

- User Experience: How could the user interface or user experience be improved?

- Integration Needs: Are there additional integrations with other tools or services that would be beneficial?

3.2 Submitting a Feature Request

You can submit feature requests through several channels:

- Microsoft Feedback Hub:

  - Open the Feedback Hub app (available on Windows).

  - Select "Feedback" and choose "Add new feedback."

  - Describe the feature you'd like to see, providing details on how it would benefit users.

  - Optionally, include screenshots or examples to support your request.

- Microsoft To Do UserVoice or Feedback Site:

  - Visit the Microsoft UserVoice or feedback site dedicated to Microsoft To Do.

- Search for existing feature requests to avoid duplicates.

- If your request is not listed, submit a new feature idea, providing a clear description and rationale.

- Community Forums:

- Post your feature request on the Microsoft Community forums.

- Engage with other users to gather support and suggestions for the proposed feature.

3.3 Engaging with the Development Team

Once you've submitted a feature request or bug report, you might receive follow-up questions or requests for additional information. Stay engaged with:

- Feedback Responses: Monitor responses to your feedback and provide any additional information if requested.

- Feature Updates: Keep an eye on updates and announcements related to new features or bug fixes. Microsoft often releases update notes and roadmaps detailing upcoming changes.

4. Best Practices for Reporting Bugs and Requesting Features

4.1 Be Constructive and Patient

When providing feedback, be constructive and patient. Developers work hard to address issues and implement new features, and it may take time for your feedback to be acted upon. Constructive feedback helps prioritize the right issues and enhances the chances of your suggestions being implemented.

4.2 Stay Informed

Regularly check for updates and announcements from Microsoft To Do. The development team often shares news about new features, improvements, and bug fixes that may address your concerns or requests.

4.3 Participate in Beta Programs

Consider joining beta programs or preview releases if available. These programs allow you to test new features before they are officially released and provide feedback on their functionality.

5. Conclusion

Reporting bugs and requesting features are crucial for improving Microsoft To Do and ensuring it meets the needs of its users. By following the guidelines outlined in this section, you can effectively contribute to the enhancement of the application and help shape its future developments. Your feedback is invaluable, and engaging with the Microsoft To Do community helps create a more effective and user-friendly tool for everyone.

CHAPTER VII
Real-World Applications and Case Studies

7.1 Case Study: Microsoft To Do in Project Management

7.1.1 Managing Project Milestones

Managing project milestones effectively is a crucial component of successful project management. Milestones are key points within a project timeline that signify the completion of major phases, deliverables, or objectives. They serve as critical checkpoints that ensure the project is on track, within budget, and aligned with overall goals. Microsoft To Do, with its intuitive task management features, can be a powerful tool for organizing and managing these milestones, ensuring that every step in the project is carefully monitored and executed.

Understanding Project Milestones

Before diving into how Microsoft To Do can be leveraged for managing project milestones, it is essential to understand what milestones are and why they are important. Milestones differ from regular tasks in that they represent significant events or achievements within a project's life cycle. These might include the completion of major deliverables, approval of a project phase, the start of a significant workstream, or the finalization of key project documentation. Unlike tasks, milestones are not about specific actions but rather about reaching certain points in the project timeline that indicate progress.

Milestones are pivotal in providing a sense of direction and accomplishment. They help project managers and stakeholders to assess whether the project is progressing as planned, allowing for adjustments in strategy, allocation of resources, or timelines as necessary. They also offer a clear framework for communication with team members, executives, and clients, highlighting when critical phases of the project have been completed.

Setting Up Milestones in Microsoft To Do

Microsoft To Do can be an invaluable tool for setting up and tracking milestones within a project. Although Microsoft To Do is primarily designed for task management, its flexibility allows project managers to adapt it to milestone management. Here's how you can set up milestones in Microsoft To Do:

1. Creating Milestone Lists: Start by creating a dedicated list in Microsoft To Do for your project milestones. This list will serve as a central hub for all the major checkpoints in your project. Name the list something descriptive, such as "Project XYZ Milestones." This will help in keeping the milestones separate from day-to-day tasks.

2. Defining Milestones as Tasks: In Microsoft To Do, you can define each milestone as a task. While this might seem unconventional since milestones are broader than tasks, this approach allows you to take advantage of To Do's task management features. For each milestone, create a task that reflects the milestone's name, such as "Complete Design Phase" or "Approval of Budget."

3. Setting Due Dates and Reminders: Assign due dates to each milestone to align with your project timeline. Microsoft To Do allows you to set reminders for these tasks, ensuring that you and your team are alerted as milestone deadlines approach. This feature is particularly useful in keeping the project team focused on the upcoming critical points.

4. Using Notes and Subtasks for Details: While milestones are high-level goals, there are often many tasks and steps involved in reaching them. Microsoft To Do allows you to add notes and subtasks to each milestone. Use the notes section to detail the criteria for milestone completion, relevant documents, or key contacts. Subtasks can be used to break down the milestone into smaller, actionable steps that need to be completed to achieve the milestone.

5. Tagging and Prioritization: Microsoft To Do's tagging and prioritization features are powerful tools for managing milestones. By tagging milestones with keywords like "Critical" or "High Priority," you can easily filter and identify the most important

milestones. Additionally, prioritization within Microsoft To Do allows you to highlight which milestones need immediate attention.

Monitoring and Tracking Milestone Progress

Once the milestones are set up in Microsoft To Do, the next step is monitoring and tracking their progress. Microsoft To Do provides several features that help project managers stay on top of milestone completion:

1. My Day Feature: The "My Day" feature in Microsoft To Do is useful for daily milestone tracking. Each day, you can add relevant milestone tasks to "My Day" to ensure that these critical points remain top of mind. This feature is particularly helpful in focusing your attention on what needs to be accomplished on any given day to move the project closer to its milestones.

2. Daily and Weekly Reviews: Regular reviews are essential in project management. In Microsoft To Do, you can conduct daily and weekly reviews to check the status of your milestones. This involves going through your milestone list and updating the progress of each milestone. During these reviews, you can adjust due dates, add new subtasks, or reprioritize tasks as needed. This ongoing review process ensures that milestones are continually monitored and that the project remains on track.

3. Collaboration and Sharing: Microsoft To Do's collaboration features allow you to share your milestone list with team members. By doing so, everyone involved in the project can view the milestones, track progress, and contribute to their completion. This shared visibility is crucial in keeping the entire team aligned and accountable for reaching the milestones.

4. Integration with Microsoft Outlook and Teams: Microsoft To Do integrates seamlessly with other Microsoft 365 tools like Outlook and Teams. By syncing your milestone tasks with Outlook, you can ensure that they appear on your calendar, making it easier to schedule milestone-related activities. Integration with Teams allows you to discuss milestones in real-time with your project team, ensuring that everyone is informed and engaged.

5. Using Filters and Custom Views: Microsoft To Do allows you to create custom views and filters based on due dates, tags, and priorities. These features can be used to create a specific view for milestones, showing only those tasks that represent critical project points. This focused view is beneficial when you need to quickly assess the status of all milestones without being distracted by day-to-day tasks.

Communicating Milestones with Stakeholders

Effective communication of milestone progress to stakeholders is a key aspect of project management. Stakeholders, whether they are clients, executives, or team members, need to be informed about milestone achievements and any potential delays. Microsoft To Do can assist in this communication process:

1. Status Reports: Using the information tracked in Microsoft To Do, you can generate status reports that detail the progress of milestones. These reports can include which milestones have been completed, which are in progress, and any that are at risk of delay. The notes and subtasks within each milestone task in Microsoft To Do provide the necessary details to inform these reports.

2. Visual Dashboards: While Microsoft To Do itself does not offer advanced dashboard features, it can be integrated with other tools like Microsoft Planner or Power BI to create visual dashboards. These dashboards can visually represent milestone progress, providing stakeholders with a clear and concise overview of the project's status.

3. Regular Updates: Schedule regular updates with stakeholders using the milestone due dates in Microsoft To Do. Reminders and notifications can prompt you to send these updates at critical points in the project timeline. Regular communication ensures that stakeholders are kept in the loop and can provide feedback or make decisions as needed.

Adjusting and Adapting Milestones

In any project, changes are inevitable. Whether due to shifting priorities, resource constraints, or unforeseen challenges, milestones may need to be adjusted. Microsoft To Do offers flexibility in adapting to these changes:

1. Revising Milestone Due Dates: If a milestone is at risk of not being met, you can easily adjust the due date in Microsoft To Do. This change will update the timeline and notify you of the new deadline, helping you manage expectations and realign project schedules.

2. Adding or Removing Milestones: As the project evolves, new milestones may emerge, or some may become obsolete. Microsoft To Do allows you to add new milestone tasks or delete those that are no longer relevant. This adaptability ensures that your milestone list remains accurate and reflective of the current project status.

3. Reallocating Resources: Sometimes, reaching a milestone requires additional resources. Microsoft To Do can help you track these resource needs through subtasks or notes within

each milestone. By monitoring resource allocation, you can make informed decisions about where to focus efforts to ensure milestone completion.

Conclusion: The Role of Microsoft To Do in Project Milestone Management

Microsoft To Do, while not a traditional project management tool, offers significant capabilities for managing project milestones effectively. Its task-oriented structure, combined with features like reminders, tagging, and collaboration, makes it a versatile solution for project managers looking to keep their projects on track.

By using Microsoft To Do to manage project milestones, you can ensure that critical checkpoints are well-defined, monitored, and communicated to all stakeholders. This approach not only helps in meeting project deadlines but also contributes to overall project success by ensuring that each phase of the project is completed as planned.

Ultimately, Microsoft To Do provides a simple yet powerful framework for managing the complexities of project milestones, helping you to achieve your project goals with greater efficiency and clarity. Whether you are managing a small team or a large-scale project, integrating Microsoft To Do into your project management practices can lead to more organized, successful outcomes.

7.1.2 Coordinating Team Efforts

Effective project management is a critical skill in any organization, and the ability to coordinate team efforts can make or break a project's success. In this section, we will delve into how Microsoft To Do can serve as a powerful tool for ensuring that team members are aligned, tasks are distributed evenly, and deadlines are met. By leveraging the features of Microsoft To Do, project managers can streamline communication, clarify roles, and foster a collaborative environment that leads to successful project outcomes.

The Role of Task Management in Team Coordination

At the heart of any successful project is the ability to manage tasks efficiently. Coordinating team efforts requires clear communication, the ability to delegate tasks appropriately, and the monitoring of progress to ensure that everyone is on the same page. Microsoft To Do offers several features that facilitate this process, allowing project managers to break down complex projects into manageable tasks, assign these tasks to the appropriate team members, and track progress in real-time.

One of the key advantages of Microsoft To Do in team coordination is its integration with other Microsoft 365 tools, such as Microsoft Teams, Outlook, and Planner. This integration ensures that tasks assigned in To Do are visible across all platforms, allowing for seamless communication and collaboration. For example, a task created in Microsoft To Do can automatically sync with a team's Planner, ensuring that everyone involved in the project is aware of their responsibilities and deadlines.

Assigning Tasks and Responsibilities

In any project, it's crucial that tasks are assigned to the right people based on their skills and availability. Microsoft To Do makes this process straightforward by allowing project managers to create tasks and assign them to specific team members directly within the application. This feature ensures that everyone knows what they need to do and when it needs to be done, reducing confusion and the risk of tasks falling through the cracks.

When assigning tasks, it's important to consider the workload of each team member. Microsoft To Do provides a clear overview of each person's assigned tasks, making it easier for project managers to distribute work evenly and avoid overloading any single team member. Additionally, tasks can be prioritized within To Do, helping team members focus on what's most important and manage their time effectively.

One of the most powerful features of Microsoft To Do in task assignment is the ability to add detailed notes, files, and links to each task. This feature ensures that team members have all the information they need to complete their tasks without needing to search through emails or other documents. For example, if a task involves drafting a report, the project manager can attach the relevant guidelines and templates directly to the task in To Do. This not only saves time but also reduces the likelihood of errors and miscommunication.

Tracking Progress and Providing Feedback

Once tasks have been assigned, the next step in coordinating team efforts is tracking progress. Microsoft To Do offers a variety of tools to help project managers monitor the status of tasks and ensure that the project is on track. The progress of each task can be easily tracked using the status indicators in To Do, which show whether a task is not started, in progress, or completed. This visual representation of task status provides a quick and easy way for project managers to assess the overall progress of the project.

In addition to status indicators, Microsoft To Do allows for the setting of due dates and reminders, ensuring that tasks are completed on time. These reminders can be customized based on the needs of the project, providing team members with notifications well in advance of their deadlines. This feature is particularly useful in projects with tight timelines, where missing a deadline could have significant consequences for the overall success of the project.

Feedback is another critical aspect of coordinating team efforts. Microsoft To Do makes it easy for project managers to provide feedback on tasks, either through the app itself or through integrated tools like Microsoft Teams. By providing timely and constructive feedback, project managers can help team members stay on track and improve their performance. This feedback loop is essential for maintaining high standards and ensuring that the project is completed to the best possible standard.

Facilitating Communication and Collaboration

Effective communication is the cornerstone of successful team coordination. Microsoft To Do integrates seamlessly with Microsoft Teams, allowing for real-time communication and collaboration between team members. This integration enables project managers to create tasks in To Do and then discuss them in Teams, ensuring that everyone is on the same page and that any questions or concerns are addressed promptly.

Collaboration is further enhanced by the ability to share lists and tasks within Microsoft To Do. Shared lists allow multiple team members to work on the same set of tasks, making it easier to collaborate on complex projects. For example, in a marketing project, a shared list could include tasks related to content creation, social media management, and campaign analysis. Each team member can see the progress of related tasks, provide updates, and make comments, fostering a collaborative environment where everyone contributes to the project's success.

Another useful feature of Microsoft To Do is the ability to attach files and links to tasks. This feature is particularly valuable in collaborative projects, where multiple team members may need to access the same resources. By attaching relevant documents directly to tasks, project managers ensure that everyone has access to the information they need, reducing the risk of miscommunication and mistakes.

Managing Changes and Adapting to New Information

One of the challenges in project management is dealing with changes and new information. Whether it's a shift in project scope, a new client request, or an unforeseen obstacle, project managers need to be able to adapt quickly and efficiently. Microsoft To Do helps project managers manage these changes by allowing for easy updates to tasks and lists.

When a change occurs, tasks can be quickly modified to reflect the new requirements. For example, if a client requests an additional feature in a software development project, the project manager can update the relevant tasks in To Do, assign new tasks as needed, and adjust deadlines accordingly. These changes are instantly visible to all team members, ensuring that everyone is aware of the new direction and can adjust their efforts accordingly.

In addition to updating tasks, Microsoft To Do allows for the creation of new lists or the reorganization of existing ones to better align with the new project requirements. This flexibility is crucial in dynamic project environments, where the ability to adapt quickly can make the difference between success and failure.

Ensuring Accountability and Transparency

Accountability is a key factor in successful team coordination. Microsoft To Do helps project managers ensure accountability by providing a clear record of who is responsible for each task and when it is due. This transparency helps prevent tasks from being overlooked and ensures that team members take ownership of their responsibilities.

To enhance accountability, project managers can use the "Assigned to Me" feature in Microsoft To Do, which provides each team member with a personalized view of their assigned tasks. This feature makes it easy for team members to see what they need to work on and track their progress. For project managers, this feature provides a clear overview of who is responsible for each task, making it easier to follow up on tasks that are behind schedule or need additional support.

Additionally, Microsoft To Do's integration with Microsoft Planner allows for even greater transparency and accountability. Tasks assigned in Planner can be viewed and managed in To Do, providing a seamless experience for team members. This integration ensures that tasks are tracked across multiple platforms and that there is a clear record of each team member's contributions to the project.

Conclusion

Coordinating team efforts in a project management setting can be challenging, but with the right tools, it becomes much more manageable. Microsoft To Do provides a comprehensive solution for managing tasks, assigning responsibilities, tracking progress, and facilitating communication and collaboration. By leveraging the features of Microsoft To Do, project managers can ensure that their teams are aligned, tasks are completed on time, and projects are delivered successfully.

In this case study, we have explored how Microsoft To Do can be used to coordinate team efforts effectively. From assigning tasks and tracking progress to providing feedback and managing changes, Microsoft To Do offers a powerful set of tools that can help project managers lead their teams to success. As you continue to explore the capabilities of Microsoft To Do, consider how you can implement these strategies in your own projects to enhance team coordination and achieve better results.

7.1.3 Tracking Project Progress

Introduction to Tracking Project Progress

In any project management scenario, tracking progress is a critical component to ensure that the project stays on course and meets its goals within the desired timeframe. Microsoft To Do, while primarily known as a task management tool, offers powerful features that can be effectively leveraged for tracking project progress. By organizing tasks, setting milestones, and keeping track of team contributions, Microsoft To Do can serve as a robust platform for monitoring the health and trajectory of your projects.

Setting Up Your Project Plan

The foundation of effective progress tracking lies in how well you set up your project plan. In Microsoft To Do, projects are typically managed by creating lists that represent different aspects or phases of the project. Each list can then be populated with tasks that need to be completed to advance the project.

1. Breaking Down the Project: Start by breaking down your project into major milestones or phases. For example, if you're managing a product launch, your milestones might include

planning, development, testing, marketing, and launch. Each of these milestones can be represented as separate lists in Microsoft To Do.

2. Adding Tasks: Within each list, create tasks that represent the individual steps required to complete that phase. These tasks should be granular enough to be actionable but broad enough to represent significant chunks of work. For instance, under the "Development" list, you might include tasks like "Design UI," "Implement Backend," and "Perform Code Review."

3. Setting Deadlines: Assign due dates to each task to establish a timeline for your project. This not only helps in prioritizing work but also in visualizing how the project will unfold over time.

4. Assigning Priorities: Use the priority feature in Microsoft To Do to indicate the importance of each task. This helps in focusing on critical tasks that are essential for keeping the project on track.

Monitoring Task Completion

Once your project is set up in Microsoft To Do, the next step is to actively monitor task completion. This involves regularly checking the status of tasks, ensuring that they are being completed on time, and making adjustments as necessary.

1. Regular Check-ins: Establish a routine for checking the status of tasks. This could be a daily or weekly review where you assess which tasks have been completed, which are in progress, and which are delayed. Microsoft To Do's interface makes it easy to see at a glance which tasks have been checked off and which remain outstanding.

2. Tracking Overdue Tasks: Pay special attention to tasks that are overdue. Microsoft To Do will automatically highlight tasks that have missed their deadlines, allowing you to quickly identify bottlenecks. Investigate why these tasks are delayed and what can be done to get them back on track.

3. Updating Task Status: As tasks are completed, make sure to update their status in Microsoft To Do. This not only keeps your project plan accurate but also provides a sense of accomplishment as you see tasks moving from "Pending" to "Completed."

4. Using Task Comments: Microsoft To Do allows you to add comments to tasks, which can be useful for tracking progress within a task. For example, if a task involves multiple steps, you can use comments to note when each step is completed.

Utilizing Task Details for Progress Tracking

Microsoft To Do's task details feature offers several tools that can enhance your ability to track progress at a more granular level.

1. Adding Subtasks: Many tasks in a project are multi-faceted, involving several smaller actions that need to be completed. Microsoft To Do's subtask feature allows you to break down a task into its component parts. As you complete each subtask, you can check it off, which gives you and your team a clearer picture of progress.

2. Using Notes: The notes section in each task can be used to provide context or additional information about the task. This could include details about what has been done so far, what needs to be done next, or any challenges that have arisen. Keeping thorough notes ensures that anyone reviewing the task can understand its current status.

3. Attaching Files: If your task requires documentation or reference materials, you can attach files directly to the task. This keeps all relevant information in one place and makes it easier to track progress on tasks that involve significant documentation, such as drafting reports or creating design documents.

4. Setting Recurring Tasks: For ongoing or recurring activities within a project, Microsoft To Do allows you to set tasks to repeat at regular intervals. This is useful for tasks that need to be revisited periodically, such as weekly status meetings or regular code reviews.

Integrating Microsoft To Do with Other Tools

While Microsoft To Do is powerful on its own, its functionality can be significantly enhanced when integrated with other tools within the Microsoft 365 ecosystem or third-party applications.

1. Integration with Microsoft Planner: Microsoft Planner is a more advanced project management tool that can be integrated with Microsoft To Do. This integration allows you to see Planner tasks in your To Do lists, making it easier to manage both simple and complex tasks from one interface. By syncing tasks between the two tools, you can track detailed project plans in Planner while using To Do for your daily task management.

2. Syncing with Outlook: Microsoft To Do seamlessly integrates with Outlook, allowing tasks to be synced with your calendar. This integration is particularly useful for ensuring that deadlines are visible within your daily schedule and that tasks are appropriately prioritized alongside meetings and other calendar events.

3. Automating Workflows with Power Automate: Power Automate allows you to create automated workflows between Microsoft To Do and other applications. For example, you can set up a flow that automatically creates a new task in Microsoft To Do whenever an email is flagged in Outlook, or when a new item is added to a SharePoint list. This automation reduces manual effort and ensures that your To Do list is always up to date.

4. Collaboration Tools: Microsoft Teams can be used in conjunction with Microsoft To Do to facilitate team collaboration. Tasks can be shared directly within Teams, allowing for better communication and coordination among team members. Additionally, team members can update task status and add comments within Teams, which syncs with Microsoft To Do.

Analyzing Progress with Smart Lists and Filters

Microsoft To Do offers several features that allow you to analyze project progress through the use of smart lists and filters.

1. Utilizing Smart Lists: Smart lists in Microsoft To Do, such as "Planned" and "Important," automatically aggregate tasks based on certain criteria. The "Planned" list shows tasks that have due dates, while the "Important" list highlights tasks marked with high priority. By regularly reviewing these lists, you can get a quick overview of upcoming deadlines and critical tasks that need immediate attention.

2. Custom Filters: Microsoft To Do allows you to create custom filters based on various criteria, such as due date, priority, or tags. These filters help you focus on specific aspects of your project, such as tasks due within the next week or tasks assigned to a particular team member. Custom filters are especially useful for project managers who need to drill down into specific areas of the project.

3. Analyzing Task Completion Rates: One of the key indicators of project progress is the rate at which tasks are completed. Microsoft To Do doesn't provide built-in analytics, but you can manually track completion rates by comparing the number of completed tasks against the total number of tasks over a specific period. By doing so, you can identify trends, such as whether the project is progressing faster or slower than expected.

4. Using Tags for Categorization: Tags are a powerful way to categorize tasks based on different dimensions, such as priority, project phase, or team member. By filtering tasks based on tags, you can analyze specific subsets of your project and ensure that all areas are progressing as planned.

Collaborating with Team Members

Effective project progress tracking requires strong collaboration among team members. Microsoft To Do offers several features that facilitate collaboration and ensure that everyone is on the same page.

1. Sharing Lists: Microsoft To Do allows you to share lists with team members, enabling everyone to see and contribute to the tasks. Shared lists are ideal for collaborative projects where multiple people are responsible for completing different tasks.

2. Assigning Tasks: While Microsoft To Do doesn't natively support task assignment to other users (this feature is more prominent in Microsoft Planner), you can still use the comments and notes sections to indicate who is responsible for each task. Alternatively, you can integrate Microsoft To Do with Planner to enable task assignments.

3. Real-Time Updates: When a task is updated, such as when a subtask is completed or a due date is changed, the updates are reflected in real-time for all team members. This ensures that everyone has the most up-to-date information and can adjust their work accordingly.

4. Communication Through Comments: The comments section within each task can be used for ongoing communication among team members. This is particularly useful for tracking discussions related to specific tasks and ensuring that all relevant information is captured in one place.

Reviewing and Reflecting on Project Progress

Regular reviews are essential for ensuring that a project remains on track. Microsoft To Do can be used to facilitate both informal daily check-ins and more formal weekly or monthly reviews.

1. Conducting Daily Check-ins: Set aside time each day to review the tasks that were completed, those that are in progress, and those that are upcoming. This daily review helps in identifying any immediate issues that need to be addressed.

2. Weekly Progress Reviews: A more in-depth weekly review can be conducted to assess the overall progress of the project. During this review, compare the current state of the project against the project plan, identify any deviations, and make adjustments as

necessary. Microsoft To Do's smart lists and filters can be used to pull up relevant tasks for this review.

3. Reflecting on Completed Tasks: Reviewing completed tasks can provide valuable insights into what worked well and what didn't. Consider using the notes section to document lessons learned for future reference. This reflection can also help in refining your project management practices.

4. Adjusting the Project Plan: Based on the insights gained from your reviews, you may need to adjust the project plan. This could involve reassigning tasks, extending deadlines, or changing priorities. Microsoft To Do's flexible task management features make it easy to adjust the project plan as needed.

Challenges in Progress Tracking

While Microsoft To Do offers robust features for tracking project progress, there are certain challenges that users may encounter.

1. Managing Complex Projects: Microsoft To Do is designed for task management and may not offer the depth of features required for managing very complex projects with multiple dependencies and resources. For such projects, it may be necessary to use Microsoft To Do in conjunction with more advanced project management tools like Microsoft Project or Planner.

2. Keeping Track of Multiple Projects: If you're managing multiple projects simultaneously, it can be challenging to keep track of progress across all of them. In such cases, it's important to establish clear workflows and regularly review all projects to ensure nothing falls through the cracks.

3. Ensuring Team Adoption: For Microsoft To Do to be effective in a team setting, all team members need to be actively using it. Ensuring that everyone is on board and consistently updating their tasks can be a challenge, especially if team members are accustomed to other tools.

4. Balancing Detail with Simplicity: While it's important to capture all relevant details in Microsoft To Do, there's a risk of overcomplicating the task management process. Strive to find a balance between providing enough detail to track progress effectively and keeping the task list manageable.

Best Practices for Effective Progress Tracking

To make the most of Microsoft To Do for tracking project progress, consider the following best practices:

1. Keep Your Tasks Organized: Regularly review and update your task lists to ensure they accurately reflect the current state of the project. Use lists, tags, and filters to keep tasks organized and easy to manage.

2. Encourage Team Collaboration: Make sure all team members are actively using Microsoft To Do and contributing to task updates. Regular communication and collaboration are key to keeping the project on track.

3. Regularly Review Progress: Set up a routine for reviewing project progress, both at the individual task level and the overall project level. Use these reviews to make necessary adjustments and keep the project moving forward.

4. Integrate with Other Tools: Leverage integrations with other tools, such as Outlook, Planner, and Teams, to enhance your ability to track progress and manage tasks effectively.

5. Focus on Continuous Improvement: Use each project as an opportunity to refine your progress tracking methods. Learn from past experiences and apply those lessons to future projects.

Conclusion

Tracking project progress is a fundamental aspect of successful project management, and Microsoft To Do offers a range of features that can be effectively utilized for this purpose. By setting up a well-structured project plan, actively monitoring task completion, leveraging task details, and integrating with other tools, you can gain a clear and accurate picture of your project's progress. Regular reviews and reflections will help you stay on course, while best practices and continuous improvement will ensure that each project is more successful than the last. Despite some challenges, with the right approach, Microsoft To Do can be a powerful ally in your project management toolkit.

7.2 Case Study: Personal Productivity with Microsoft To Do

7.2.1 Organizing Daily Tasks

In our fast-paced world, managing daily tasks effectively is crucial for maintaining productivity and achieving personal goals. Microsoft To Do, with its intuitive design and robust feature set, provides an excellent platform for organizing daily tasks. This section delves into the practical application of Microsoft To Do for daily task management, exploring how it can be used to streamline routines, prioritize important activities, and maintain a balanced, productive life.

The Foundation of Daily Task Management

Before diving into the specifics, it's essential to understand the foundational principles of daily task management. Effective task management involves identifying what needs to be done, prioritizing those tasks, and then executing them efficiently. Microsoft To Do offers several features that support these principles, such as task creation, prioritization, and reminders.

Setting Up Your Daily Tasks

To begin organizing your daily tasks in Microsoft To Do, start by creating a new list dedicated to your daily activities. This list will serve as a central hub where you can add, manage, and prioritize tasks. Here's a step-by-step guide to setting up your daily tasks:

1. Creating a Daily Tasks List:

   - Open Microsoft To Do and click on "New List."

   - Name your list "Daily Tasks" or something similar.

   - Customize the list by choosing an appropriate theme or color to make it visually appealing.

2. Adding Tasks:

  - Click on the list you just created and start adding tasks.

  - Break down larger tasks into smaller, manageable subtasks. This makes it easier to track progress and ensures that no steps are overlooked.

  - For example, if you have a task like "Prepare for presentation," you can break it down into subtasks such as "Research topic," "Create slides," "Practice presentation," and "Gather feedback."

3. Setting Due Dates and Reminders:

  - For each task, set a due date to ensure that it gets done on time.

  - Use the reminder feature to get notifications when a task is due. This helps in staying on track and avoiding procrastination.

  - If you have recurring tasks, set them to repeat daily, weekly, or at any other interval that suits your schedule.

4. Prioritizing Tasks:

  - Assign priority levels to your tasks using the built-in priority feature. You can mark tasks as "Important" to highlight those that need immediate attention.

  - Arrange tasks in the order of priority. Microsoft To Do allows you to drag and drop tasks to rearrange them easily.

Using Smart Lists and My Day

One of the standout features of Microsoft To Do is "My Day." This feature helps you focus on what needs to be done today without getting overwhelmed by your entire task list.

1. Populating My Day:

  - Each morning, review your Daily Tasks list and select tasks that you plan to complete today. Add these tasks to "My Day" by clicking on the "Add to My Day" button.

  - This practice helps in setting daily goals and maintaining focus.

2. Smart Lists:

   - Microsoft To Do automatically creates Smart Lists, such as "Important," "Planned," and "Flagged Email," based on your tasks and settings.

   - Utilize these Smart Lists to get an overview of your tasks. For example, the "Important" list shows all tasks marked as important, while the "Planned" list displays tasks with upcoming due dates.

Integrating Microsoft To Do with Other Tools

To further enhance productivity, consider integrating Microsoft To Do with other tools and applications you use daily. Microsoft To Do seamlessly integrates with several Microsoft 365 apps, as well as third-party applications.

1. Outlook Integration:

   - If you use Microsoft Outlook for email, you can flag emails, and they will automatically appear in your Microsoft To Do as tasks.

   - This integration ensures that important emails don't get lost and are followed up on time.

2. OneNote Integration:

   - For note-taking and more detailed task planning, integrate Microsoft To Do with OneNote.

   - You can create tasks in OneNote and sync them with Microsoft To Do, allowing you to keep detailed notes while managing tasks efficiently.

3. Using Cortana:

   - If you use Cortana, Microsoft's digital assistant, you can add tasks to Microsoft To Do using voice commands.

   - This feature is particularly useful when you need to capture tasks quickly on the go.

Daily Review and Reflection

A crucial aspect of maintaining productivity is the daily review and reflection process. At the end of each day, spend a few minutes reviewing your completed tasks and planning for the next day.

1. Reviewing Completed Tasks:

   - Check off tasks that you have completed. This not only provides a sense of accomplishment but also helps in tracking progress.

   - Reflect on what you achieved and identify any tasks that need to be carried over to the next day.

2. Planning for Tomorrow:

   - Look at your upcoming tasks and start populating "My Day" for tomorrow.

   - Adjust priorities based on any new developments or changes in your schedule.

Overcoming Common Challenges

While Microsoft To Do is a powerful tool, users may face some common challenges in daily task management. Here are some tips to overcome these challenges:

1. Procrastination:

   - Break tasks into smaller, manageable steps to make them less daunting.

   - Use the reminder and due date features to stay on track and avoid putting tasks off.

2. Overloading Your Day:

   - Be realistic about what you can accomplish in a day. Avoid adding too many tasks to "My Day."

   - Prioritize essential tasks and leave some buffer time for unexpected interruptions.

3. Staying Motivated:

   - Use the "Completed Tasks" view to see what you have achieved. This can boost motivation and provide a sense of progress.

   - Celebrate small wins and reward yourself for completing tasks.

Maintaining Work-Life Balance

Managing daily tasks effectively also involves maintaining a healthy work-life balance. Microsoft To Do can help you organize both professional and personal tasks, ensuring that you allocate time for work and relaxation.

1. Separating Work and Personal Tasks:

   - Create separate lists for work and personal tasks. This helps in maintaining focus and avoiding overlap.

   - During work hours, focus on your work list, and switch to your personal list during your free time.

2. Scheduling Downtime:

   - Include personal activities and downtime in your daily tasks. Scheduling time for relaxation, hobbies, and family ensures that you don't neglect these important aspects of life.

   - Use reminders to take breaks and avoid burnout.

Customizing Microsoft To Do to Fit Your Style

Everyone has a unique way of managing tasks, and Microsoft To Do offers several customization options to tailor the experience to your preferences.

1. Themes and Backgrounds:

   - Personalize the appearance of your lists by choosing different themes and backgrounds. A visually appealing interface can make task management more enjoyable.

2. Custom Sorting and Filtering:

   - Customize how your tasks are sorted and filtered. For example, you can sort tasks by due date, priority, or creation date.

   - Use filters to view tasks based on specific criteria, such as all tasks due this week or tasks tagged with a particular label.

Real-World Example: A Day in the Life with Microsoft To Do

To illustrate the practical application of Microsoft To Do in daily task management, let's look at a real-world example. Meet Sarah, a marketing manager who uses Microsoft To Do to organize her busy day.

Morning Routine:

- Sarah starts her day by reviewing her Daily Tasks list and adding tasks to "My Day." She includes tasks like "Team Meeting at 10 AM," "Draft Email Campaign," and "Review Social Media Analytics."

- She sets reminders for important tasks, such as the team meeting, to ensure she stays on schedule.

Work Hours:

- Throughout the day, Sarah uses Microsoft To Do to track her progress. She marks tasks as complete once they are done and adjusts her priorities if new tasks come up.

- She uses the Outlook integration to add flagged emails as tasks, ensuring that important follow-ups are not missed.

Afternoon Check-In:

- After lunch, Sarah conducts a quick review of her tasks. She identifies any tasks that need to be carried over to the next day and adjusts her plans accordingly.

- She uses the "My Day" feature to refocus on the most critical tasks for the remainder of the day.

Evening Reflection:

- Before ending her workday, Sarah spends a few minutes reflecting on what she accomplished. She checks off completed tasks and updates her lists.

- She then switches to her personal tasks list, planning activities for the evening, such as "Grocery Shopping" and "Yoga Session."

Conclusion

Organizing daily tasks with Microsoft To Do can transform the way you manage your day. By leveraging its features—such as task creation, prioritization, reminders, and integrations—you can stay organized, focused, and productive. Whether you're managing professional responsibilities or personal activities, Microsoft To Do provides the tools you need to get things done efficiently. Through careful planning, regular reviews, and customization to fit your unique style, you can achieve a balanced, productive life.

7.2.2 Managing Personal Goals and Habits

Managing personal goals and habits is an essential aspect of leading a fulfilling and productive life. Whether it's developing a new skill, improving health, or working towards a significant life milestone, setting and tracking goals can help you stay focused and motivated. In this section, we'll explore how Microsoft To Do can be leveraged to manage personal goals and habits effectively, ensuring that you make consistent progress and achieve the outcomes you desire.

Understanding the Importance of Goals and Habits

Before diving into the practical application of Microsoft To Do, it's crucial to understand the significance of setting goals and cultivating habits. Goals give direction to our efforts, while habits create the structure necessary to achieve those goals. Together, they form the backbone of personal productivity and success.

Goals are the milestones you aim to achieve, whether they're short-term, such as completing a course, or long-term, like running a marathon. Goals should be specific, measurable, achievable, relevant, and time-bound (SMART). By clearly defining your goals, you set a clear path toward what you want to accomplish.

Habits are the repeated actions that contribute to achieving your goals. For instance, if your goal is to improve your physical health, developing habits like regular exercise and healthy eating will be instrumental. Habits are powerful because they automate behavior, reducing the mental effort required to perform tasks and making it easier to stay on track.

Setting Up Goals in Microsoft To Do

Microsoft To Do is an excellent tool for setting up and tracking your personal goals. The first step in using Microsoft To Do for goal management is to define your goals clearly. Here's how you can do that:

1. Create a Dedicated Goals List: Start by creating a new list in Microsoft To Do specifically for your goals. This will serve as your central hub for all the goals you are working on. Name the list something meaningful, like "Personal Goals" or "2024 Goals."

2. Break Down Goals into Tasks: Once you have your goals list, add each goal as a task within that list. For instance, if your goal is to "Run a Marathon," this would be a task in your goals list.

3. Set Due Dates and Reminders: Assign due dates to your goals to give them a timeline. Microsoft To Do allows you to set reminders, so you can receive notifications as deadlines approach, ensuring that you stay on track.

4. Use Subtasks for Milestones: Break down each goal into smaller, manageable milestones or steps. These can be added as subtasks under the main goal. For example, under "Run a Marathon," you might have subtasks like "Complete a 5K race," "Run 10 miles," and "Join a marathon training group." These milestones help you monitor progress and provide a sense of achievement as you tick them off.

5. Prioritize Your Goals: Microsoft To Do allows you to mark tasks as important. Use this feature to prioritize your most critical goals, ensuring they remain at the forefront of your daily focus.

6. Use Tags for Categorization: To further organize your goals, use tags to categorize them by type, such as "Health," "Career," or "Personal Development." This helps in quickly filtering and reviewing your goals based on different aspects of your life.

Tracking Habits with Microsoft To Do

Tracking habits is a slightly different process than managing goals, as habits require daily or regular attention. Microsoft To Do can be adapted to monitor and reinforce your habits effectively.

1. Create a Habits List: Just as you did with your goals, create a new list in Microsoft To Do dedicated to your habits. You can name it "Daily Habits" or "Habit Tracker."

2. Add Habits as Recurring Tasks: Enter each habit you want to develop as a recurring task in your habits list. For instance, if one of your habits is to "Exercise for 30 minutes," set it as a daily recurring task. Microsoft To Do will automatically regenerate the task each day, keeping it on your to-do list.

3. Set Specific Times for Habits: For habits that are time-sensitive, such as "Meditate for 10 minutes in the morning," you can set specific times for these tasks. Microsoft To Do will remind you at the designated time, helping you incorporate these habits into your routine.

4. Track Progress: As you complete your habits daily, mark them as done in Microsoft To Do. The satisfaction of checking off a task can be a powerful motivator. Additionally, seeing a streak of completed tasks can encourage consistency.

5. Review and Reflect: Periodically review your habits to assess how well you're maintaining them. If you notice you're struggling with certain habits, consider breaking them down into smaller steps or adjusting your approach. Reflection is a key component of habit formation, allowing you to refine your methods and increase success rates.

6. Visualize Your Success: Use the "My Day" feature in Microsoft To Do to visualize your habits for the day. By adding your daily habits to My Day, you get a clear view of what needs to be accomplished, keeping you focused and motivated throughout the day.

Integrating Goals and Habits

One of the most powerful aspects of using Microsoft To Do for personal productivity is the ability to integrate your goals and habits. Since habits are the building blocks that lead to goal achievement, it's essential to align them with your goals. Here's how you can do that:

1. Link Habits to Goals: When setting up your habits, consider how each habit contributes to your broader goals. For example, if your goal is to "Improve Mental Wellbeing," habits like "Daily Meditation" and "Journaling" can be directly linked to that goal. This connection reinforces the purpose of your habits and provides a stronger motivation to maintain them.

2. Review Progress Together: At the end of each week or month, review both your goals and habits together. Microsoft To Do allows you to see all tasks completed over a period,

giving you an overview of your progress. Assess whether your habits are effectively contributing to your goals and make adjustments as needed.

3. Adjust Goals Based on Habit Performance: Sometimes, the performance of your habits might indicate that a goal needs to be revised. For instance, if you're consistently unable to maintain a daily exercise habit, you might need to modify your fitness goals or explore alternative habits that are more achievable.

4. Celebrate Milestones: As you reach milestones within your goals, celebrate them by acknowledging the habits that helped you get there. Microsoft To Do allows you to add notes and comments to tasks, so you can document your achievements and reflect on the habits that contributed to your success.

Practical Examples of Goal and Habit Management

To further illustrate the application of Microsoft To Do in managing personal goals and habits, let's explore a few practical examples:

Example 1: Improving Physical Fitness

- Goal: "Run a 10K Race"

- Subtasks/Milestones: "Research 10K Training Programs," "Complete a 5K Race," "Increase Weekly Running Distance to 20 miles"

- Habits: "Run 3 Times a Week," "Stretch for 15 Minutes After Each Run"

- Integration: The habit of running 3 times a week is directly linked to the milestones of completing a 5K race and increasing weekly running distance. Regular stretching supports injury prevention, ensuring consistent progress toward the 10K race.

Example 2: Enhancing Professional Skills

- Goal: "Become Proficient in Python Programming"

- Subtasks/Milestones: "Complete an Online Python Course," "Build a Python Project," "Contribute to an Open Source Python Repository"

- Habits: "Study Python for 1 Hour Each Day," "Practice Coding Challenges on Weekends"

- Integration: Daily study sessions and weekend coding challenges build the skills needed to complete the milestones, such as finishing a Python course and working on a project. These habits ensure steady progress toward becoming proficient in Python.

Example 3: Improving Mental Wellbeing

- Goal: "Reduce Stress and Improve Mindfulness"

- Subtasks/Milestones: "Attend a Mindfulness Workshop," "Incorporate Meditation into Daily Routine," "Track Stress Levels Weekly"

- Habits: "Meditate for 10 Minutes Each Morning," "Journal Before Bed," "Avoid Screen Time for 1 Hour Before Sleep"

- Integration: The daily habit of meditation and journaling directly contributes to the goal of improving mindfulness and reducing stress. Tracking stress levels weekly provides feedback on the effectiveness of these habits.

Overcoming Challenges in Goal and Habit Management

While Microsoft To Do is a powerful tool, managing personal goals and habits can still present challenges. Here are some common obstacles and strategies to overcome them:

1. Losing Motivation: It's natural to lose motivation over time, especially with long-term goals. To counter this, regularly revisit your reasons for setting the goal and remind yourself of the benefits. Use Microsoft To Do's notes feature to write motivational messages or review your progress to reignite your drive.

2. Inconsistent Habit Maintenance: Maintaining consistency in habits can be difficult, particularly with busy schedules. If you find yourself struggling, consider adjusting the frequency or duration of the habit. For instance, if daily exercise feels overwhelming, try reducing it to three times a week and gradually increase it as you build momentum.

3. Feeling Overwhelmed by Multiple Goals: Managing multiple goals simultaneously can lead to overwhelm. To address this, prioritize your goals and focus on one or two key goals at a time. Use Microsoft To Do to temporarily archive less urgent goals, allowing you to concentrate your efforts where they are most needed.

4. Difficulty in Measuring Progress: Some goals and habits may have less tangible progress, making it hard to measure success. In such cases, break down these goals into smaller, more specific tasks or milestones. For example, instead of a vague goal like "Improve Health," specify "Lower Blood Pressure by 10 Points" and create related habits to support that goal.

Conclusion

Microsoft To Do is a versatile tool that, when used effectively, can transform the way you manage personal goals and habits. By integrating goal setting with habit tracking, you can create a cohesive system that keeps you focused, motivated, and on track to achieve your personal aspirations. Remember, the key to success lies in consistency and reflection. Regularly review your progress, adjust your strategies as needed, and celebrate your achievements along the way. With Microsoft To Do, you're well-equipped to get things done and make meaningful strides toward a more productive and fulfilling life.

7.2.3 Planning Events and Activities

Planning events and activities can be a complex task, requiring attention to detail and a well-structured approach. Microsoft To Do offers a powerful set of tools that can help streamline this process, making it easier to manage all the elements involved. In this section, we will explore how Microsoft To Do can be used to plan various types of events and activities, from small gatherings to large-scale events, and how it can help ensure that everything runs smoothly.

Understanding the Scope and Objectives

Before diving into the specifics of planning an event or activity using Microsoft To Do, it's essential to understand the scope and objectives of the event. Whether you're organizing a family reunion, a corporate retreat, or a community fundraiser, knowing the goals and expectations will guide your planning process.

1. Defining the Event Purpose and Goals

- Identify the primary purpose of the event.

- Establish clear goals and objectives.

- Determine the target audience and their needs.

2. Setting the Event Date and Location

- Select a suitable date and time.

- Choose an appropriate venue or location.

- Consider logistics such as accessibility and capacity.

Creating a Master Task List

Once the scope and objectives are clear, the next step is to create a master task list in Microsoft To Do. This list will serve as the foundation for all your planning activities.

1. Breaking Down the Event into Tasks

- List all the major components of the event (e.g., venue, catering, invitations).

- Break each component down into smaller, manageable tasks.

- Prioritize tasks based on their importance and deadlines.

2. Using Subtasks for Detailed Planning

- Add subtasks to provide more detail for each main task.

- Assign deadlines and reminders to ensure timely completion.

- Use tags to categorize tasks and enhance organization.

Utilizing Lists and Groups

Microsoft To Do allows you to create multiple lists and groups, which can be particularly useful for event planning. By organizing tasks into specific lists and groups, you can maintain a clear and structured approach.

1. Creating Event-Specific Lists

 - Create separate lists for different aspects of the event (e.g., logistics, marketing, guest management).

 - Use descriptive names for each list to enhance clarity.

 - Share lists with team members or collaborators as needed.

2. Grouping Lists for Comprehensive Oversight

 - Group related lists under a common category (e.g., "Event Planning").

 - Use groups to track overall progress and identify any gaps.

 - Move tasks between lists and groups as the planning progresses.

Setting Deadlines and Reminders

Timely execution is critical when planning events and activities. Microsoft To Do's deadline and reminder features ensure that tasks are completed on time and nothing is overlooked.

1. Assigning Deadlines to Tasks

 - Set realistic deadlines for each task based on its priority.

 - Use the calendar view to visualize deadlines and avoid overlaps.

 - Adjust deadlines as necessary to accommodate changes.

2. Utilizing Reminders for Key Milestones

 - Set reminders for important milestones and deadlines.

 - Use recurring reminders for ongoing tasks (e.g., weekly check-ins).

 - Customize reminder notifications to suit your preferences.

Collaborating with Team Members

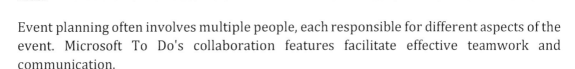

Event planning often involves multiple people, each responsible for different aspects of the event. Microsoft To Do's collaboration features facilitate effective teamwork and communication.

1. Sharing Lists and Assigning Tasks

- Share event-specific lists with team members or collaborators.

- Assign tasks to individuals and track their progress.

- Use comments to communicate and provide updates on tasks.

2. Tracking Team Contributions and Progress

- Monitor task completion and overall progress in real time.

- Provide feedback and support to team members as needed.

- Use the activity log to review changes and updates.

Using Smart Lists for Enhanced Organization

Smart Lists in Microsoft To Do offer automated organization based on specific criteria. These lists can simplify the planning process and help you stay on top of critical tasks.

1. Utilizing the "Important" Smart List

- Mark high-priority tasks as important to include them in the "Important" list.

- Use this list to focus on tasks that require immediate attention.

- Regularly review and update the "Important" list to maintain accuracy.

2. Leveraging the "Planned" Smart List

- Automatically include tasks with deadlines in the "Planned" list.

- Use this list to visualize your schedule and upcoming tasks.

- Adjust task deadlines directly from the "Planned" list as needed.

Tracking and Reflecting on Progress

Effective event planning involves continuous tracking and reflection. Microsoft To Do provides tools to monitor progress and ensure that everything stays on track.

1. Monitoring Task Completion

- Regularly update task statuses as they are completed.

- Use the progress bar to visualize overall completion.

- Celebrate milestones and achievements to maintain motivation.

2. Conducting Post-Event Reviews

- Reflect on the planning process and identify areas for improvement.

- Gather feedback from team members and participants.

- Document lessons learned for future events.

Case Study: Planning a Community Fundraiser

Let's explore a practical example of how Microsoft To Do can be used to plan a community fundraiser.

1. Defining the Purpose and Goals

- The primary purpose of the fundraiser is to support a local charity.

- Goals include raising $10,000 and engaging the community.

2. Creating a Master Task List

- Major tasks include securing a venue, coordinating volunteers, and promoting the event.

- Subtasks for securing a venue include researching options, negotiating contracts, and confirming bookings.

3. Organizing Tasks with Lists and Groups

- Separate lists are created for logistics, marketing, and volunteer management.

- All lists are grouped under the "Community Fundraiser" category.

4. Setting Deadlines and Reminders

- Deadlines are set for key tasks, such as finalizing the venue and launching marketing campaigns.

- Reminders are set for weekly check-ins with the planning team.

5. Collaborating with Team Members

- Lists are shared with volunteers, and tasks are assigned based on individual roles.

- Comments are used to communicate updates and provide feedback.

6. Using Smart Lists for Enhanced Organization

- Important tasks, such as securing sponsorships, are marked and reviewed regularly.

- The planned list is used to track upcoming deadlines and ensure timely execution.

7. Tracking and Reflecting on Progress

- Progress is monitored through regular updates and team meetings.

- A post-event review is conducted to gather feedback and identify areas for improvement.

Case Study: Organizing a Family Reunion

Now, let's consider how Microsoft To Do can be used to organize a family reunion.

1. Defining the Purpose and Goals

- The primary purpose is to bring the extended family together for a memorable gathering.

- Goals include confirming attendance, organizing activities, and creating a keepsake album.

2. Creating a Master Task List

- Major tasks include sending invitations, planning activities, and arranging accommodations.

- Subtasks for sending invitations include collecting contact information, designing invitations, and tracking RSVPs.

3. Organizing Tasks with Lists and Groups

   - Separate lists are created for invitations, activities, and accommodations.

   - All lists are grouped under the "Family Reunion" category.

4. Setting Deadlines and Reminders

   - Deadlines are set for tasks such as sending invitations and finalizing activity plans.

   - Reminders are set for regular check-ins with family members helping with the planning.

5. Collaborating with Family Members

   - Lists are shared with family members, and tasks are assigned based on their availability and preferences.

   - Comments are used to share updates and coordinate efforts.

6. Using Smart Lists for Enhanced Organization

   - Important tasks, such as booking accommodations, are marked and reviewed regularly.

   - The planned list is used to track upcoming deadlines and ensure timely execution.

7. Tracking and Reflecting on Progress

   - Progress is monitored through regular updates and family meetings.

   - A post-event review is conducted to gather feedback and identify areas for improvement for future reunions.

Conclusion

Planning events and activities can be a demanding task, but Microsoft To Do provides a comprehensive and flexible solution to help manage every aspect of the process. By utilizing its features effectively, you can ensure that all tasks are organized, deadlines are met, and events run smoothly. Whether you're planning a community fundraiser, a family reunion, or any other type of event, Microsoft To Do can help you stay on top of everything and achieve your goals with ease.

7.3 Real-World Examples

7.3.1 Using Microsoft To Do in Education

In the fast-paced and dynamic environment of education, managing tasks, assignments, and projects effectively is crucial for both educators and students. Microsoft To Do offers a powerful and flexible toolset that can significantly enhance productivity and organization in the educational context. This section explores how Microsoft To Do can be utilized in various educational settings to streamline workflows, improve time management, and foster better academic outcomes.

1. Organizing Academic Assignments and Deadlines

For students, managing multiple assignments and deadlines can be challenging. Microsoft To Do provides a structured approach to keep track of academic tasks. By creating separate lists for different subjects or projects, students can categorize their work and prioritize tasks based on deadlines and importance.

Example: A student can create lists for each subject—such as Math, Science, and History. Within each list, they can add individual tasks like "Complete History Essay," "Prepare for Science Lab," or "Finish Math Homework." Setting due dates and reminders ensures that tasks are completed on time and helps in avoiding last-minute cramming.

2. Developing Study Plans

Effective study planning is essential for academic success. Microsoft To Do allows students to create study plans by breaking down their study sessions into manageable tasks. Students can set up recurring tasks for regular study sessions, create checklists for study materials, and use reminders to stay on track.

Example: A student preparing for finals might create a list called "Study Plan for Finals" with tasks such as "Review Chapter 1," "Complete Practice Problems," and "Attend Study Group." By scheduling these tasks over the weeks leading up to the exam, students can manage their study time more effectively and ensure comprehensive preparation.

3. Collaborating on Group Projects

Group projects are common in education and require effective coordination among team members. Microsoft To Do facilitates collaboration by allowing students to share task lists and assign tasks to each other. This feature helps in managing group responsibilities, tracking progress, and ensuring that all members contribute to the project.

Example: In a group project for a research paper, students can create a shared list where each member is assigned specific tasks such as "Research Topic," "Draft Outline," and "Prepare Presentation." The ability to see updates and check off completed tasks helps in keeping the project on track and ensures that everyone is aligned with the project goals.

4. Managing Extracurricular Activities

Balancing academics with extracurricular activities requires careful planning. Microsoft To Do can help students keep track of their commitments outside the classroom, such as club meetings, sports practices, and volunteer work. By creating separate lists for these activities, students can manage their time more effectively and avoid scheduling conflicts.

Example: A student involved in various extracurriculars might have lists for "Basketball Practice," "Debate Club," and "Volunteering." Adding tasks like "Attend Team Meeting" or "Prepare Debate Speech" with appropriate deadlines and reminders helps in maintaining a balanced schedule and staying on top of commitments.

5. Streamlining Lesson Planning for Educators

For educators, lesson planning is a critical aspect of their role. Microsoft To Do can be used to organize lesson plans, track curriculum progress, and manage teaching materials. Educators can create lists for different classes or subjects, breaking down lesson plans into specific tasks and scheduling them throughout the semester.

Example: A teacher might create a list titled "Lesson Plans for English 101" with tasks such as "Prepare Week 1 Lesson," "Create Homework Assignments," and "Review Student Submissions." Setting deadlines for these tasks and using reminders ensures that lesson planning is organized and completed in a timely manner.

6. Tracking Professional Development

Educators often engage in professional development to enhance their teaching skills and knowledge. Microsoft To Do can assist in managing professional development goals by creating lists for workshops, courses, and certifications. Tracking progress and setting deadlines for completing professional development tasks helps in staying committed to continuous learning.

Example: An educator pursuing a certification might create a list called "Professional Development" with tasks such as "Complete Online Course," "Attend Workshop," and "Submit Certification Application." By scheduling these tasks and setting reminders, educators can effectively manage their professional growth and stay updated with the latest teaching strategies.

7. Facilitating Parent-Teacher Communication

Effective communication between parents and teachers is crucial for student success. Microsoft To Do can help in organizing and tracking communication tasks such as parent meetings, progress reports, and follow-up actions. Educators can create lists to manage these tasks and ensure timely and effective communication with parents.

Example: A teacher might have a list titled "Parent Communication" with tasks like "Schedule Parent-Teacher Conferences," "Send Progress Reports," and "Follow Up on Student Concerns." Using reminders and due dates helps in managing communication tasks efficiently and maintaining a positive relationship with parents.

8. Handling Administrative Tasks

In addition to teaching, educators often handle various administrative tasks, including grading, organizing classroom resources, and managing school events. Microsoft To Do can streamline these administrative duties by creating lists and tasks for each area of responsibility.

Example: A teacher might create a list called "Administrative Tasks" with items such as "Grade Midterm Exams," "Organize Classroom Supplies," and "Plan End-of-Year Party." By breaking down administrative duties into manageable tasks and setting deadlines, educators can handle these responsibilities more effectively and stay organized.

9. Utilizing Microsoft To Do for Remote Learning

With the rise of remote learning, managing online classes and virtual assignments has become increasingly important. Microsoft To Do can support remote learning by organizing online class schedules, tracking virtual assignments, and managing digital resources.

Example: A student engaged in remote learning might use a list titled "Remote Learning" to track tasks such as "Attend Zoom Class," "Submit Online Assignment," and "Review Class Materials." Setting deadlines and reminders helps in staying on top of virtual coursework and maintaining a structured remote learning experience.

10. Leveraging Microsoft To Do for Special Education

For educators and students in special education, Microsoft To Do offers tools to support individualized learning plans and accommodations. Creating custom lists and tasks can help in managing specialized educational needs and tracking progress toward individualized goals.

Example: An educator working with a student with special needs might create a list titled "Special Education Plan" with tasks such as "Develop Individualized Learning Plan," "Monitor Progress," and "Coordinate with Support Staff." Using Microsoft To Do to manage these tasks ensures that individualized education plans are effectively implemented and monitored.

By incorporating Microsoft To Do into educational settings, both students and educators can enhance their productivity, organization, and overall effectiveness. Whether managing academic assignments, coordinating group projects, or handling administrative duties, Microsoft To Do provides a versatile and valuable tool for achieving educational goals and fostering a more organized and productive learning environment.

7.3.2 Microsoft To Do for Small Businesses

Small businesses often face unique challenges when it comes to managing tasks, projects, and team coordination. Limited resources and manpower mean that every tool and strategy must be used efficiently to ensure productivity and success. Microsoft To Do, with its user-friendly interface and robust features, can be a game-changer for small businesses looking to streamline their operations and enhance team collaboration. In this section, we'll explore how small businesses can leverage Microsoft To Do to overcome common challenges and achieve their goals effectively.

1. Setting Up Microsoft To Do for Small Businesses

To get started with Microsoft To Do, small businesses need to set up a few key components to tailor the tool to their specific needs. The setup process involves creating lists, tasks, and projects that align with the business's operations and goals.

- Creating Business Lists and Projects: Small businesses can start by creating lists for different departments or functions within the company, such as "Marketing," "Sales," "Operations," and "Customer Service." Each list can then be subdivided into projects or task categories that are relevant to the specific needs of that department.

- Assigning Tasks and Setting Deadlines: Once the lists and projects are set up, tasks can be assigned to team members with specific deadlines. Microsoft To Do allows users to set due dates, reminders, and priorities for each task, ensuring that important deadlines are met and tasks are completed on time.

- Using Shared Lists for Collaboration: For teams working on the same projects or tasks, shared lists are a valuable feature. By sharing lists with team members, businesses can ensure that everyone is on the same page and has access to the latest updates and changes.

2. Streamlining Task Management

Effective task management is crucial for the success of any small business. Microsoft To Do provides several features that can help businesses streamline their task management processes.

- Creating and Managing Tasks: Tasks can be easily created and managed within Microsoft To Do. Users can add tasks with detailed descriptions, attach files, and set due dates and reminders. This helps ensure that all tasks are tracked and nothing falls through the cracks.

- Prioritizing Tasks: Prioritizing tasks is essential for managing workload and ensuring that critical tasks are completed first. Microsoft To Do allows users to assign priority levels (important, medium, or low) to tasks, helping businesses focus on what matters most.

- Tracking Progress with My Day and Completed Lists: The "My Day" feature allows users to focus on their most important tasks for the day. By selecting tasks from various lists and adding them to "My Day," users can create a daily focus list that helps them stay organized and productive. Additionally, the "Completed" list provides a record of finished tasks, which can be useful for tracking progress and reviewing achievements.

3. Enhancing Team Collaboration

Collaboration is a key component of any successful small business. Microsoft To Do offers several features that facilitate team collaboration and communication.

- Sharing Lists and Assigning Tasks: Teams can share lists with each other to work on common projects or tasks. By sharing lists, team members can see updates in real-time and collaborate more effectively. Tasks can also be assigned to specific team members, ensuring clear responsibility and accountability.

- Using Tags for Task Organization: Tags can be used to categorize tasks and make it easier to find and manage them. For example, tags like "urgent," "client request," or "follow-up" can help businesses organize tasks and prioritize them based on their significance.

- Integrating with Microsoft 365 Apps: Microsoft To Do integrates seamlessly with other Microsoft 365 apps, such as Outlook and Teams. This integration allows for better communication and coordination between team members. For instance, tasks can be created from emails in Outlook, and team members can discuss tasks and projects directly within Microsoft Teams.

4. Managing Projects and Deadlines

Project management is a critical aspect of running a small business. Microsoft To Do provides several tools and features that can help businesses manage projects and meet deadlines.

- Creating Project-Based Lists: Businesses can create separate lists for each project, allowing them to track tasks and milestones specific to that project. This helps ensure that all aspects of the project are covered and progress is monitored effectively.

- Setting Deadlines and Reminders: Deadlines and reminders are crucial for keeping projects on track. Microsoft To Do allows users to set due dates and reminders for tasks, ensuring that important deadlines are not missed and tasks are completed on time.

- Tracking Project Milestones: For larger projects, tracking milestones is important for monitoring progress and ensuring that key objectives are met. Microsoft To Do can be used to create milestones as tasks and track their completion to ensure that the project stays on schedule.

5. Using Microsoft To Do for Customer Management

Customer management is another area where Microsoft To Do can be beneficial for small businesses. By using Microsoft To Do to track customer interactions, follow-ups, and tasks, businesses can improve their customer service and build stronger relationships with their clients.

- Tracking Customer Interactions: Businesses can create lists or tasks to track customer interactions, such as meetings, calls, and emails. This helps ensure that follow-ups are timely and that customer needs are addressed promptly.

- Managing Follow-Ups and Requests: Customer follow-ups and requests can be managed using Microsoft To Do's task features. Tasks can be assigned to team members, set with deadlines, and tracked to ensure that customer requests are handled efficiently.

- Organizing Customer Information: Microsoft To Do's tagging and list features can be used to organize customer information and categorize tasks based on client needs or projects. This helps businesses stay organized and provide better service to their customers.

6. Tips for Maximizing Microsoft To Do for Small Businesses

To get the most out of Microsoft To Do, small businesses should consider the following tips:

- Regularly Review and Update Lists: Regularly reviewing and updating lists helps keep tasks and projects organized and ensures that nothing is overlooked. Set aside time each week to review your lists, update tasks, and make any necessary adjustments.

- Utilize Keyboard Shortcuts: Microsoft To Do offers keyboard shortcuts that can help you navigate and manage tasks more efficiently. Familiarize yourself with these shortcuts to save time and improve productivity.

- Leverage Integration with Other Tools: Take advantage of Microsoft To Do's integration with other Microsoft 365 tools to enhance your workflow. For example, integrate with Outlook to manage tasks from emails or use Teams to collaborate on tasks with your team.

- Train Your Team: Ensure that your team is trained on how to use Microsoft To Do effectively. Provide training sessions or resources to help team members understand the features and best practices for using the tool.

7. Conclusion

Microsoft To Do offers a range of features and capabilities that can significantly benefit small businesses. By setting up tasks and lists, streamlining task management, enhancing team collaboration, managing projects and deadlines, and improving customer management, small businesses can improve their efficiency and productivity.

With its user-friendly interface and integration with Microsoft 365 apps, Microsoft To Do provides a powerful tool for small businesses looking to stay organized and achieve their goals. By leveraging the features and best practices outlined in this section, businesses can make the most of Microsoft To Do and drive their success.

7.3.3 Non-Profit Organization Task Management

In the realm of non-profit organizations, effective task management is crucial. Non-profits often operate with limited resources and need to maximize their efficiency to achieve their missions. Microsoft To Do can be a powerful tool for non-profit organizations, helping them organize their tasks, coordinate activities, and ensure that their goals are met effectively.

This section explores how Microsoft To Do can be utilized by non-profits, with a focus on task management, project coordination, and enhancing overall productivity.

1. Organizing Tasks and Projects

For non-profit organizations, managing tasks can be complex due to the variety of activities involved, from fundraising and outreach to program implementation and administrative duties. Microsoft To Do provides several features that can streamline this process:

- Creating and Managing Lists: Non-profits can use Microsoft To Do to create separate lists for different projects or functions. For example, a list for fundraising activities, another for volunteer coordination, and one for program development. This helps in organizing tasks based on priority and type, ensuring that team members can focus on their specific responsibilities.

- Utilizing Tags and Categories: Tags can be used to categorize tasks based on their nature or urgency. For instance, tasks related to urgent fundraising events can be tagged with "Urgent," while routine administrative tasks might be tagged with "Routine." This categorization helps in quickly identifying and addressing high-priority tasks.

- Setting Due Dates and Reminders: Non-profit organizations often work on tight deadlines, whether it's for grant applications, event planning, or program reports. Microsoft To Do allows users to set due dates and reminders for tasks, ensuring that deadlines are met and no task is overlooked.

2. Coordinating Team Efforts

Effective team coordination is essential for non-profit organizations, especially when managing large projects or events. Microsoft To Do supports team collaboration through several features:

- Sharing Lists: Lists can be shared with team members, allowing everyone to view and contribute to the same task list. This is particularly useful for collaborative projects, such as organizing a community outreach event or managing a volunteer drive. Team members can update tasks, add comments, and check off completed items, ensuring everyone stays on the same page.

- Assigning Tasks: Within shared lists, tasks can be assigned to specific team members. This feature helps in clearly defining responsibilities and tracking who is working on what. For example, one team member might be responsible for logistics, while another handles communication with stakeholders.

- Collaborative Task Management: Microsoft To Do integrates with other Microsoft 365 tools, such as Microsoft Teams and Outlook, enhancing collaboration. Team members can discuss tasks in Teams chats, attach relevant files, and link tasks to calendar events. This integration ensures that all team communication and task management are centralized and accessible.

3. Enhancing Productivity and Efficiency

Non-profit organizations can significantly benefit from the productivity features offered by Microsoft To Do:

- Customizable Views and Filters: Microsoft To Do allows users to customize their task views and filters, which can help non-profit organizations focus on what's most important. For example, team members can create a "My Day" view to focus on tasks they plan to complete today, or use filters to view tasks by due date or priority.

- Recurring Tasks: Non-profits often have recurring activities, such as monthly reports, regular meetings, or annual events. Microsoft To Do's recurring task feature allows users to set up tasks that repeat at specified intervals, reducing the need to manually recreate these tasks each time.

- Task Progress Tracking: Tracking task progress is crucial for non-profits to ensure that projects are moving forward as planned. Microsoft To Do provides visual indicators of task completion, such as progress bars and completed task lists. This helps organizations monitor their progress and make adjustments as needed.

4. Case Studies and Examples

To illustrate the practical application of Microsoft To Do in non-profit settings, let's look at a few real-world examples:

- Example 1: Community Food Bank

A community food bank uses Microsoft To Do to manage its daily operations, including food drives, volunteer scheduling, and inventory management. By creating separate lists for each area of operation and using tags to categorize tasks, the organization can efficiently track and manage its activities. The ability to set reminders and deadlines ensures that critical tasks, such as coordinating with suppliers and organizing distribution events, are completed on time.

- Example 2: Environmental Conservation Group

An environmental conservation group leverages Microsoft To Do to plan and execute various conservation projects, such as tree planting initiatives and wildlife monitoring programs. Shared lists and task assignments enable team members to collaborate effectively, while recurring tasks help manage ongoing activities like regular field inspections. The group also uses the integration with Outlook to schedule project meetings and track progress.

- Example 3: Educational Non-Profit Organization

An educational non-profit organization utilizes Microsoft To Do to manage its programs, including curriculum development, teacher training, and student workshops. The organization creates detailed task lists for each program and uses tags to track different types of activities, such as curriculum updates or training sessions. The ability to share lists and assign tasks helps ensure that all team members are aligned and working towards common goals.

5. Best Practices for Non-Profit Task Management

To maximize the benefits of Microsoft To Do, non-profit organizations should consider the following best practices:

- Regularly Review and Update Lists: Ensure that task lists are regularly reviewed and updated to reflect any changes in priorities or new developments. This helps maintain an accurate overview of ongoing activities and ensures that no tasks are missed.

- Encourage Team Collaboration: Foster a collaborative environment by encouraging team members to actively use shared lists and contribute to task management. Open communication and regular check-ins can help keep everyone engaged and informed.

- Utilize Integration Features: Take advantage of Microsoft To Do's integration with other Microsoft 365 tools to streamline workflows and enhance productivity. For example, link tasks to calendar events in Outlook or use Teams for project discussions and file sharing.

- Monitor and Adjust: Continuously monitor task progress and make adjustments as needed. Use the insights gained from task tracking to identify areas for improvement and optimize task management processes.

By applying these practices and leveraging the features of Microsoft To Do, non-profit organizations can enhance their task management, improve team coordination, and ultimately achieve their mission more effectively.

Conclusion

As we conclude "Getting Things Done with Microsoft To Do," we hope that you now have a comprehensive understanding of how to leverage Microsoft To Do to optimize your productivity and achieve your goals. This book has been designed to provide you with practical, actionable insights into harnessing the full potential of this powerful task management tool, grounded in the principles of the Getting Things Done (GTD) methodology.

Microsoft To Do is more than just a digital to-do list—it's a dynamic, intuitive platform that integrates seamlessly with your daily routine, helping you stay organized and focused. By implementing the strategies outlined in this book, you can transform how you manage tasks, projects, and personal goals. Whether you're a busy professional juggling multiple projects, a student managing coursework, or anyone seeking to improve their personal productivity, Microsoft To Do offers a flexible solution to meet your needs.

In the chapters of this book, we've explored various facets of Microsoft To Do, from setting up your task lists and prioritizing your workload to integrating the GTD methodology and customizing your experience. Here's a brief recap of the key takeaways:

1. Getting Started: We began with the basics, ensuring you had a solid foundation for using Microsoft To Do. Understanding the core features, setting up your account, and navigating the interface were essential first steps.

2. Task and List Management: We delved into creating and managing tasks and lists, emphasizing the importance of organization and prioritization. You learned how to set due dates, add reminders, and use tags to categorize your tasks effectively.

3. Integrating GTD: One of the most powerful aspects of Microsoft To Do is its ability to support the GTD methodology. We covered how to capture, clarify, organize, and review your tasks using GTD principles, enabling you to maintain a clear and actionable task list.

4. Advanced Features: Customizing your Microsoft To Do experience was another key focus. From personalizing your task views to integrating with other Microsoft 365 apps, you now know how to tailor the platform to fit your unique workflow and productivity needs.

5. Best Practices: We provided insights into optimizing your task management system and maintaining productivity. Techniques for prioritizing tasks, setting realistic goals, and managing your workload effectively will help you stay focused and achieve your objectives.

6. *Troubleshooting and Support: We addressed common issues and provided resources for support. Understanding how to troubleshoot problems and access help will ensure a smoother experience with Microsoft To Do.*

7. *Real-World Applications: By exploring case studies and real-world examples, you've seen how Microsoft To Do can be applied in various contexts, from project management to personal productivity. These insights should inspire you to implement similar strategies in your own life.*

8. *Future Outlook: Finally, we discussed the future of Microsoft To Do, highlighting upcoming features and enhancements. Staying informed about these developments will help you continue to make the most of the tool as it evolves.*

As you move forward with Microsoft To Do, remember that productivity is an ongoing process. The principles and techniques outlined in this book are meant to be adapted and refined according to your personal and professional needs. The goal is not just to get things done, but to do them efficiently and effectively, freeing up time for what truly matters.

Thank You for Your Support

We extend our heartfelt thanks for choosing "Getting Things Done with Microsoft To Do." Your decision to invest in this book reflects a commitment to enhancing your productivity and achieving your goals. Writing this book has been a rewarding experience, and we are grateful for the opportunity to share our insights and knowledge with you.

Your support and feedback are invaluable. We hope that the strategies and best practices shared in these pages will serve as a valuable resource in your journey toward greater organization and efficiency. If this book has helped you, we encourage you to share your thoughts and experiences. Your feedback will not only help us improve future editions but also inspire others who seek similar solutions.

We also invite you to connect with the wider community of Microsoft To Do users. Engaging with others who are on the same journey can provide additional insights, support, and motivation. Whether through online forums, user groups, or social media, sharing your experiences and learning from others can enhance your productivity even further.

In closing, we wish you the best of luck as you continue to use Microsoft To Do. May it help you stay organized, manage your tasks effectively, and achieve your goals with greater ease.

Remember, productivity is a journey, not a destination. Embrace the process, stay focused, and keep moving forward. Thank you once again for your support and for being a part of this journey.

Happy planning, and here's to your continued success!

www.ingramcontent.com/pod-product-compliance
Lightning Source LLC
LaVergne TN
LVHW081332050326
832903LV00024B/1127